THE HIGHEST EXAM

THE
HIGHEST
EXAM

How the Gaokao
Shapes China

o o o

Ruixue Jia and Hongbin Li
with Claire Cousineau

THE BELKNAP PRESS OF
HARVARD UNIVERSITY PRESS
Cambridge, Massachusetts, and London, England
2025

EU GPSR Authorised Representative
LOGOS EUROPE, 9 rue Nicolas Poussin, 17000, LA ROCHELLE, France
E-mail: Contact@logoseurope.eu

Library of Congress Cataloging-in-Publication Data

Names: Jia, Ruixue, author. | Li, Hongbin, author. | Cousineau, Claire.
Title: The highest exam : how the gaokao shapes China / Ruixue Jia and
    Hongbin Li ; with Claire Cousineau.
Description: Cambridge, Massachusetts : The Belknap Press of Harvard
        University Press, 2025. | Includes bibliographical references and index.
    Identifiers: LCCN 2025000656 (print) | LCCN 2025000657 (ebook) | ISBN
    9780674295391 (cloth) | ISBN 9780674301832 (epub) | ISBN 9780674301849 (pdf)
Subjects: LCSH: Gaokao (Educational test)—Social aspects. | Universities
    and colleges—China—Entrance examinations. | Educational tests and
    measurements—Social aspects—China.
Classification: LCC LB2353.8.C6 J53 2025 (print) | LCC LB2353.8.C6
    (ebook) | DDC 378.1/660951—dc23/eng/20250407
LC record available at https://lccn.loc.gov/2025000656
LC ebook record available at https://lccn.loc.gov/2025000657

CONTENTS

THE HIGHEST EXAM

Introduction

o   o   o

For two days every year in June, China comes to a standstill. Unusual sights abound: men put on qipaos, traditional dresses typically worn by women, as a symbol of luck; police stand on street corners, silencing drivers to ensure minimal disturbance; temples overflow with relatives sending out final prayers; crowds, unusually quiet, gather in hushed vigils outside thousands of schools. State media in all forms zero in on the one event affecting millions of students and their many family members who have invested time, money, and, above all, hope in the outcome of these two days. The gaokao, China's national college entrance exam, grips the country.

As students emerge from the second and final day of testing, the nervous quiet dissipates, and the roar of activity begins. Social media buzzes with speculation; some families lament that the math on their version of the exam was more challenging than that of neighboring provinces while others puzzle over the best answer to this year's essay question. Many adults are even curious to take this year's version of the exam themselves—could they do as well as they did in the past?—or, at the very least, explore the test content distributed by the government.

At the same time, an army of professors mobilized by the government trades places with the students. Sequestered in hotel rooms across the country, they grade a flurry of exams flying across their desks. They are to complete their task in just under two weeks, and then scores are released to the public. The highest scorers in each province are practically guaranteed a spot at an elite university and the life-changing power that comes with it. In just a month, they will face the pull of university recruiters, who will try to corral these students into their classes. In some provinces, the highest scorers, lauded for their hard work and discipline, are treated as newly crowned celebrities. Their smiles on local television seem to say, *if you study as hard as I did, you too can end up here.* In other provinces, legal measures now shield the identity of the highest scorers to protect them from overexposure.

But whether people know the identity of the top scorer in the province isn't important: the fact that highest scorers might even *need* protection says enough. Armed with the knowledge that their child could one day utterly transform their social standing, families are willing to do whatever it takes to facilitate success within the education system. For twelve years or more, schoolchildren take the hundreds of exams and practice tests for the gaokao that define the student experience in China. Precious time outside of school is spent in the company of tutors organized by their parents. For some, the decade-long obsession is enough to earn them a seat at one of China's most prestigious universities. For others, a single missed point—perhaps their own fault, perhaps just the tired eyes of a professor grading their exam—is enough to knock them down the ranks, obligating them to attend a second- or third-tier university. This reality is a painful one: it is well understood that their gaokao score will follow them for the rest of their life.

The gaokao marks one of the few opportunities in China to prove your worth to society, and even more consequentially, to the government. In truth, few across China are left untouched by the country's education system. Whether you dropped out of school before taking the gaokao, or took the gaokao ten, twenty, or forty years ago, this annual reminder inevitably evokes memories: some good, others painful, but above all else, nearly impossible to escape. Few can afford to be indifferent to the exam.

This is the gaokao, literally translated as the "highest exam" of China. But the gaokao is just one exam among hundreds if not thousands of exams that students sit for throughout the years. Nor is the gaokao the last test that these students will take in their lives: undergraduate and graduate programs, in addition to certain career paths (such as the state bureaucracy), also require countless exams. Of course, exams are a fact of life in many places around the world. But China stands alone as a country thoroughly governed by exams and the scores that they produce. It is the education system's exams that serve as the underlying framework of China's society, both reflecting and reinforcing its particular societal structure.

In the past several decades, the influence of China's exam culture has also quietly expanded far beyond its borders. Indeed, if you are a reader in the United States, you might not realize just how significant a role China's exam system plays in your own life. Decades of unprecedented development have secured China a corner in the US's national consciousness; its presence is everywhere, from the clothes on your back to the technology powering your devices. Some even project that China will unseat the United States as the world's largest economy over the next decade, and the US Congress has focused on containing various aspects of China's economic dominance. In the process, China's education system has rightfully captured their attention. For years, economists have understood the connection between education and the economy: a more highly educated population is associated with labor productivity improvements that drive innovation and long-term economic growth. It is education that determines which country can produce the most creative scientists, the most innovative business leaders, and ultimately the most capable labor force. Together, these factors are responsible for driving economic productivity and raising the gross domestic product (GDP).

Beyond national politics, the extensive relationship between China and the United States also means that China's education system has come to affect the dynamics of the US's own schools. As those schools see increasing numbers of first-, second-, and third-generation Chinese American and other Asian American students, clashes in values connected to education have become increasingly hard to ignore. A court case filed against Harvard University that effectively dismantled a decades-long legacy of affirmative action may be the most high-profile story. But smaller, quieter debates of the same ilk are playing out across the US in suburbs and cities alike. What happens when students and families who look at education through different lenses find themselves sharing the same school system? And what happens when success and achievement are defined in fundamentally different ways?

Despite the importance of China's education system to international power struggles and its pertinence to families across the United States, the inner workings of that system are still largely a mystery, even to those responsible for crafting policies meant to contain or address it. Congress has convened panels of expert testimonies on the topic, but while these have been illuminating in many respects, presenting a cohesive portrait of a vast and complex system in just a few hours is an impossible task. We came to realize that no single body of work effectively explained how China's education system functions and what far-reaching effects it has on China's entire society. And so, a few years ago, we decided to explore the findings of over two decades of research and share a lifetime of personal experience in this book.

· · ·

Unofficially, our research began when we set foot in our first classrooms in China. Though a decade apart, Ruixue and Hongbin traveled through elementary, middle, and high school classes that culminated in the gaokao and subsequently enrolled at universities in Beijing. Our time in China's education system, first as students and later as professors, provided us with the context and relationships through which we were able to conduct our more official research in China and the United States, even in the face of increasingly stringent restrictions on academic work. Hongbin's understanding has also deepened over the past two decades as he raised and educated his two children. During his time in Beijing, Hong Kong, and California, each new day brought with it decisions about his children's education in a rapidly changing landscape.

Growing up in China's planned economy during its transition to a market economy, Hongbin naturally developed an interest in the country's reforms. Today, his research spans a range of topics that are all connected by a central question: how do individuals navigate their lives and how does the economy function within China's centralized, state-dominated system? In his work, education is not merely a product of the state-dominated system but a key force shaping labor market outcomes, social equity, politics, and China's economic development. Hongbin sees education as one of China's most defining institutions, and even more broadly, one that captures the essence of what China is today.

But it quickly became clear that obtaining data to empirically analyze China's economy, including its education system, would present significant challenges. In response, Hongbin founded and directed the Tsinghua China Data Center, dedicated to collecting social and economic data for the academic community studying China. The center, which operated from 2009 through 2016, made numerous official datasets accessible to researchers around the world. While these data were extensive in both scale and scope, they were primarily intended for government reporting rather than academic research. Recognizing the need for more nuanced insights, Hongbin also conducted extensive fieldwork to collect original data. Together with colleagues from Tsinghua, he launched the Chinese College Student Survey, gathering data from universities across China to examine how college education and gaokao scores influence a student's labor market outcomes. Additionally, he founded the China Employer-Employee Survey, focusing on the dynamics of China's manufacturing sector and labor market, with an emphasis on how education shapes labor outcomes and drives economic performance.

Ruixue, as an unwanted daughter, had been sent to live with an adoptive family in a small rural village in China shortly after she was born. She had never traveled by train or airplane until she attended college in Beijing. Her knowledge of the world was drawn from the dusty books she read as a child, each of which sparked her imagination. The cultural shock she felt upon moving from her village to Beijing at age sixteen was more profound than anything she would later experience while studying in Sweden or teaching in California and London. This initial experience ignited a curiosity about political economy: Why are some groups more powerful than others? Why did people in her village seem content within such an unequal system? Why did the authors of the books she read often come from privileged, cultured families with captivating histories, while her family and friends' lives seemed relegated to the realm of fiction? These formative questions ultimately guided her path into political economy.

One area of Ruixue's research examines the development and evolution of China's institutions and power structure. Among these, the centralized examination system for elite recruitment—originating in the Sui Dynasty around 600 AD—stands out. Her research reveals how this examination system has historically influenced governance, political stability, and societal values. Given that China's contemporary education system retains many foundational elements from the imperial exams, studying these historical dynamics sheds light on the modern system's structure and its impact on society. By digitizing extensive historical archives and utilizing administrative datasets, Ruixue has illustrated how China's current education system mirrors its historical counterpart, highlighting significant parallels in their roles within state and society.

In her field, many influential scholars argue that China will ultimately struggle in science and innovation due to its nondemocratic institutions. However, China's advancements in science and technology so far seem to challenge this assumption. These contradictions drive

Ruixue's second line of research: the political economy of science and technology. As US-China tensions increasingly shape the global landscape of science and technology, these geopolitical dynamics hold significant implications for the two nations and others as well. This research has also led her to reflect on structural and cultural differences between US and Chinese education systems and how these differences may shape scientific progress and national strategy.

Employing one-of-a-kind data sources and a variety of different perspectives, the two of us have published studies in some of the top academic journals on a subject that is increasingly challenging to research. And though we intuited as much through growing up and working within the system, this research has led us to more formally describe the setup of China's education system: it is a *centralized hierarchical tournament*. This framework can help us understand much not only about education in China but also about China's governance, society, and its influence on education systems beyond its own.

. . .

What does it mean to have an education system that resembles a *tournament*? After twelve years of sitting for hundreds of exams, China's pre-tertiary education culminates in one final exam: the gaokao. The gaokao is the tournament's final match, from which students emerge either victorious or defeated. Administered in June across all of China, the gaokao is taken by over ten million students each year. Every student's score on the gaokao is compared to the score of every other student within their province; it is only by knowing how well others are performing that one can gauge one's own performance. And college admission is entirely determined by a student's performance relative to their peers. In this way, China's education system is a zero-sum game: if your neighbor wins, in all likelihood you lose. Such a system stands in contrast with college admissions in the United States, where standardized tests like the ACT and SAT are just one of many factors considered by an admissions office, and each college typically has a wide range of accepted scores. Perhaps unsurprisingly, the tournament-like setup fosters a highly competitive atmosphere across China's education system.

What does it look like to have a *centralized* system of education? China's education system is in large part organized by the central government. There is only one avenue through which students can gain admission to an institution of higher education: passing the gaokao. The government designs each question on this exam, determines the dates on which it is administered, assigns regional quotas, and decides strict cutoff scores for admission to each of China's universities for every region. A student's success and failure is contingent on how well they can perform within these boundaries. For most students, there is practically no alternative method for matriculation, no test-optional box that students can check, no choice between the ACT or SAT. It all boils down to the gaokao, the one exam for which students train their entire pre-tertiary educational career, and it is the central government that draws up the rules. Students are required to sit for the exam if they hope to attend any one of China's universities.

What does it look like to have a *hierarchical* education system? China's higher education system resembles a pyramid. At the top of the pyramid are China's most exclusive elite colleges, which receive priority over all other universities in government funding and resources. Only students whose exam scores are at the very top of the score distribution in each province can gain admission to these schools. Below the elite colleges are the remaining four-year universities. These universities also differ substantially in terms of their reputation and government-allocated financial resources, and are divided further into Tier 2, Tier 3, and Tier 4 schools. Finally, at the bottom of the pyramid sit two- or three-year vocational colleges, which are similar to community colleges in the US. But while students in the US can go on to develop prestigious careers for themselves after graduating from almost any college, and can transfer from a community college to a flagship state or private college or university, in China many doors are slammed shut for all but the few who attend the most elite of China's universities at around eighteen years of age.

. . .

With this framework in mind, we embark on our exploration of China's education system. In Part I, "Family," we explore the relationship between the individual and the education system. Our point of departure is this: education is a top priority for families of all types across China's society, so much so that we characterize their behavior as an obsession. But this behavior is in fact extremely rational. Somebody who goes to college in China receives on average a 40 percent higher income relative to somebody who did not go to college. And what matters even more is getting into an *elite* college. This is in part because those who attend an elite college in China earn an additional 40 percent more than those who attend a non-elite four-year institution. But bundled with an elite college degree is the real prize: tacit admission to the top of China's social hierarchy. Without the prerequisite elite college degree, it is extremely challenging to advance in China's society. A position in the state sector, for example, is almost impossible to secure without such a degree. And a position at the top of the social hierarchy grants China's citizens access (or maintains their access) to hidden benefits that make it possible to conquer three "mountains" of expenses: the costs of education, medical care, and housing. An elite college degree is well worth the grueling price of admission. Families across China compete in the tournament year after year with the understanding that the lucky 5 percent will earn the coveted prize of social status and prosperity.

But the price of admission to an elite college is steeper for some than for others. At birth, every person in China is given a *hukou,* a household registration card that serves as a residence permit. Each citizen's hukou card carries with it a slew of facts and figures. Most important among these, for our purposes, is birthplace, both the province and exact location. According to the quota system maintained by the central government, each province is allocated a specific number of seats for admission at each university. Provincial-level cities like Beijing or Shanghai, which have the highest concentration of China's political and business elites, are given the most seats. Regions that are considered important politically, like Xinjiang, also have a higher quota. In this way, the central government carefully dictates what percentage of individuals from each province are allowed access to the upper echelons of China's society. But just as important as one's province for calculating the odds of elite college admission is whether a student is born in an urban or rural part of their province. Lack of resources and lower quality of schools put rural hukou holders at an extreme disadvantage, making them far less likely than their urban peers to gain access to a life-changing elite college degree. But even in the face of such inequalities, our analysis suggests that China's education system provides far more social mobility than that of the education system in the United States.

Still, the systemic inequalities of the gaokao are undeniable, and a low score not only affects college admission but life outcomes. Note here that we're emphasizing the gaokao itself, not the quality of college education that the score enables. According to several studies that compare global academic achievement, China's high school students perform better than those of any other country on measures like critical thinking, reading, and math. But *during* their four years in college, evidence indicates that the skills of the average student in China stagnate, or perhaps even decline. This suggests that attending an elite college serves as a signal of ability rather than a stepping stone to learning. Indeed, a student's gaokao score can predict their income years down the line with a high degree of accuracy, likely because of the strong signal the gaokao score sends to potential employers. But to return to our original point, people in China are obsessed with education for precisely this reason: there are few other avenues that will allow them to change their socioeconomic fate. And, of course, there are the social implications often associated with a low gaokao score, particularly for those who come from a higher socioeconomic bracket and see doing well on the test as a requirement for maintaining their social status. So many life outcomes depend on a test that students sit for when they are eighteen. For families, education—or more specifically, raising their child's score on the gaokao—is thus necessarily of paramount importance.

After establishing the relationship between China's education system and its families, we turn our attention to the role of education in China's political power in Part II, "State." Today's exam system in China is the most modern iteration of one invented more than a thousand years ago. Since its inception, the system has been a political one. In a country as vast as China, the emperor needed a method to find and select some of the most talented individuals in his kingdom to work under him. This also served as a control mechanism: with the most talented individuals owing their position of power to his exam, the likelihood of such men rebelling against the emperor shrank. Ultimately, several rounds of highly competitive testing determined who would join the ranks of government officials, the most elite positions anyone could hold at the time. Though the imperial examination system has since been abolished, the goal of the modern iteration of the exam system remains to develop the next batch of talented individuals working for and loyal to the central core of the Chinese Communist Party. Through over a thousand years of trial and error, the education system has evolved to include a host of cleverly designed features. In large part by providing a reliable channel for social mobility, these features have collectively served as a stabilizing force for China's society—with one exception. Each new regime inevitably attempts to impose its new priorities on the education system, but as with any tournament, no one likes it if you change the rules of the game mid-competition. Both in the more distant past and more recently, change has given rise to notable instances of social unrest.

In practice, the central government manages the exam system to best serve its political agenda in two key ways: it controls the number of positions available in the education system, all of which are a part of the state sector, and it assigns power to these positions depending on their rank. Because China's education system is enormous, the central government cannot control all of it directly, and instead opts to delegate power to governments at the local level through a carefully designed hierarchical incentive structure. Centralized control also grants the government a monopoly over one of the key resources underpinning development in every country around the world: its people. China's central government thus ensures that its people acquire the *type* of skills that they need to further drive economic development, by lavishing resources on and assigning higher quotas to certain fields. In the past ten years, for example, the government has significantly enlarged the quota for STEM majors at elite universities and directed funds toward some of the best universities to bolster strategic programs in response to the US-China technology competition.

Part of the reason why China's education system is so centralized is that the government is keenly aware of its role in shaping China's economic power. When China's reform period began in the late 1970s, the education system was one of the leadership's top priorities. What followed was an unprecedented wave of higher education expansion and overall upgrading of the system, one that took place alongside a period of startling economic growth. An analysis of the interplay of education and GDP reveals that education can explain up to one-third of China's economic growth. China's education expansion also facilitated the country's remarkable technological progress, helping it make things better, faster, and cheaper. Education has not been the only factor, of course: domestic market-friendly policies and growing integration with the global ecosystem have also been important to China's progress. And now that China is at the research frontier and tasked with innovating independently, some of the characteristics of its education system that initially allowed it to succeed—its centralized, hierarchical, tournament-style approach—may hinder the system's ability to propel China past the United States in its technological capabilities.

After exploring education's central role for China's families and government, in Part III, "Society," we look at how the education system can be used to understand China's societal values, and the debates that these values have brought to discussions of education in the United States. In China, the notion that personal advancement is dependent on merit is at the heart of many social phenomena. Several public opinion surveys indicate a belief that merit is a result of intelligence and hard work. Though survey respondents in China were generally more extreme in their answers, the surveys also revealed that US citizens view merit in a similar light. But despite their parallel value systems, the US and China have chosen very different approaches to their education systems. This is particularly evident as it relates to college admission, where US institutions base their decision on a host of factors, while China bases admission exclusively on gaokao scores. What explains this difference? We suggest that in China, weak institutions—ones that are easily influenced by connections and corruption—have driven citizens to buy into a single-score system to reliably ensure transparency and objectivity. When other areas of life can be influenced by connections and corruption, transparent and objective scores have become the standard for success.

Intended to counteract China's weak institutions, such meritocratic scoring systems can be found across China's society. So, too, can the idea of centralized hierarchical tournaments. Among the most notable of these can be found within China's government. In the political tournament, a government official's success is primarily evaluated based on a single-score metric set by the central government: GDP growth. Officials compete against each other for promotion, as individual performance on GDP growth is assessed relative to their predecessor and to every other provincial leader. In addition, academics in China continue to compete for promotion in an endless university hierarchy that is also based on a single-score metric: their publication score count. Though we focus on these two examples, our experience indicates that this model can be found throughout China's society.

Finally, we turn our attention to the tournament's arrival in the United States. After US president Richard Nixon and Chairman Mao Zedong's historic meeting in 1972 facilitated an era of reform in China, Chinese students began seeking education abroad. For over two decades now, China has been the most important foreign supplier of scientists, many of whom work for US universities and firms. Chinese students educated in the US have also returned to China, benefiting China's development. But this mutually beneficial arrangement is increasingly facing political and social backlash as the exam empire expands beyond China's borders. Because many US immigrants from China are those who thrived in China's tournament-style education system, it is only natural they would wish to instill in their own children similar lessons for success. Indeed, in the US, Asian Americans consistently excel on standardized exams. But universities in the US do not base admissions exclusively on test results. They also include intangible and subjective measures in college admission. Despite rising to the top on all *objective* measures that colleges consider, Asian American families still face headwinds in gaining admission to the nation's top schools. Realizing this, they have sought to promote score-based systems, championing objectivity and transparency in the years leading up to college application and in the college admission process itself. This tactic has reshaped national and local politics, and at times even contributed to heightened social divisions, as many parents who do not subscribe to the tournament mentality try to escape it altogether.

• • •

In China, exam scores represent the ultimate measure of success. The centralized hierarchical tournament underlying the education system has both reflected and reinforced the structure and values of China's politics and society for well over a thousand years. This model follows many of China's citizens from cradle to grave.

When a citizen receives their hukou assignment at birth, their initial placement in the social hierarchy is set. The education system is among the very few ways to change that initial determination. But whether or not one chooses to sign up for the education tournament, one is still subject to the model that the system perpetuates: in the presence of a hierarchy, individuals are inevitably made to compete. The lowest-level employees in the warehouses of a Chinese grocery store chain, who likely never finished high school, have their packing efficiency ranked and displayed on TV screens. At a major Chinese tech firm, when asked whether the employees were ranked against one another, the manager responded with some puzzlement: "Of course." For its most celebrated citizens, the hierarchy remains alive even in death: revolutionary heroes, high-ranking government officials, and other individuals central to China's development are required to be buried in Ba Bao Shan Cemetery in Beijing. Even when some prominent leaders have voiced their desire to be buried elsewhere, they are nonetheless laid to rest in Ba Bao Shan.

Before we explore these phenomena and the role of the exam system in shaping it all, it's important that we acknowledge that we are stepping somewhat beyond our role as traditional economists. In our line of research, we usually do our very best to establish clear lines of causality. Many of the conclusions here, on the other hand, though they derive from decades of research, are also based on an intuitive understanding of the system. As students and professors of education—and, in Hongbin's case, as a parent—we're supposed to have all the answers. But we too are still figuring out just what drives the behavior of families and students both within and beyond China's borders. By offering our own stories to better illuminate several decades of quantitative research, we hope that this book can not only summarize what we have learned so far but also help our readers—including those who survived the system, those who succeeded within it, and, perhaps most important, those who are only beginning to explore China as a country—to understand China's exam empire.

PART I

FAMILY

1

Obsession

o   o   o

"Is there anyone born to be a king, a duke, a general, or a minister?"

—Shiji

"王侯将相, 宁有种乎? "   —《史记》

On a crisp spring morning in May 1972, Little Li took his first breath in a factory hospital. Just three months prior, US president Richard Nixon had come to China to meet Chairman Mao, marking the beginning of a new era for China and its people. For over two decades prior, China had been virtually isolated from Western countries. Little Li was born at just the right time. Far from the borders of his home province of Jilin, Little Li would come to witness economic transformation and reap outsized benefits from the changing tides of the country's history. But for now, that state-owned factory was to be his childhood home. The snow in Jilin was still melting, making for a muddy season at the factory.

Little Li spent his early years crawling up, over, and around heavy machinery producing graphite electrodes. With a population of around 100,000, this particular factory community, like many communities under Chairman Mao's planned economy, was akin to a small city, producing specialized goods according to government demand. From the moment of his birth, Little Li's fate was nestled soundly in the walls of the factory: one day, he was to assume his father's position as a crane operator. At the time, factory-affiliated positions—ones that ranged from the factory's elementary school teacher to an assembly-line man— were some of the best jobs anyone could hold, and some of the only reliable jobs in the area. Guaranteed a comfortable position with a government-allocated wage, Little Li was one of the lucky ones. His community contained hundreds of factory-constructed and -allocated apartment buildings, a kindergarten, elementary, middle, and high school, plus a hospital and a food ration "store." All Little Li knew— and all he seemed destined to know—was factory life. But with only one coupon per person for half a pound of pork and four eggs per month, Little Li also knew hunger.

Under Mao, China operated as a planned economy. In other words, there was no market. In many ways, Little Li's factory served as a microcosm for the rest of the country. Transactions were carried out through an allocation system: commands were made at the very top of the system, and people at the very bottom of the system followed accordingly. Those at the top of the system—the central government— made every decision: what to produce, how much to produce, and where to produce it; what goods people could consume, how much each person could consume, when they got to consume it . . . the list was endless. The factory workers did what they were told. If they were told to produce a thousand pipes, they produced a thousand pipes. If they were given half a pound of pork to eat for the month, they ate half a pound of pork for that month and no more. Alternatives were practically nonexistent. Similarly, the price of everything in the whole country, including the price of labor, or one's wages, was also determined by the central planning agency in Beijing. Wages were set low, but more importantly, they were set equally for people with varying degrees of education. Wages mainly increased with seniority or age, not at all based on one's qualifications. Education was not a factor.[1]

While the intricacies of the planned economy weren't high on Little Li's priority list, food was. Every month, Little Li and his older brother were tasked with bringing their coupon to the food ration store to pick up whatever items they were allocated for the month. One day a year—the factory's only vacation day of the entire year apart from public holidays—his family and the rest of the factory workers would collectively make their way to the state-owned food ration store to pick up an enormous supply of cabbages. Those cabbages were to last them the whole winter, the only vegetables they would see for six months.

In preparation for winter, factory members would pickle and preserve their cabbage in enormous, human-sized jars. The remaining fresh cabbage was carefully placed in an underground cellar and covered with a quilt to protect it from Jilin's bitter cold. Little Li and his brother were always tasked with retrieving a cabbage on the rare days their mom decided to cook fresh cabbage. Little Li's brother would always take the leap into the cellar: *Catch!*, his brother would yell, tossing the cabbage from the cellar up to Little Li. This was always Little Li's favorite chore. Despite the cold, winter did have its perks.

In 1975, toddling hand-in-hand with his brother on their monthly visit to the food ration store, Little Li and his brother stumbled upon a scene—two men from the factory, their hands tied, wearing tall, skinny hats, with shameful words written up and down the hats' five-foot length. Little Li recognized them. Those men were the same people his parents seldom spoke to, ones they scornfully referred to as "the intellectuals." Helpless, they kneeled in the town center as people yelled at them, berating them for the harm they inflicted upon society. Little Li's brother looked down at him and explained in words Little Li would later recall: "Chairman Mao says these are the bad men." Little Li was just coming of age during what would later be known as China's Cultural Revolution, so he had a hard time grasping how the scene before him was related to China's leader. Nonetheless, that day in Jilin's town center, Little Li was witnessing history unfold.

From toddling with his brother to walking confidently on his own two feet, Little Li came to notice pockets of factory workers on their breaks, chain smoking, huddled over makeshift tables or pieces of lined paper on the ground, moving wooden discs around on tattered chessboards. At four years old, Little Li won the first round of Chinese chess he ever played against his father. Emboldened by his victory, Little Li sat cross-legged in the factory workers' shadows and challenged them to a game. They delighted in—and often cursed—his unusual mastery of the game. The only thing that seemed to quell his hunger was chess. Watching a good match would consume him, from the opening move to checkmate. The rules were set and the goal was clear. Since there were three shifts of workers keeping the factory moving around the clock, there was always somebody to play with. What they knew about the game didn't come from books or formal teaching, but from years of playing one another after they got off work. Little Li would play with anyone who was willing—even if they were the intellectuals, the ones who had supposedly graduated from college—just so long as his parents didn't see him. Since the workers moved their bodies all day at the factory, he knew they wanted to work their minds after hours. From his very first match, Little Li dreamed of becoming a professional chess player, joining the national team, and sweeping tournament after tournament in China's capital, Beijing. All he'd ever known about Beijing came from the few adults in the factory who had visited the capital, or frayed books containing old, blotchy pictures of the vast expanse of Tiananmen Square. The city seemed like a different universe. He imagined that Beijing's successful citizens must feast on platters of dumplings and meat at each meal, luxuriating in gleaming cars that chauffeured them around town. Indeed, if China's citizens could somehow be sorted into a pyramid, Little Li was certain that it would be Beijing's citizens who would find themselves at the top. While he wasn't exactly sure where he would be situated in that pyramid, he did know that he'd find himself looking up at the Beijingers.

Just a few months later, in September 1976, the life that Little Li had become so accustomed to screeched to a halt. Sobs rose in the throats of adults around the factory. Flooded with alarm, he wondered: *Why are they crying? What happened?* Soon enough, some of the kids started crying too. Suddenly, he looked down—a little white flower, those worn at memorial services, had appeared in his hands. The lady who ran his daycare shuffled around the room, distributing flowers to each of the small children. She announced to them, tears pouring down her face—"Chairman Mao is dead. Chairman Mao is dead." Chairman Mao is dead? This didn't mean much to him. But for the rest of the country, this was monumental.

In the wake of Chairman Mao's passing, a sense of inexplicable unease set in at the factory. The wrinkles lining the faces of the factory workers with whom he played chess appeared deeper, more pronounced, their hushed conversations echoing eerily across the machinery. The old radio in the family kitchen buzzed with news of reform, a formal education system, and of Deng Xiaoping, who Little Li later discovered was to be China's next great leader. And then, in 1978, Little Li's mom sat him down, stating with little room for argument: *You're going to school.* The next day, for the first time in his life, Little Li attended school.

In the years that followed, both before and after school, Little Li's focus revolved almost exclusively around scrounging for food and playing chess. By the time he graduated to middle school, it had become clear that what he would learn wouldn't take place in the classroom. He often knew the answers to math questions before his teachers did. He finished the homework in a matter of minutes and understood the textbook concepts after just one read. But he didn't mind: more time for chess. It was all he could think about.

While it was true that few lessons in his middle school textbook had the power to divert his attention away from chess, one in particular stood out to him: the story of Fan Jin, the fifty-four-year-old peasant who devoted his life to trying—and failing—to pass the first round of the imperial exams during China's Ming Dynasty (1368–1644). This tale utterly mystified Little Li. He found himself reading and rereading Fan Jin's story in disbelief:

"How old are you this year?"

"I gave my age as thirty. Actually, I am fifty-four."

"How many times have you taken the examination?"

"I first went in for it when I was twenty, and I have taken it over twenty times since then."

"How is it you have never passed?"

"My essays are too poor," replied Fan Jin, "so none of the honorable examiners will pass me."[2]

Over *twenty* times? This commitment was unfathomable to Little Li: who would ever dream of taking an exam over and over again? And more importantly, why? While there were neither limits on age nor on the number of attempts to pass the imperial exams, Fan Jin invested an unthinkable amount of time and money in preparing for an exam that required rote memorization and recitation of Confucian classics, forgoing all else in the process. But, according to Little Li's shabby textbook, if Fan Jin passed, he would be transformed practically overnight from a farmer into an esteemed official.

One exam could change your fate—but at what cost? Years and years of life spent studying, it seemed. Little Li marveled at the stakes of such an exam. This account of the Ming Dynasty's social order read more like fiction than fact: in the factory, it was the intellectuals, the educated workers, who had been considered the lowliest sort since the day he was born, not the other way around. And, while he didn't much mind—his father's position as a crane operator at the factory promised comfort and safety for Little Li—his fate was almost inextricably bound to the factory. No amount of school, or chess, seemed likely to change that. As he closed his textbook, he wondered how he would have fared on the imperial exams. Days passed in a blur of chess games, and Fan Jin's story faded further each day from Little Li's mind.

Near the end of his middle school career, Little Li found that the chess competition at the factory was no longer what it used to be. There were few who could beat him, and it was becoming harder and harder to ignore the grumble in his belly. Finally, at age fourteen, the day arrived when he was to take the vocational high school exam, one that would determine whether he had the skills to assume his father's position at the factory. As he sat down to take it, he couldn't help but recall Fan Jin's commitment to his studies. He smiled wryly to himself. He was fortunate to have been born in today's China; otherwise, he may have been stuck taking one exam for the rest of his life. Luckily, the vocational high school exam proved easy for Little Li. Though passing the exam was no guarantee, he felt sure of a sufficient score. Sure enough, when the scores came back, his name was at the top of the city rankings. He was one step closer to fulfilling his destiny at the factory.

Little Li's uncle, however, had other plans for him. Little Li's uncle was the only person he knew who had attended college. Other than that, all Little Li knew about his uncle was that he had a very prestigious job in the faraway city of Beijing.

It just so happened that his uncle was visiting the week before another exam, one that Little Li had no intention of taking: the highschool entrance exam. As his eyes drifted shut, Little Li couldn't help but hear urgent whispers in the living room through the paper-thin factory walls. "Sister, things are changing. Education—Deng thinks it's important. If your boy goes to high school, he could go to college. He could be like me. He could escape. You must let him take the exam." Although his uncle's words echoed the new content he often tuned out in his factory's politics class, Little Li couldn't understand why it would matter for him. The new leader's education reforms had little to do with his life at the factory.

The very next week, a disgruntled Little Li found himself sitting for the high school exam, which he passed with flying colors. Little Li became the factory's star: they hung a big, red banner decorated with traditional Chinese calligraphy congratulating him so that everyone coming and going through the factory gate would read his name. While many of the factory workers couldn't yet fully appreciate the value of education in the wake of the Cultural Revolution, they still applauded high scores on exams, especially coming from one who had beat them time and time again in chess matches. That little kid, the one who grew up hovering around the elders, obsessing over chess—he was going to high school: Jilin No. 1 High School. And he was one of very few. At his factory, just eight out of roughly a thousand kids attended Jilin No. 1 High School. In a city of 4 million, the school was one of the few elite high schools in the province, and the only one in the city. Suddenly, his future at the factory seemed anything but certain.

CHANGING THE GAME: FROM CHESS TO GAOKAO

Things were a little different in high school. On his first day, Li walked into a cloud of smoke. Like the factory workers huddled around the chess boards, his teachers chain-smoked all day. But unlike the factory workers, these teachers had just graduated college. They were young, liberal, idealistic, and very unlike the uneducated teachers at the factory. They lived in the city, near the school, and knew things that Little Li couldn't have even dreamed of. They spoke of the wealth in Beijing, the newfound value that Deng Xiaoping placed on a college education, and the fantastic potential for China to reclaim its former greatness. They were strict, too. Every day, the teacher examined his students' uniforms from the front of the classroom: all the students, girls and boys alike, were required to have their hair cut short. One day, Li's classmate was asleep on the desk next to him. A teacher walked up to him, yanked him up by his hair, and dragged him into the next room for a haircut. His classmate's nap had exposed the long hair bunched at the nape of his neck, otherwise hidden from the teacher during inspection.

Eagerly listening to his teachers' stories each day, Li began to dream of life in Beijing. As he rode the creaky state-run bus in the dusky evenings, his dream of becoming a professional chess player dimmed. His mother and father no longer allowed him to play chess with the factory workers after school, demanding he focus on his studies, as they, too, began to recognize what Li's education might mean for his future. Around them, the educated workers, the intellectuals, who had been ostracized for many years, were now earning higher wages—bonuses, even—and were promoted to manage the other workers. The names of kids who attended university in Beijing began to appear at the gate of the factory. Education, it seemed, was becoming something worthy of respect. Li's parents wanted that respect for their son.

To dodge his parents' watchful eyes, Li snuck out during his free periods at school to play chess, a task that became more challenging with each passing day as his teachers zeroed in on him as a rising talent. His teachers never failed to scoff at Little Li when he took out his chessboard. "Forget these hobbies, boy, and pick up your books. There is no time for games here." Having nearly been caught sneaking out earlier that week, Li, with a heavy heart, arrived at an indisputable truth: the probability of making it to Beijing through chess was close to zero. He didn't even know if rumors of the existence of a national chess team were true, let alone how to win his way onto the team. But perhaps by graduating high school, he, like his uncle, would be chauffeured around, feasting on unlimited meat at every meal, working an important job. Perhaps he would no longer feel hunger. Perhaps he could ensure that none of his family would feel hunger either. After two years of attending high school in the city center, Li felt compelled to put aside his passion for chess. He would do whatever his teachers asked of him—they knew how to get to Beijing.

But it would take more than just graduating high school to get there. He needed to pass China's college entrance exam, the gaokao— "the highest exam"—and score high enough to earn a seat at a prestigious college in the nation's capital. Passing required mastery of six or seven subjects. All students had to take Chinese, math, politics, and English. Students in the social science track would take history and geography, whereas students in the natural science track would take physics, chemistry, and biology. Li always knew he would choose the science track. During his first year of high school, a history class left him struggling to understand its underlying logic. History seemed to be a collection of stories about emperors, but one question lingered: Why was one emperor praised as a beloved ruler while his successor was condemned as a tyrant? When Li learned that emperors often hired scholars to write official histories, it raised another question: if rulers shaped the narrative to glorify themselves and discredit others, how could anyone trust that those histories, as we read them today, are objective or true? In contrast, the clarity, structure, and objectivity of science made far more sense.

Those first two years in high school consisted of memorizing all the material that would appear on the exam. In year three, the curriculum shifted from memorizing content to taking practice tests. Each day, his teachers drilled him relentlessly on each subject. Any energy that Li might otherwise have spent on chess he quickly redirected to the exam: much like the game he knew and loved, the gaokao offered clear rules and an obvious goal—score higher than anyone else in your class. Test after test after test. Day after day after day. Never had Li been more prepared for anything in his life. Chess, for the first time in his life, was far from his mind. There was no more time for hobbies—only studying.

The science and math questions were easy. But since his parents didn't register the importance of reading, he never had books laying around his home. As a result, Little Li's Chinese test scores—particularly his essay scores, which represented half of the total score—lagged behind those kids in his class whose parents had gone to high school or college. Much to Little Li's confusion, almost every exam included some reading question or some essay prompt that asked him what he was doing for his country. *What am I doing for my country?* This perplexed him. *How can my classmates be doing anything for our country when they are as hungry as me? What am I missing?* Practice test after practice test, he failed the Chinese portion of the exams. But he remained hopeful, for his scores on the other subjects outranked everyone else's.

But then in April, not two months before he was scheduled to take the exam, his teachers stopped showing up to school, and the creaky buses—the ones that barely made it to and from the city center in the first place—stopped showing up altogether. Li sat in front of the black-and-white TV, the most expensive asset his family owned, and quickly gathered that people were protesting. Excitement bubbled up in him—he'd never seen protests before. His teachers, some local college students—they were all in the streets, speaking out against apparently corrupt government officials. But one thought persisted in his mind: what if he wouldn't make it to Beijing? What if he would never have the chance to leave the factory? What if all his time had been wasted studying for this exam? For all he knew, the exam that would decide his future would be canceled. Suddenly, the rules he relied on seemed anything but clear.

For a month, thoughts of Beijing completely consumed him. He couldn't tear himself from the TV, as news of the 1989 student movement and protests at Tiananmen Square flashed across the screen. Even in his tiny city, far away from the country's capital, he was experiencing the collective outrage of millions of China's youths. From his high school in the city center, Li would watch seas of protesters, his teachers among them, swarm familiar haunts. But almost as quickly as it had begun, Li watched those TV hosts disappear from the screen. Their replacements spoke of the strength and power of the Communist Party. No longer were protestors occupying the streets. While Li couldn't begin to understand what had taken place, he suddenly began to feel hope again, and with good reason. Shortly thereafter, the government released a particularly consequential announcement: the gaokao was now scheduled for July 7 through July 9, 1989.

On the morning of July 7, to support his son on the most consequential three days of his life to date, Li's father pedaled his son on the family bike all the way to the city center. He wasn't willing to rely on the creaky bus—not for those three days. Before he walked up the stairs to the test center, Li's father slipped something into Li's palm, whispering, "this will help fuel your mind through the gaokao." As he walked up the stairs, Li opened his hand to a bar of chocolate, tucked safely away in gleaming tin foil. Li could only guess where his father had acquired such a luxury. But with two to three subjects per day over the course of three eight-hour days, seventeen-year-old Li would need all the help he could get. He gratefully ate a small bite of the bar, saving some for the next two mornings. Hour after hour, he ground through each answer, from multiple choice to essay questions and everything in between. With each question he conquered, Li repeated to himself over and over again: this will get you to Beijing.

Unsurprisingly, Li struggled with the Chinese essay. His heart sank as he read the prompt: "You want to study history in college. Write a letter to a relative explaining why you want to study history." Panic set in, as he thought to himself, *I've barely taken any history in high school. I'm not one of those kids in the social sciences track. What am I supposed to say?* Even before seeing his score, Li knew deep down that he had failed that part of the test.

His father had taken three full days off work—unprecedented at the time—and waited patiently outside of the exam site. After each day, Li would join his father on the steps in front of the exam site, too exhausted to smile, and Li's father would pedal him back home on the family bike. Those three nights, Li's mom prepared beautiful meals for him, procuring some of the best food—a stewed whole carp fish caught fresh from the nearby Songhua Lake—for Li to eat. So much was riding on this exam.

Three days later, Li savored his last bite of the chocolate. Hours passed before he set his pen down once and for all. The exam he had obsessed over, the one that had consumed his life, forcing him to abandon his passion for chess, the one that was going to get him to Beijing, was suddenly no more. He was done. Emerging from his testing site, his thoughts flitted once again to Fan Jin. How ironic it seemed—just years ago, he had scoffed at Fan Jin's story and the idea of one all-powerful exam. And here he was, waiting for the news of a score that had the potential to change his life as he knew it. Perhaps his life wasn't as far from Fan Jin's as he once thought.

Then, the waiting began. Students' scores were publicly posted at school a month later, ranked from top to bottom. As soon as Li and his seven peers from the factory learned the scores were up, they rushed to school to see where they ranked. Eager to find his name, Li's heart soared when he finally spotted it. As expected, he had completely failed the Chinese test, earning a score he would never forget—67 out of 120—one of the lowest among over 600 students in his class. But Li didn't dwell on it. Despite the low score in Chinese, he had achieved one of the top scores in the province, securing his place at one of the thirty best universities in the country. His dream was within reach—he was going to Beijing.

· · ·

As he emerged from his testing site that fateful day, Li inadvertently stumbled upon an unlikely truth: he, like Fan Jin, had become obsessed with one of China's many exams. Fan Jin was persistent in his pursuit of success. Though Li could at first only laugh at Fan Jin, he eventually came to pursue success with a similar single-minded determination. And while both Fan Jin and Li wanted more than anything to pass their respective exams, what they really sought was this: a chance to move up China's social hierarchy. Though separated by the centuries, it was still the exam that would allow both of them to achieve their goal. But what is this so-called hierarchy that the pair obsessed over ascending? And why does the exam play such a critical role in doing so?

HIERARCHIES AND THE EXAM SYSTEM, PAST AND PRESENT

In ancient times, China's society could be split into four distinct classes, or the four occupations (士农工商). The gentry (士) ranked highest in the social order, followed by the peasants and farmers (农)—those who were seen to work for an honest living—the artisans and crafts-men (工), and finally, the merchants and traders (商)—those who sup-posedly used sordid tactics like marketing and cheating to make a living. No matter the class, none of these positions were hereditary. Initiated around 600 AD, and expanded around 1000 AD, the imperial exam system offered a pathway to join the gentry. Such a pathway meant that any man in China, regardless of his family background, had the power to change his social standing—or, at least, the illusion of it.[3] It was simple: he just had to get an education to pass the imperial exam. Becoming "educated" in ancient times would not teach a merchant the skills necessary to become an artisan, nor would it help a craftsman learn a farmer's trade. No—in ancient times, the "educated" were those who could literally memorize, from start to finish, several ancient texts deemed important by the emperor. An education served as preparation for only one task: taking the imperial exam. A passing mark on the imperial exam would move a person from any rank in the social hier-archy all the way to the top. In other words, one could be a farmer one day and an esteemed official the next. And yet, while there were no limits on age or the number of attempts to pass the imperial exams, test takers needed to invest an enormous amount of time and money to prepare for an exam heavily dominated by Confucian texts, forgoing work opportunities in the process. Like Fan Jin, many men devoted their entire lives to study. Most poor families could not afford to do so, even though they were technically eligible to sit for the exam.[4]

Men who had the resources obsessively devoted their entire lives to passing one of three exam levels. During the mid-Qing era (circa 1800), about 2.5 percent of the entire male population between fifteen and forty-five—at least 2 million men—would register for the first level of exams.[5] The higher the exam level, the more promising the rewards—from being exempt from paying taxes to earning a position in the emperor's inner circle. But each exam required candidates to memorize an increasingly large body of Confucian texts, which could take between a few years to several decades to accomplish, if they wished to pass. And usually, they didn't—during the mid-Qing era, China's male population was around 200 million. Given that the number of passing marks available for the entry-level exam was predetermined, even assuming a man could try to pass the exam ten times, the probability that he would pass was a measly 0.27 percent.[6] Nonetheless, the payoff was remarkable, driving hopeful men of means to sit for the exam. There was always more to study, always another level of the hierarchy to ascend. For that reason, there was no clear finish line for the majority of those attempting to pass the exams—lives were spent obsessing over the next rank. For the few who succeeded, passing one level was only the beginning.

When Fan Jin ultimately passed the exam himself, provincial officials flocked to his house, praising him for his ascent to the upper class. As promised, Fan Jin's life, along with his family and community, changed for good. Even though he was one of few, Fan Jin served as a poster child for the riches that passing the exam could bring. Everyone knew of somebody like Fan Jin. Just one story was enough to bring people back year after year, no matter how slim the odds.

And so, for over 1,300 years, the imperial exams served a far greater purpose than giving China's people a shot at wealth—they served as a societal ladder, allowing mere peasants like Fan Jin the opportunity to join the ranks of the high-level state bureaucrats. If only they tried hard enough, studied enough hours, and memorized enough classical texts, it seemed that they, too, could ascend the ranks. One of the most important institutions in Chinese history, the exam system influenced not only the competence of the bureaucracy but also the circulation of elites and the allocation of talent in society. It reinforced China's social hierarchy too, dictating who rose to the top and who remained at the bottom. Perhaps most important, it created the perception of social mobility among average citizens. The mere possibility of passing fostered a frenzied hope—an obsession—bringing millions of men back year after year.

That exam system persisted for over a millennium, but after years of mounting criticism, the Qing government abolished it. Shortly thereafter, the Qing dynasty itself fell in 1911. China entered a period known as the Republic Era, one marked by decades of political turmoil governed by changing factions.[7] In 1949, this came to an end when the Chinese Communist Party (CCP), chaired by Mao Zedong, established the People's Republic of China (PRC). This was the beginning of the China we know today.

After the momentous founding of the PRC, China's leaders faced a predicament: the new government lacked a social ladder, a channel through which officials could identify young individuals of promising talent, bureaucrats who could govern China. So, leaders built a new ladder: the gaokao, closely modeled after the historical imperial exams. While passing the imperial exams ensured men direct access to the bureaucracy, the gaokao worked a bit differently. The few who were able to successfully prepare and pass the exam would simply attend college. After that, however, the natural step for most was the government, or similarly prestigious work in the state sector.

But just shy of two decades later, China faced yet another critical juncture. Chairman Mao had become deeply distrustful of the elite intellectuals surrounding him—those who had gotten an education to take and pass the gaokao. While they had helped him rise to power in 1949, the elite began openly criticizing Mao, faulting his policies and the planned economy for triggering the Great Chinese Famine (1959–1961). Fearful of being overthrown, Mao decided he no longer needed their support. To delegitimize them, all he had to do was turn the social hierarchy on its head. What better way to rebel against the existing political order than to disrupt education, China's traditional avenue to the elite?[8]

By making use of his unique charismatic standing, Mao resorted to mass mobilization for political support. A spontaneous organization, the Red Guard was established in 1966 by college, middle school, and high school students who dropped out of school to answer Mao's call to rebel against the existing social order. This marked the beginning of the Cultural Revolution, a period characterized by a complete upheaval of the social hierarchy that had effectively organized China's people for over a thousand years. [9] Mao largely succeeded in suspending the social order: he shut down practically all aspects of the education system, from kindergarten to college. [10] Along with it, he suspended the gaokao. It was precisely for this reason that Little Li, his family, and the rest of the factory workers were entirely uninterested in education. During Mao's time, being educated was just short of a curse. The Red Guard raided the intellectuals' homes, burned their books and manuscripts, and subjected them to painful sessions of "study and criticism," much like the one Little Li witnessed that day in Jilin's town square. Many of them were arrested, jailed, or sent to labor camps in remote rural areas. Scientific research was paralyzed by political fear and lack of equipment and supplies; research in the social sciences and humanities had all but stopped. [11]

Having lived through the very end of the Cultural Revolution, Li was intimately familiar with a highly unusual time in China's history. Mao's Cultural Revolution established and enforced an alternate social order: for the first time since the emperors created the imperial exam system, an education was a one-way chute to the *bottom* of the social hierarchy.

The education system and the gaokao remained almost entirely defunct until Mao's passing, which marked the end of the Cultural Revolution. China trudged forward under Deng Xiaoping's leadership, but by the late 1970s, the planned economy of the Maoist era had left China in dire straits. The lack of incentives to work depressed productivity, smothered innovation, and led to widespread resource misallocation. Deng Xiaoping and his administration recognized the seriousness of the situation and promptly initiated a series of drastic reforms. Deng, like Mao and each emperor before him, turned to education to lay the groundwork for his agenda: almost right away, Deng's administration reinstated a formal education system. Along with it, they reinstated the gaokao. It was around this time that Li's family pushed him to go to high school, and later to take the gaokao. This decision changed Li's life and provided the government with another success story, another anecdotal bit of evidence to support the obsessive drive toward educational success. Half a century later, the gaokao remains at the heart of China's education system. With each passing year, students like Little Li hear of the exam system's promise: you too can change your future life path—you simply need to pass.

Passed from emperor to emperor, from Mao to Deng, from Fan Jin to Little Li, from then to now: China's steadfast obsession with their education system and the social hierarchy it supports has remained a historical tradition, despite a brief upheaval during Mao Zedong's rule. In dynastic times, the imperial examinations created a perception that education could change your fate, even though success stories were few and far between. But when the imperial exams were abolished, so too were the dynasties. Later, when Mao recognized just how powerful the education system had come to be—and the power of those who had successfully passed through the system—he turned it upside down, refusing to bow down to those who had sacrificed everything for a system he loathed. But Deng and his colleagues, realizing the centrality of the education system in China's society, reinstated an exam system. It is that same exam system that governs the lives of students today.

Few institutions stand the test of time—a millennium, no less. And yet, except for a very brief period during which Mao completely upended the social order, the promise of a life-changing passing mark has drawn countless individuals to obsess over the opportunities offered by the exam. From the imperial exams of China's dynasties to the gaokao of today, exams have, and continue to be, one of the most fundamental pillars supporting China's society.

RETURNS TO EDUCATION

Having just read the stories of Little Li, Fan Jin, and the hierarchies so central to China's history, it's likely that you're in the majority of the

global adult population, having received some sort of education—
you're literate. Many societies around the world have devoted exorbi-
tant amounts of time, money, and resources to their education systems.
Clearly, we've all agreed that education is important, and that more
education is better. Economists wanted to understand *why*. They found
two underlying reasons: consumption and investment.

"Consumption" is how an idealist might view education: students
enjoy going to school, and so their incentive for attendance is exactly
that—joy. They don't care about the possible financial outcomes associated with education down the line. But did Li attend school because
he enjoyed it? Throughout most of his career as a student, only a sliver
of his attention was devoted to learning. His passion was unquestionably for chess. And when he did begin to care about education, it was
not because he suddenly found joy in it. It was because he understood
its eventual payoff.

So, the more plausible explanation for many students—Li being one
of them—is investment. Although consumption is important—a kid
who loves reading and writing is likely to exhibit higher levels of moti-
vation in Chinese class than a peer who despises cracking open a book—
investment is the primary incentive behind receiving an education.
Students invest their time and energies today in order to benefit in the
future, like investing in and later selling a stock, ideally at a higher price.

For education, the sacrifice is twofold: money and time. Parents and
students around the world collectively invest tens of thousands of dollars in education, from preschool classes to doctoral degrees. As for
time, students certainly could have spent the many years of education
necessary for any sort of degree in a variety of other ways (like playing
chess or learning how to run machines at the local factory). Yet, despite
the monumental investment of time and money that go into eventually
receiving a degree, so many of us continue, year after year, to make
these sacrifices. This must mean that it's worth it—right?

To explain the "why" behind education, economists have settled on
a model known as "returns to education."[12] To estimate one's returns to

education, economists calculate how much each year of education is worth. This is calculated based on one measure alone: how much additional labor income (one's salary) each year of education can bring about. In the United States and most other developed nations, returns to one year of higher education are around 10 percent.[13] To understand what this number means, consider this example: a twenty-five-year-old college graduate in the labor market makes a hypothetical $1,400 dollars a month. Meanwhile, a twenty-five-year-old high school graduate makes $1,000. In this example, the college graduate makes about 40 percent more than the high-school graduate. This means that the returns to a four-year college education would amount to 40 percent, or 10 percent for each year of college.

Economists started to estimate returns to China's education starting in the 1990s. Until the mid- to late twentieth century, however, there were no official data available that allowed researchers to estimate the returns to education throughout the hundreds of years of the imperial exams. Based on the sudden change in Fan Jin's fortune, it's natural to assume that the returns would be high. In the twentieth century, Mao's disdain for education so painfully taken out on the so-called intellectuals during the Cultural Revolution brought returns to education to a resounding zero, if not a negative number. Even after nearly a decade of Deng and his colleagues emphasizing the importance of education, one year of schooling in 1986 would still only increase earnings by 1–4 percent.[14] And yet, beginning in 1988, returns to education began to rise until they leveled out with the returns of developed countries in 2001: 10 percent.[15] As is the case in most developed countries, they have remained at 10 percent since.

With rising returns to education has come renewed interest: the percentage of those between eighteen and twenty-four years old attending college per year has grown from about 1 percent in 1977, when Little Li's uncle took the gaokao the very first year it was reinstated, to 67 percent in 2021.[16] Among those who graduate high school and take the gaokao, 93 percent of students pass and go on to attend college. For these students, returns to education are on par with the rest of the world. But signs of the obsession with education are still everywhere in China.

In China today, returns continue to rest at around 10 percent. And yet, while China is by no means an outlier in terms of the effects that the education system exerts on postgraduate salaries, China's families *are* an outlier in their behavior. Hongbin and his team's research also shows that, on average, China's families put a staggering 17.1 percent of their entire household earnings toward education.[17] This is five times that of the global average.[18] And a fifty-five-country comparison indicated that China's students spent almost the most time studying after school—27 hours per week. US students studied 20.4 hours, and UK students studied 17.[19] Books like Amy Chua's *Battle Hymn of the Tiger Mother* have been acclaimed for revealing how Chinese and Chinese American families strive to instill the value and importance of an education in their child at a young age and drive their children to succeed above all else.[20]

As such behavior might suggest, with a 93 percent admission rate and 67 percent of students aged eighteen to twenty-four going to college, it is not a college education that students clamor for. No—now, it is an *elite* college education and the hidden benefits that come with it. Like China's society, the higher education system in China is its own hierarchy, resembling a five-tier pyramid designed by the government. At the top of the education hierarchy sit China's elite universities, which receive priority in government funding and resources over other universities. Below them are several thousand other four-year universities. These universities, designated Tier 2, Tier 3, and Tier 4, differ substantially in terms of their reputation and government-allocated financial resources. Finally, at the bottom of the pyramid sit two-year or three-year vocational colleges, which are similar to community colleges in the United States. Tier eligibility is determined by one factor alone: students' scores on the gaokao.

Within China's government-designated elite Tier 1 are the one hundred hallowed colleges to which all students taking the gaokao hope to be admitted.[21] The rate of admission to elite colleges in China is tragically low, falling somewhere around or below 5 percent. This is close to the rate of admission to Stanford University, one of the most exclusive universities in the United States. Note, however, that Stanford is one of many excellent colleges in the US. Hundreds of other excellent (and elite) schools admit a far higher proportion of applicants. UCSD, for example, has an admission rate of 25 percent. In China, however, *all* elite colleges—all one hundred of them—have this low acceptance rate. Of the 10 million students that take the gaokao, 5 percent of them—500,000—will gain admission to an elite college. And without that elite undergraduate college diploma, opportunities to climb China's social hierarchy are few and far between, a reality that we'll continue to expand upon throughout this book.

Given the extent to which students push themselves to earn a spot at an elite university, they and their families clearly recognize the importance of attending an elite college. Our research backs up what these families know to be true: students who attended one of China's 100 or so elite colleges have up to a 40 percent higher monthly average wage than students who earned the average 40 percent return earned by attending a non-elite college, Tier 2 and below.[22] However, the additional labor income from elite college education still cannot explain the degree to which China's families obsess over their child's education—indeed, even China's government is aware of the obsession and has taken steps to mitigate its power. From the tutoring industry to the real estate market, education and its many expenses have extended far beyond the four walls of the classroom. In the summer of 2021, top leadership issued a policy essentially outlawing tutoring, decimating an industry worth billions of dollars. The policy's explicit goal was to relieve the pressure on overworked students and families. And yet, anecdotal evidence suggests that the policy did little to achieve its goals.

Beyond China's borders, global news outlets continue to report on the obsession. In the *New York Times*, the *Wall Street Journal*, the

Washington Post, and on the BBC and CNN, headlines over the last ten years have read: "China's College Entry Test Is an Obsession"; "In Flooded China Town, Students Cling to Tractors to Get to College Entrance Exam"; "China's Cutthroat School System Leads to Teen Suicides," "Gaokao Season: China Embarks on Dreaded National Exams," and "10 Million Students in China Are Facing the Toughest Exam of Their Lives in a Pandemic."[23] One student posted a video detailing her test prep schedule. She woke up at 7 a.m. and outlined her studies for the day, taking breaks only to eat. She wrapped up her studies at 10:30 p.m. It was a Saturday.[24]

Considering both returns to elite and non-elite college education, the extent of China's families' behavior suggests that there is something more at play. Our many years of research on China's education system have indeed led us to another conclusion: it may just be the case that the returns-to-education model so carefully outlined in the economics literature cannot quite capture the real returns to education in China, a problem that we've come to believe is rooted in the way returns are measured. The economics literature focuses on one output only: labor income, or one's salary. In China, however, returns to education simply cannot be quantified in terms of income alone.

Consider our initial example: in the United States, or in most countries that have a market economy, education does indeed work like buying a stock. You buy the stock, and years later, you sell the stock. What you earn (or lose) is the difference between what you bought it at and what you sold it at. In China, selling the stock isn't as simple. What you get back does include the difference between what you bought it at and what you sold it at. This difference is what the returns-to-education model captures: your labor income. What it fails to capture, however, is a series of hidden returns that are far more challenging to measure. And though at first glance these hidden returns may not seem financial, they do ultimately translate into financial gain, albeit in a roundabout way. We believe that it's these "hidden returns" that explain why China is such an outlier in behavior despite the conventional returns-to-education model indicating that returns are on par with those of other countries.

Using this lens, we analyzed returns to education during Fan Jin's time with fresh eyes. It became clear that the returns-to-education model wasn't all that applicable. Today, returns to education are calculated using the number of years of education, with the underlying assumption that each year is valuable for one's labor income. Yet, during Fan Jin's time, years had very little to do with the return. Fan Jin's studying one year versus twenty years would make no difference to the return he eventually would receive if he one day passed the exam. When he *did* end up passing the exam, while Fan Jin's life may have changed, evidence suggests that his income, along with the income of others who also passed, changed only modestly. Instead, Fan Jin's father-in-law went from beating him to regarding him as "one of the stars in heaven," while the villagers, out of respect for the new elite in their midst, began funneling a steady stream of gifts into his home. These anecdotes alone are telling: the villager's respect for Fan Jin and generous behavior is rooted in their expectation that Fan Jin would be both powerful and useful in his newfound position. In other words, passing the exam gave individuals the power and resources, though not necessarily an enormous salary, that come with life as a bureaucrat at the top of the social hierarchy. That's not to say that Fan Jin wouldn't have acquired a relative bounty of resources thanks to his new status—it just wasn't by way of a large, formally bestowed income.

The economists' model of educational returns seems similarly ill-equipped to capture the returns associated with education today. Take, for example, a high-ranking bureaucratic job at an office in one of Beijing's state-owned enterprises. Such a position would come with a reasonable salary appropriately correlated with the years and prestige of education received. That income is what the returns-to-education model would capture. But it wouldn't capture the following hidden benefits.

First, finding a job in Beijing's state sector means immediate access to the Beijing hukou—effectively, a residence permit, and one of the most valuable permits one can hold in China. The Beijing residence permit is the only way that one can access local public welfare, including public school districts, housing purchase eligibility, and medical care. Holding a job in Beijing's state sector also amplifies those benefits that are attached to the residence permit. Instead of a house costing 10 million RMB, its market value, a state employee in Beijing would receive a discount and pay only 3 million RMB. Instead of needing to buy a multi-million-dollar apartment to secure the best schools for one's children in the most elite housing district, the benefits associated with a state job would waive school district requirements, admitting the employee's children to exclusive schooling with no extra effort from the employee. Benefits also include free medical care. In other words, a position at the top of the hierarchy—available only to one with a top-tier education—mitigates three of the largest expenses for most of China's families: housing, education, and medical care. Those employed in the state sector enjoy the hidden financial returns of an education in China.

And as you'll recall, it is nearly impossible for the average person to end up anywhere near the top of China's social hierarchy without the prerequisite of an *elite* education. Indeed, considering the hidden benefits—those that go well beyond labor income—it's clear that obsession with China's education system is a perfectly rational response. With the support of both anecdotal evidence, such as the stories of Fan Jin or Little Li, and a long historical tradition, the perception that education can change your fate runs deep in China—centuries deep.

EXCAVATING THE SYSTEM

For over a millennium, a testing system has prevailed, both reflecting and supporting China's social hierarchy. For Fan Jin and the few who conquered their exam, passing completely changed their lives. While the benefits of education and the social hierarchy the system upheld were briefly dismantled during the Cultural Revolution—which, ret-rospectively, is a blip on the radar of China's long history—they quickly returned after Mao's death, giving students like Li the opportunity to change his fate, too. Receiving—or not receiving—an education served as one of the most important deciding factors in one's life. This is no less true today.

Indeed, by receiving a college education, Little Li did change his fate. I, Hongbin Li, have witnessed economic transformation and reaped the benefits of the changing tides of leadership. One of very few among my peers—and among the 2 percent of those in my age group who went to college—I successfully earned my way to an elite college in the late 1980s without even recognizing what exactly it might mean for my future.[25] I just wanted to get to Beijing, to escape hunger, and to experience the opulence I had only ever dreamed about. After arriv-ing in Beijing in 1989, I began to recognize the power that the educa-tion system and the hierarchy it upheld wielded in China. I went on to earn a PhD from Stanford and wound my way back to China to work at Tsinghua University before returning to Stanford as a faculty mem-ber, struggling to understand the system that had given me my life and that shapes the lives of so many in China today.

In this pursuit, my co-authors and I have published over two dozen papers on various aspects of China's education system, many of which apply the returns-to-education model. Yet, a model that performs well in explaining the economic logic of a well-functioning labor market in the United States fails to capture the deep-rooted obsession with edu-cation and exams in China. For the model to actually be useful, it must be assumed that the returns represent true market returns—that is, income earned while working within the labor market. As economists studying China, however, we know that China has never operated as a true market economy, even though a large part of it has been converted from a planned economy to a market economy over the last forty years. This discrepancy—a market versus planned economy—is what accounts for the inability of the conventional model to capture the full returns. As far as we can tell, at least two features of the economy are not market based.

The first is that China does not have a Western-style labor market—indeed, the state still very much influences employment and employees' income, with over 36 percent of the urban labor force working in the state-owned sector as of 2021.[26] The second is that China's hierarchy has been defined for over a thousand years by the ruler of the era, a fact which is as true today as it was in the time of the emperors. The rulers dictate hukou, the universities, and later, the employment opportunities that are at the top of the hierarchy and the benefits associated with such status. This hierarchy exerts tremendous influence over people's behavior, preventing the market from running on supply and demand alone. And by sorting students into college tiers based on their gaokao score, China's education system is effectively a ranking system, or even a tournament. It is one of the first tools that the government wields in sorting its people into the hierarchy.

For these reasons—all of which we will expand on throughout the course of the book—we should exercise caution when applying the returns-to-education model. Despite the fact that we have spent the last few pages disavowing the traditional returns-to-education model, we will still refer to the model throughout this book, as it provides us with a useful framework through which we can analyze so much of the system, just so long as we keep these caveats in mind.

I was fortunate to be born at a time when getting into a good college in China was still possible, even with a failed Chinese test—not like today, when every point counts. I also had the freedom to spend most of my teenage years playing the game I was passionate about, rather than grinding through sixteen-hour study days seven days a week, as so many do now. This experience gave me the confidence to pursue what I love, without worrying about following the crowd. In hindsight, failing my Chinese test might not have been such a bad thing. Much of what we were taught in high school never really resonated with me, leaving space for me to explore society through my own lens. Ironically, the first Chinese history book I read at Stanford became one of my favorites—not because it provided straightforward answers, but because it offered a logical narrative and alternative hypotheses, with historians carefully building evidence to support one hypothesis over another. For the first time, history truly made sense.

Whether I like it or not, I was one of China's students who benefited from this system, leveraging it to climb the social hierarchy so carefully designed and maintained by the government. And yet, not everyone was able to reap the system's rewards. Take, for example, my own sister. She went to the factory's vocational high school and succeeded my mother in her position at the factory, just as I was meant to succeed my father. She married a middle-school classmate of mine. Today, they both still work grueling hours with little pay at the same graphite electrode factory where I grew up. What money they do have goes to educating their only child; they recognize what a good education will mean for their son's future. And while I followed in the footsteps of my uncle, my nephew is following in the footsteps of his. A tradition, passed down from generation to generation.

I, and Ruixue Jia, one of my co-authors whose story you'll hear in the next chapter, are a few of the lucky ones. Like many steeped in China's culture, we, too, are obsessed. So much more than money followed as we climbed the social ladder. Realizing that the available models couldn't explain our change in life outcome, we have devoted much of our professional lives to understanding the shape, contours, and nuances of our obsession. Through it all, we've come to believe that to understand the first thing about China today, from its families, government, and society to its role on the global stage, it's critical to excavate one of the foundational pillars that has supported the country for over a thousand years, one that survived and thrived at each critical juncture of the country's history: China's exam system.

2

Rules of the Tournament

o   o   o

"My boyhood was a pretty rough passage. . . . I came through it, yes. But that was luck, luck, luck! Think of the others!"

—Robert F. Wagner

Ruixue was adopted in a rural village of Shandong province, a twelve-hour drive south of Hongbin's hometown, shortly after her birth in 1984. Marked by poverty and its role as a Red Army revolutionary base, the surrounding area was shaped by its hilly terrain and relative isolation. Ruixue's nose was never far from a book, even as she trailed behind her grandparents while they toiled in the field. No matter how ragged the book or how many pages were missing, Ruixue carefully pored over the complex strokes that made up the characters, each worth their weight in gold. And one day, they practically would be.

The knowledge Ruixue gleaned from the words would serve her well. At age five, she enrolled in first grade at the local village primary school, nestled in a grove of old cottonwood trees. In the eyes of the villages' parents, the primary school informally doubled as a daycare center. About twenty of the village's children from grade 1 to grade 3 sat cramped together in a one-room schoolhouse, one that stubbornly remained upright despite years of turmoil. Dark and musty, the schoolhouse's windows had long ago been shattered. Planks of wood functioned as de facto glass, blocking sunlight or fresh air that may otherwise have filtered in. When classes ran into the evening, usually during independent study time, the teacher lit kerosene lamps. Since there was no light on the street, she and her peers trudged home with the lamps in hand. Ruixue woke with black soot lining the inside of her nose.

Ruixue attended school only when one of the three village teachers called for class. As farmers themselves, each teacher worked part-time, so the school didn't follow a set schedule. An unexpected storm meant that each student would find themselves in the field the next day, diligently picking cabbage for their teachers. Ruixue picked extra hard, hoping to gain recognition as a particularly dedicated pupil. And earn their recognition she did, both in and out of the classroom. She was faster than any other student in her class, picking up the lessons even faster than the cabbages. Recognizing her as a pupil with potential, the teacher would hover around her desk, patiently correcting each character stroke that she wrote out of line.

During summer vacations, she worked in the village fields. When she had any extra time, she gathered wheat or peanuts from other people's fields after the harvest. Without two coins to rub together, gleaning allowed her to continue attending school each year: the wheat and peanuts, after being dried, were accepted as tuition by the village teachers. But as three summers' harvesting passed and she graduated from third grade, she began to wonder what came next. While her teachers had barely graduated from middle school, she dreamed of more, though she knew not what that might entail. Her father had mentioned vocational school when she last saw him—was she destined to become a school teacher or a nurse?

Ruixue grew up alongside a big group of friends—the elderly folks in the village. After long hours working in the field, they'd all come together and sit down for a game known to the villagers as "stones and branches." Ruixue was often tasked with gathering the pieces necessary from the street. She would painstakingly lay out the board with branches she'd found, then give her elderly opponent the stones, as she always opted for the familiar, smaller twigs for her pieces. After each game Ruixue won, one of her closest friends would say, "We know you must be very clever to win so often. Though you never met him, know that your great-grandfather was a learned man. You remind us so much of him." Although she knew that she was adopted by her grandparents and their son at a very young age, and thus bore no resemblance to her great-grandfather, she accepted these kind words with a smile. She wondered whether she might one day also become a learned person.

Her passion for learning drove her to sit for the middle school entrance exam. Passing that exam would be her only chance to move forward in her pursuit of education. Luckily for Ruixue, this was not an obstacle. For many of her classmates, however, the exam ended their academic career—especially for the girls with younger brothers. Most of the village families only earned enough to send one child through school, and their sons would be prioritized without question, even if the girls had earned a passing mark. Without Ruixue's drive to succeed at tests or the special attention and words of encouragement from teachers, however, her classmates' education in that dark schoolhouse proved too meager to satisfy many of their prospects.

The middle school was too far to bicycle every day from Ruixue's village. Luckily for her, Ruixue's adoptive father was a teacher at the middle school. More than most, her father knew how few of the village students, especially girls, could enroll at the middle school, owing to the poor quality of their primary school education. Noting her talent for testing, he looked seriously at Ruixue, who stood wide-eyed on the steps of the middle school. *What would you like your future to look like? Would you like to attend vocational school? High school? The choice is yours.* For Ruixue, the answer was clear. Like the people she'd spent years reading about in the dusty old books, she, too, wanted to escape the countryside and travel to cities, to keep pursuing the knowledge she felt sure was just beyond her fingertips in the rural countryside. While she didn't understand the rules of the game she was playing, her father did: if she, a poor girl from the rural countryside, was to opt for high school over vocational school, she might be able to attend university. But it would be an uphill battle. First, she'd have to graduate middle school and earn a sufficiently high mark on the high school entrance exam to attend high school, preferably the best of the two county high schools. Then, after making her way through three years of high school, she'd have to beat out everyone in the province on one final test that would decide her fate: the gaokao. But achieving these scores would be no easy feat: all the king's men and all the king's horses crossing a single-plank bridge. That is how her father—and so many in the country, as she later learned—described the gaokao. And as he reminded her, time and time again, the only way she would ever cross that single-plank bridge was through hard work and effort. Only those who invested everything they had in the exam could succeed.

From that day onward, Ruixue persisted with a single-minded determination: she wanted nothing more than to lead the king's army. She conquered the first challenge, passing the middle school entrance exam at the top of her class, which ensured her a spot at the No. 1 High School in the county. With that passing mark, she left many of her classmates behind, even those who had also earned top marks—their families needed their income as soon as possible, and vocational school guaranteed that in just two years.

She was also forced to move yet again, away from her middle school to the high school. Her grandparents were a little over an hour away by bike, and she couldn't afford to waste any valuable study time on commuting. She chose to live in the dorms like all her other classmates from rural villages. And with a short haircut and a simple tracksuit uniform that matched that of every other student in her school, her morning and evening routines occupied as little time as possible. Every moment of her day, from dawn to dusk, was spent on practice problems. The crimson red government banners draped around her school advertised the benefits of hard work and effort in preparing for the exam, which only further reminded Ruixue of her father's words at every turn: if only she tried hard enough, could she lead the king's army.

The first two years of high school revolved exclusively around learning all the material included on the gaokao. But instead of three part-time teachers assigned to teach three grades of every subject, there was one teacher per subject in each grade. Instead of a middle school education, these teachers had graduated from colleges with degrees designed specifically for teaching. Ruixue quickly noticed that each teacher thought their subject was the most important. At the top of the high school's hierarchy were the teachers whose subjects were featured on the gaokao, and at the top of *that* hierarchy stood the teachers whose subject represented the largest proportion of exam points. Ruixue seldom attended physical education class, though not by choice. Her math teacher held them over every day, scoffing at the other subjects—they would do them no good on exam day. While Ruixue would have appreciated the exercise, she couldn't help but agree. Noticing how she excelled, the teachers spent extra time going over the few questions she missed, taking care to ensure she understood. Student scores on the gaokao were released each year to the entire province by subject matter, and teachers' promotions depended on their students' scores.

Constantly looking to improve her scores, to work harder wherever she possibly could, Ruixue would devour the small booklets that the teachers distributed for extracurricular reading. The contents of those booklets were nearly identical: students who had passed the gaokao and attended the most elite universities in all of China wrote about their experiences, highlighting the myriad benefits of their newfound knowledge and status. Each of their stories reiterated the power of hard work. Ruixue dreamt of one day receiving an invitation to write about her own experience.

After two years of painstakingly learning the content that would appear on the gaokao, Ruixue and her classmates took practice tests nearly every week. On the first full-length practice exam, Ruixue scored second in her entire high school. After the test, each student's scores were publicly ranked and printed, one for each student who had taken the exam. The teacher of the class walked around, distributing the same sheet of paper to each student, taking special care as usual to stop at the students who had scored particularly well. That day, the rankings sheet looked more like a golden ticket—a ticket to the vibrant cities Ruixue had only ever read about in her dusty old books. In order for any of it to matter, she realized she'd have to remain in second for the final year of high school, right up until she took the real gaokao. The girl ranked first must be working harder, which only drove Ruixue to find more minutes to study where there were seemingly none. Since the last year of high school exclusively focused on exam practice, there would be no new material. She worried constantly—would one of her classmates breeze past her? Since she was competing with the entire province in the rankings, if she wasn't leading the king's army at her own school— even though it was seemingly the best one—she worried that there was someone just miles away investing more time, more effort. And so she only strove harder in her studies.

Day after day, test after test, Ruixue firmly held her position at the front of the king's army. The local tractor company offered to sponsor the first-place winner's college tuition, and she was determined. But when the big day came, she scored fourth. While not the first place seat she was angling for, it proved good enough: she was going to leave her rural village behind, escaping the shadow of the cottonwoods once and for all. She had secured a seat at an elite university in the heart of Beijing.

Her neighbors and friends in the village gathered to congratulate her: soon, they joked, she would earn her place among the "sitting" jobs. The villagers divided jobs into the "standing" ones and the "sitting" ones—if one worked in the field or the factory, they would stand; if one worked a white-collar job, they sat. Of course, a sitting job—one in a government office no less—would be the best of the best. Her days of picking cabbages were behind her.

On a muggy morning in late August, the summer after the gaokao, Ruixue boarded the train to Beijing, waving goodbye to her grandparents. Every one of her years up to that moment was imbued with purpose: excel on her tests, climb the rankings, go to college. And now? She was leaving it all behind to reap the rewards of her hard work.

The train raced past countless villages just like hers—mud-brick homes, fields, and trees, as far as the eye could see. She couldn't help but remember a story she'd read in middle school out of the faded pages of a worn magazine. In the story, "The Child from the Forest," Sun Changning lived a grueling life in the forest among the trees but chose to travel thousands of miles to Beijing where his musical talent would finally get recognized. While she might not have had a talent like his, Ruixue had escaped those trees too. She was bound for the city.

· · ·

When I, Ruixue, took the gaokao, China's meritocratic testing system seemed to promise students like me equality in facing the gaokao, equality in accessing the brighter future that higher education all but guaranteed to students from all walks of life—the rural poor to the urban rich, and everyone in between. While there was little consistency in my earlier years, one message followed me wherever I went, practically becoming my own personal mantra: if only I tried hard enough, if only I invested enough hours—more than my competitors, at least—I could succeed. From the government banners draped around my school to the encouragement from everyone I trusted, my deep belief in the equality of the exam was only confirmed by my success. Indeed, there seemed to be a clear one-to-one correlation: hard work and effort directly translated into success. I had no reason to think the system was anything but fair. In retrospect, I had no time to consider an alternative.

And yet, a niggling suspicion began to take root in those early days as I reflected on the students walking Beijing's university sidewalks by my side. It was over the course of those four years that I was suddenly exposed to the realities of a system I had felt so certain were designed to help students like me succeed. But I couldn't prove what I began to suspect—not then, at least.

· · ·

Among the skyscrapers of Beijing, the first year passed in a blur. Ruixue stood out like a sore thumb everywhere she went. The price of everyday goods was unimaginably high: a haircut cost twenty times what it cost in the village, so she learned how to cut her own. When there was a talent show, her peers sang pop songs that she'd never heard of. Ruixue recited a long poem she learned from a dusty magazine. Where her classmates wore their trendy new clothes, Ruixue stuck to her trusty high school uniform tracksuit. When her classmates went out on the weekend, Ruixue went to the library. One of her good friends was the librarian, and she introduced Ruixue to the existence of internet activism. There, she discovered a whole corner of the internet devoted to dismantling the one-child policy. For the first time, she wondered if such a policy had led to her adoption.

Very soon, her classmates picked up on her knack for the material—a knack that certainly surpassed their own abilities, and even most of the other rural students'—and would come to her with their questions. Ruixue was happy to oblige. As usual, Ruixue's high exam scores and knowledge about obscure books protected her, earning her status and respect among her peers. It was because of her willingness to help that her classmates didn't make fun of her when she asked who they were always talking about—Princess Diana? She'd never even heard of her.

It seemed that the rural students comprised a measly percent of the population at her school. They were easy to spot. Like Ruixue, they were timid, and often appeared to be somewhat lost amid the sea of colossal buildings around campus. Ruixue quickly noticed that one of the girls in her dorm hailed from a rural county in southern China. Unlike Ruixue, however, the girl was of the Zhuang ethnic minority. When Ruixue introduced herself, the girl was quick to point out—*I didn't get the extra points on the gaokao*. Her words made Ruixue recall a lecture from one of her high school teachers, during which he encouraged students who belonged to an ethnic minority to indicate the fact on their college application files. She knew that students would automatically receive a small number of extra points if they did so, and every point counted. However, according to her friend, the Zhuang ethnic minority was not considered "minor" enough—it was one of the biggest ethnic minority groups in China—and thus the girl was not eligible for the bonus points in college admission. Either way, Ruixue didn't care. She and the girl became fast friends, bonded by their shared rural background.

One day, recognizing her as a student in need of some spare change (her high school uniform may have given her away), a professor approached Ruixue about tutoring a high school girl. Tutoring? She assumed that the girl was exceptionally behind in her studies; maybe she had gotten sick and missed some class. But Ruixue needed the money and the family was paying: one session alone paid as much as one week of Ruixue's high school living expenses.

On her way to the tutoring session, Ruixue meandered by an impressive-looking high school, well-dressed parents and uniformed students gathering around its imposing entrance. Ruixue wondered— was that where all urban students attended high school? It was hard to believe—her high school was a fraction of the size, and utterly lacked the pomp that this school exuded.

Minutes later, Ruixue found herself in front of an enormous gate guarding an equally enormous apartment complex. Keeping her eyes down, trying to avoid drawing too much attention, Ruixue quietly knocked on the door. Her knocks were soon answered by a tall, unassuming girl: Nan Nan. Ruixue was there to teach Nan Nan English.

Right away, Nan Nan explained the situation at hand: many of her classmates had studied or traveled abroad. This put Nan Nan at a disadvantage in her school's rankings—her classmates would outperform her on the English portion of the gaokao. Obviously, she had to have an English tutor to bring her to their level. Right now, she ranked in the middle of her class, but her parents believed that she could achieve more. That is where Ruixue came in. Besides, practically all Nan Nan's classmates had an English tutor, regardless of whether they'd gone abroad. But given Ruixue's rural background, how could Ruixue teach her English? As it happened, the English portion of the gaokao focused largely on grammar. Although Ruixue had never met any foreigners, let alone native English speakers, before coming to Beijing, she had memorized the grammar.

Ruixue could hardly believe her ears—Nan Nan's family had hired somebody—her—to boost Nan Nan's scores on the gaokao? Nan Nan hadn't missed school? While it all seemed so laughably frivolous in comparison to the scant resources at her fingertips prior to taking the gaokao herself, Ruixue quickly realized that Nan Nan and her family were not alone. Soon enough, Ruixue began frequenting job posting boards, finding no shortage of tutoring requests. Almost daily, Ruixue found herself in homes tutoring wealthy urban students whose stories so closely resembled Nan Nan's: they simply wanted to get ahead of all the other students in the rankings and needed some extra help to do so. They had money, which gave them access to the best possible pool of tutors: students at the local elite universities who had just taken the gaokao and clearly performed quite well.

Not only that, but Ruixue soon noticed that all these families were concentrated in some of Beijing's wealthiest neighborhoods. Without fail, these students attended the nearby high schools, which were usually in close proximity to the elite universities. Ruixue began to piece together that it was these high schools that sent students to the best universities in all of Beijing. When Ruixue asked Nan Nan what this was all about, Nan Nan whispered that her parents had paid to buy a house in the prestigious local middle school district, which gave her the education she needed to test into the best high school.

Her head spinning, Ruixue somehow sympathized with Nan Nan and the rest of the urban students: the options to improve upon their scores—from buying a house to hiring tutors across every subject area featured on the gaokao—almost seemed to be a burden for some of these urban families, though at least they had the option to do so. Meanwhile, Ruixue's rural peers had no options at all. As that year passed, each day marked a new discovery, some new rule that governed the game she had played without even realizing it.

That summer, Ruixue returned to her village. Wandering the streets in the shadow of the cottonwoods, she found herself noticing how cracked the mud-and-brick homes seemed, and how weathered many of the villagers appeared. Life here was far harder than she had ever realized. Rounding a corner, she bumped into her old friends, who still played the same game, though with different stones and branches. They cajoled her into joining—*what, have you forgotten how to play our game?* Ruixue smiled, and joined. As they set the pieces up, Ruixue asked after her former classmates. Most of them, she learned, still lived in the village, having started families of their own. Some, however, had ventured to nearby cities to find jobs working in a factory. They looked at her, their tone suddenly serious: *don't forget your grandparents once you make it big in Beijing.*

• • •

In recent years, a Chinese slang term, "small-town swot" (小镇做题家), has emerged on social media, shedding light on the hidden side of success for rural students like me. The term is much like the English idiom "to be a big fish in a small pond," though perhaps crueler. The small-town swots are known for their exceptional test-taking abilities, which grants them access to elite universities far outside their rural ponds. But when they depart from their little rural pond as big fish, they believe they will maintain their status as big fish, rising to prominence and success in a pond far bigger than they had ever anticipated. But their hopes and dreams are for naught—in the eyes of the urbanites, those small-town swots are nothing in the big pond, lacking the social sophistication, resources, and experience necessary to succeed.

While the term itself may not have circulated on social media when I first attended college, the underlying attitude toward rural students was one I had internalized. In retrospect, I recognize that as a college student, I unconsciously sought to distance myself from this demeaning stereotype. I read extensively, provided assistance to my peers in their studies, and engaged in policy debates organized by the librarian, hoping to become an intellectual akin to those found within the pages of my books. Now that I am older, I embrace my identity as a small-town swot with a deep sense of connection. In fact, I wish that all rural children could have the opportunity to first become small-town swots, as it implies that they, too, can access an elite college education.

And yet, it was painfully obvious how I was one of the few small-town swots at my university. As I gradually became equipped with the tools necessary to build the case that perhaps China's education system was not as it seemed, a realization that had dawned on me as I flitted in and out of the homes of Beijing's wealthiest families, one question in particular drove me: how accessible could the system be, when I was one of very few to leave our village?

As Hongbin and I began our research, one thing became increasingly apparent: China's gaokao is relatively *inaccessible,* a far cry from a system sold by the government and understood by those around me as fair and equal. Indeed, we soon came to see those three days of testing in June as the final game in a countrywide tournament that China's students spent the majority of their lives up until that point preparing for. For those playing, it's less about learning and more about winning, climbing the ranks whenever possible.

The gaokao is the tournament's playing field. Over the course of several testing days, students either emerge victorious or defeated—there's hardly any in-between. Administered on the same few days across all of China, the gaokao is taken by over 10 million students each year. Each student's score on the gaokao is compared to every other student's score in their province, and it is only by knowing how well others are performing that one can gauge one's own performance. This is because the government determines the cutoff score for college admission after students take the gaokao, ensuring that only around 4–5 percent of China's top-scoring students can gain admission to elite colleges. As such, students' admission is entirely determined by their performance relative to how their peers score on the gaokao. This means that to guarantee their own seat at the college of their choice—one of China's most elite universities—each student must score higher than at least 95 percent of all test takers. Like every good game, that tournament—the biggest tournament in the world—has its rules.

The rules are neither fair nor publicly acknowledged—it was only in retrospect that I began to understand what the rules were. Yet, with the information disadvantage growing ever smaller owing to the technology connecting rural and urban platforms, most playing the game today—those students opting to take the gaokao (or the parents playing on behalf of their children)—largely understand what they're getting into. It's this playbook that governs the only tournament that can effectively allow players to climb China's hierarchy.

After reading my and Hongbin's stories, it's likely that you now understand some of these rules. Our experiences differed in some ways, with over a decade of remarkable change separating us. Hongbin lived an urban factory life in the midst of China's dramatic social and economic changes, and I, a small-town swot, helped my family farm in rural fields. But Hongbin and I both found ourselves playing relatively trivial games in the streets as we bided our time until our next exam. While we chose to play those games on the street corners of our youth, we also found ourselves unwittingly participating in another game—part of the most widely played tournament in all of China: the gaokao. While the rules of childhood games are clear and fair no matter your background, we cannot say the same for the exams. We're here to explicitly open the playbook, rule by rule.

THE REGIONAL QUOTA SYSTEM

One of the most important sources of education inequality today is rooted within an age-old system: the regional quota system. But to understand the quota system, you have to first understand the hukou system with which the quota system is deeply intertwined. China's hukou system is complex, intimately governing the lives of every single one of China's 1.4 billion citizens.[1] The hukou serves as a household registration system assigned at birth; it is often likened to a caste system. The system assigns social benefits based on one's place of birth. Though we'll explain the implications of the system at length, what's important to note is this—every student across China is mandated to take the gaokao within their hometown province written on their hukou. As such, Ruixue was mandated to take the gaokao within Shandong province.

Within China, the Ministry of Education decides what percentage of students each university is allowed to admit from China's thirty-one provinces. Contrary to what one might expect, the quotas are not based on population. Instead, all colleges set higher admission quotas for local students. For example, as indicated by the administrative gaokao data Hongbin collected when working at Tsinghua University, while the population of Shanghai represents less than 2 percent of the entire country, Fudan University in Shanghai admits 53 percent of their students from Shanghai. But, as with China's primary, middle, and high schools, China's colleges are unevenly allocated across the country, and every single one of China's elite universities are in a few provinces with major urban centers. As such, students living in major urban centers with a higher concentration of elite universities have a significantly better chance of gaining admission to China's elite universities.

Beside the typical urban bias, the quota system also favors provinces with a sizable ethnic minority population, a reality that reflects the political consideration of the central government. Coupled with the fact that minority students receive bonus points for their minority status, such a policy has often stigmatized minority students at elite universities. Indeed, conversations around affirmative action are charged and explain why Ruixue's friend was eager to explain that she did not enjoy the benefits associated with some minority groups.

Taken together, the urban bias and the government's political considerations imply that the most disadvantaged provinces in the quota system are those in the middle of the country, far from major urban centers. They have few colleges, even fewer elite colleges, and are not regions with high concentrations of ethnic minorities. Yet, these provinces still have some of the largest populations in the entire country. While the logic behind the allocation system has never been formally disclosed to the public, some data show that the five highest admission rates of China's top-100 colleges are in Beijing, Shanghai, Tibet, Tianjin, and Qinghai, while the "middle" provinces—Henan, Anhui, and Ruixue's home province of Shandong—are among the lowest. Hailing from one of the "middle" provinces, Ruixue's success was highly unlikely from the moment she was legally registered as a citizen of Shandong province.

This also means that students in Beijing and students in Shandong are held to a different standard. According to data from the Ministry of Education, while the top 14 percent of students' scores from Beijing and Shanghai are accepted by elite universities (China's top 100), only the top 3–4 percent of scores are accepted from Ruixue's province, Shandong. Naturally, such a standard contributes to a highly competitive atmosphere. Each student is competing against the student next to her—and every other student in her province—to earn one of the coveted seats at the top. The room for error is negligible—every point counts.[2]

Ruixue and her coauthor Torsten Persson's research revealed that this is true to the extent that individuals are willing to change their legal ethnic identity.[3] In an online forum group, a father lamented his experience,

> I went to register the birth of my child a while ago. I am a Han man and my wife is a minority. I told the police that I want my child to be a Han. The police kindly suggested that I choose minority [status] for the child. She said that one extra point means surpassing thousands

of competitors in the gaokao, and that I should bear responsibility for my child's future.

Especially for those living in the middle provinces that are at a more extreme disadvantage like Ruixue, the extra points available for students with ethnic minority status are, to many parents, worth their child's identity, even though an ethnic minority distinction may carry discrimination down the line.

Taking all this into account, another rule becomes abundantly clear: where you are born will determine your chance of accessing China's colleges. But perhaps equally as important as your province is where you were born in that province, or rather, whether you were born in a rural area or in an urban area. Note that while students in Shandong province are competing against every other student in Shandong province, they are *not* competing against students in any other province. This also means that Ruixue and Nan Nan were never actually competing against one another—they belonged to different provinces within the quota system. However—and this is the important bit—if Nan Nan was born in Shandong province in a relatively wealthy city, she would likely still have access to resources beyond that of Ruixue's wildest dreams. In that case, Nan Nan, a Shandong urbanite, and Ruixue, a Shandong small-town swot, would be competing with each other. This exposes another one of the rules of the tournament: the rural-urban divide.

THE RURAL-URBAN DIVIDE

One of the fundamental rules of the exam system's playbook became increasingly clear as Ruixue wound her way through the education system all the way to university: rural students are at an extreme disadvantage when it comes to accessing a college education. While Ruixue was testing at the top of her class in the rural Linshu County, what she didn't realize was that students in Beijing, Shanghai, and every other urban center, including in Shandong, were playing what seemed to be an entirely different game with top-of-the-line resources. So many urban students had the opportunity to attend high school, even the ones scoring lowest in their class. This wasn't even in the realm of possibility for Ruixue and her classmates—unless you were the best of the best in a rural area, middle school, high school, and college were out of the question. But even if Ruixue's father had taken her to the city of Linyi to attend elementary or middle school to study with Shandong's urban students, Ruixue still wouldn't have been able to register as a student in even the worst of Beijing's schools, the ones that Nan Nan and her parents wouldn't even consider attending, owing to the hukou system. While the hukou system legally identifies individuals based on the province of their birth, it goes one step further, cleaving China's people into two distinct groups—agricultural and nonagricultural, rural or urban.

Every citizen in China has either an urban hukou or a rural hukou. Until she attended college, at which time the government granted her a temporary urban hukou that would last the duration of her college career, Ruixue held a rural hukou. With few exceptions, rural hukou holders can only access schooling, healthcare, pensions, and other social services in rural areas, which is why Ruixue wasn't eligible to attend school in an urban area. Clearly, services offered in cities to urban hukou holders tend to be much better than those offered in rural areas to rural hukou holders. In this context, consider the elite institutions to which Nan Nan's parents battled to secure Nan Nan a seat. Like Ruixue, rural students have no such choice; most students are eliminated from the game before it even begins.

Despite the outsized influence the hukou system exerts on China's people today, it is a relic of reforms under the planned economy implemented by Chairman Mao in 1958 to support urbanization and industrialization. By heavily taxing China's poorest—the rural peasants—the government subsidized urban people and industrialization throughout the planned economy.[4] The government knew who to tax—the farmers—because farmers were those who held rural hukous. Naturally, the urban workers were able to dodge this fate. Despite economic reforms that render the rationale behind the original system moot, the hukou system remains in place today, affecting hundreds of millions of rural students' chances at climbing the hierarchy vis-à-vis college education.

Though they can face the unlikely odds of testing into an urban high school if they can afford to buy property in an urban city center in their province, students with a rural hukou like Ruixue are mandated by law to attend a rural elementary and middle school. The quality of rural education lags far behind the quality of urban schools in more ways than one—where Nan Nan's teachers were well educated, often holding a master's degree, Ruixue's primary school teacher had barely graduated middle school; where Nan Nan attended class in beautiful, well-lit buildings, Ruixue and her classmates were sequestered to a one-room, lantern-lit schoolhouse. As a result, even if a student's parents secured property in an urban center in the province on their hukou, such circumstances make it exceedingly unlikely that a rural student could stack up to an urban student on testing day. Unsurprisingly, urban students have higher attendance rates, higher academic performance scores, and higher rates of educational attainment than their rural counterparts by significant margins. Not only that, but many rural students face a health crisis—they are undernourished and lack basic necessities, like health care. How are rural students expected to perform against urban students twelve years later on the gaokao?[5]

Simply put, unless many factors pan out in their favor—or, like Ruixue, they are exceptional test-takers—they cannot compete. Indeed, unless students test into one of the nation's most elite high schools, a process that requires buying property in an urban area, excellent scores, and sky-high tuition fees, rural students are guaranteed one thing: they cannot attend the nation's most prestigious colleges. Research by

Hongbin and his coauthor Binzhen Wu estimated that the chance of getting into two of China's top universities—Peking University and Tsinghua University—is close to zero if the student did not attend one of the top 10 percent of high schools in China.[6] Recall that rural hukou holders are, in most cases, legally ineligible to attend the top 10 percent of high schools in China precisely because they do not hold an urban hukou, as nearly every one of those schools are situated in urban centers.

In addition, an urban student like Nan Nan has options if she scored lower than she anticipated. Why? Higher-income urban families can afford to send their children to an extra year of high school so that they have a chance to retake the gaokao. Repeat takers typically score higher, and within China's top two universities, over 10 percent of admitted students are repeat gaokao takers, as shown by Hongbin and Binzhen Wu. For rural students like Ruixue paying their tuition in dried peanuts, repeating a year is out of the question.

Bearing all this in mind, it is no wonder that fewer rural students will end up taking the gaokao than their urban counterparts. Remember, in Ruixue's county, only the students who attended high school in the two available high schools were eligible to attend college. Meanwhile, urban students are faced with remarkably fewer obstacles in accessing a high school education.

The statistics look grim for rural students. In 2003, just three years after Ruixue took the gaokao, only 7 percent of rural youth from poor counties took the gaokao and accessed any college. The 93 percent who didn't take the gaokao likely dropped out of school before accessing high school, having failed one of the entrance exams, or because they failed to be accepted by colleges once they did take the gaokao. For urban students, that number amounted to 48 percent. In other words, urban students were a staggering six times more able to access any college in China than their rural counterparts. Meanwhile, access to elite colleges—the true game-changer for students—is even more unattainable for rural students: in 2003 only 0.6 percent of rural students were able to access China's elite universities, as shown by Hongbin and his colleagues.[7] In 2015, these statistics did not look much better—while the disparity has shrunk, still only a meager 35 percent of all rural students could access college, which stands in contrast with the 51 percent of urban students who could do so.[8] Ruixue defied the odds in accessing an elite college education, overcoming the powerful rule that has held rural students back for decades. For better or for worse, her story became one that provided hope for the next generation of rural students.

THE COSTS OF PLAYING THE TOURNAMENT

As it often seems, our final point boils down to money: which groups have it and which groups don't. In 1986, China's government introduced its compulsory education system. The policy effectively mandated that students across China would receive nine years of education—the equivalent of a primary and middle school education—paid in full by the government. While the government's slow rollout of the policy meant that Ruixue wasn't able to reap the benefits of the new system, it may not have changed all that much in the end: for students and families today, China's education system is one of the most costly in the world.

Shortly after taking office in 2012, China's new administration promised to alleviate the "three mountains" plaguing China's people: education, housing, and health. Research by Hongbin and colleagues has supported the reality behind one of those metaphorical three mountains: on average, families with students enrolled in China's education system contribute approximately 17.1 percent of their entire household earnings to education and 7.9 percent of household expenditures.[9] For context, families around the world contribute roughly 2–3 percent of their household expenditures to education. These numbers suggest that China's families spend more money on their child's education than most anywhere else in the world. But with a compulsory education system in place for decades and relatively low high school and university tuition, why?

While primary and middle school are free, as mandated by the compulsory education system, students must pass both the middle school entrance exam and the high school entrance exam if they want to attend college. As Ruixue's father knew thirty years ago, even matriculating to high school is a highly competitive process. And if everyone across the country is supposedly receiving the same government-designed nine years of education, the only way to surpass everyone else is to do something different, something extra. That's where tutoring comes in.

For urban students, tutoring is nonnegotiable. In urban China, there are typically three avenues through which to matriculate into a particularly desirable elementary school: 1) by living in the corresponding residential school district, 2) by paying a large one-time fee, or 3) through a special connection. Roughly a third of students are enrolled by parents paying the fee, easily half a million RMB in Beijing, or 75,000 USD, to ensure their child a seat. But because there are more parents willing to pay the fee than spots for their children, there's an additional obstacle to overcome: an entrance exam. For these students, the elementary school entrance exam marks the beginning of their journey in China's exam system. As such, their parents slate them to begin the tutoring grind at age four or five before even entering elementary school at age six in order to boost their test-taking abilities in time for the exam. Today, rural families are eager to participate in the tournament and take advantage of resources like tutoring that were completely out of reach for rural students like Ruixue, thanks to technology and higher levels of mobility. Nonetheless, given that an average urban family has more resources at their disposal, urban families continue to dominate the demand for tutoring. As of 2018, urban students are tutored at nearly four times the rate that rural students are.[10]

Perhaps equally as important to the urban education tournament are the housing districts that Nan Nan alluded to. If parents are unable to secure their student a seat in an elementary school by way of a one-time up-front fee, living in a desirable housing district is another route through which students in urban areas can matriculate to their family's target elementary school. Simply put, if families live in School A's district, they can send their student to School A for their elementary years. However, if School A is one of the most prestigious districts, living in School A's district comes at a price. With the intensity of urban competition and wealth of resources at families' disposal in areas like Beijing, families are willing to pay for such a guarantee—7.5 million RMB for a 550-square-foot apartment, to be exact. For context, 7.5 million RMB shakes out to roughly 1.2 million dollars, or 2,230 dollars per square foot. This is more expensive than the average unit price in Palo Alto, one of the most expensive neighborhoods in America. Buying an apartment to secure their child's position in the tournament is not out of the question—in fact, it is common practice for some of the wealthiest families in Beijing and other urban centers.

It is important to note that parents are willing to pay this much to ensure a place at *elementary* school. With the popular phrase "don't let your children lose at the starting line" ringing in their head, how could they not? Remember, the chance of getting into two of China's top universities—Peking University and Tsinghua University—is close to zero if the student does not attend one of the top 10 percent of high schools in their province. In order to attend a top high school, a student must be a top tester in one of the best middle schools. And in order to get into one of the best middle schools, students must be a top tester in one of the best elementary schools. While it may seem like we're belaboring our point, it's important to understand that the tournament's starting line has inched closer and closer to some of the earliest years of students' lives. If students don't start out on a good foot, our research shows that they're unlikely to end up at an elite college. Obsessing over the starting line and every benchmark up until the gaokao is perfectly rational: unless they do so, families have little chance of succeeding within the system.

Urban or rural, if students can effectively leverage their tutoring, and for some, their housing district, they will matriculate to high school. Nonetheless, once students do make it to high school—only after passing the high school entrance exam, of course—they must focus on preparing for the gaokao. But students and their families have aged out of the compulsory education system, and must now pay tuition, uniform expenses, and for some students who can't directly access their school, room and board.

For many families in lower socioeconomic brackets, the transition to high school is a painful one. Although lower-income households spend significantly less on children's education, Hongbin's research shows that it amounts to a considerably larger share of their earnings. For China's highest-earning households, those in the top quartile, parents earn on average 118,197 yuan per year, or 13.6 times that of China's lowest-earning households, those in the bottom quartile, earning 8,666 yuan on average per year. More importantly, however, is that while lower-income households spend significantly less money on children's education by virtue of their overall smaller income, it amounts to a considerably larger share of their earnings: 57 percent compared to 11 percent for the wealthiest families. In other words, China's poorest families spend five times that of China's wealthiest households, which represents over *half* of their household earnings.[11] Such results essentially point to what we've determined to be a tax on China's poor, underscoring the excessive financial burden imposed by education, particularly on families in the lower income bracket. Education expenses are indeed a mountain plaguing so many of China's most vulnerable.

But why do poorer households spend a larger proportion of their income on education? Hongbin and his team found that families invest in education as a way to improve or maintain their social status within China's competitive hierarchy. In this way, higher inequality not only raises the perceived benefits of achieving and maintaining higher status but also elevates the financial threshold needed to attain it, pushing all families to invest more in education. As a result, the impact of income inequality on education spending is stronger for poorer and younger households, as they have a greater need to move up the social ladder.[12]

Together, our findings lead us to another rule of China's tournament. Closely following the importance of one's location—the determining factor for one's hukou status and quota allocation—comes one's socioeconomic status. As is true in most countries around the world, wealth places individuals at a notable advantage. Among those between twenty-seven and thirty-seven in China right now, the wealthy and affluent—those in the top 20 percent of China's socioeconomic bracket—are fully twice as likely to get into any college in China than those in the bottom 20 percent of China's socioeconomic bracket. Having money sets you up to play this game.[13]

TAKING DOWN THE MOUNTAIN?

How can such inequality in educational opportunity exist in a country that emphasizes socialist ideals? Wouldn't such a gap between principle and practice threaten the foundations of China's society? In recent years, the government has taken pains to tackle inequalities in the exam system. In the summer of 2021, in a remarkable display of unilaterality, China's government outlawed all forms of tutoring. Within one month, stock prices of China's most prominent tutoring agency listed in Nasdaq plummeted by 90 percent.

While the policy targeted students and families struggling with expenses, it did nothing to change the underlying reality of the system—the demand for higher scores exists precisely because the gaokao still exists. More resourced individuals can now simply hire private tutors instead of contracting with bigger companies. Meanwhile, other tutoring companies have gone underground, which only drives up the expenses and limits access for students already struggling with limited resources. But Hongbin's research shows that over the course of a child's educational career, tutoring amounts to 12 percent of a family's education expenses.[14] The vast majority of other expenses go toward school fees. In other words, banning tutoring won't eliminate the expenses. Instead, it may just further exacerbate pre-existing inequalities.

To the government's credit, efforts to reduce private spending on education extend beyond the tutoring crackdown. Since 2012, the government has boosted their education budget to over 4 percent of its GDP, which matches global averages of 4.3 percent. They have also turned their focus to housing districts in major urban centers, instituting a lottery system to grant students access who live beyond the borders of a prestigious school district. But with the system as competitive as ever and the starting line as early as it is, these efforts have done little to address individual expenses. Ask any family in China today: the mountain remains as tall as ever.

• • •

One standardized test represents the final round in a twelve-year-long tournament, one that seems to promise equality for all students. But keeping in mind systemic barriers—the hukou system and the quota allocation system—coupled with basic socioeconomic realities, it is safe to say the following: no, China's education system is not "fair," or at the very least, not *as* fair as the system might have you believe.

And yet, the reality is this: education systems around the world are not fair. As debates escalate surrounding the inequalities and sustainability of China's college entrance system, some have even suggested abolishing it all together. But really—is there a better alternative? One absent of tutoring, housing districts, and all the window dressing associated with the intensity of a tournament? Consider the United States, where college admission is based on a variety of factors: high school GPA, standardized testing, extracurricular activities, awards, personal essays, supplementary essays, and recommendation letters. Colleges also take into account hopeful students' residential address, high school

quality, family backgrounds and, in particular, parents' education background, such as being an alumnus of a college. Proponents of this
system argue that college admission officers can see the whole student
this way—student admission amounts to more than just a number on
a test—and that students are rewarded for their sense of personal creativity and individuality in a way not possible under a standardized
testing system with one test alone.

The results of a head-to-head comparison of the two country's systems yielded surprising results. As inaccessible as China's system may
seem, the US's may be worse. In China, children from the richest 20
percent of families—in other words, the upper class—are 2.3 times
more likely to go to an elite college than those from the poorest 20
percent of families—the lower class. Meanwhile, in the United States,
students from wealthy families are fully eleven times more likely to
attend elite institutions than those from poor families.[15]

This disparity returns us to our original point: China's system may
be unfair, but accessing elite colleges in China is no more difficult than
in the United States. Accessibility, or lack thereof, is undeniably a problem around the world. And yet, no matter how unfair the system may
be, the payoff in winning China's tournament—the biggest tournament in the world—is remarkable. Year after year, it is stories like mine
and Hongbin's that inspire a steadfast belief in and return to the system. Families continue to invest time and money with the understanding that they, too, may be able to access the riches at the top of the
hierarchy. But as we've proven throughout this chapter, in almost every
respect, our cases were the exception, not the rule. China's system is
unfair, with obstacles around every corner for the country's most
vulnerable.

3

The Payoff

o   o   o

"The college entrance exam was our own 'peak of life's knowledge.' Back
then, we knew everything from astronomy to geography, and could both
calculate trigonometric functions and write chemical equations."

—Social media post

The experiences of Hongbin and Ruixue make the significance of
exams in China's tournament-style education system challenging
to overstate. Throughout the course of the last two chapters, we have
referred to China's education system as an exam system. This is not just
because there are a lot of exams, though there certainly are. Rather, it's
related to a lesser-known aspect of any education system around the
world: its utility in selecting individuals at each stage of education.

Within a single education system, there are multiple routes through
which individuals are selected at each stage of their education. Exams are
often an important one, and not just in China—India, Vietnam, South
Korea, Turkey, and Chile all use exams to select individuals. Other countries, like Iran, consider both exam scores and high school performance
in their college selection process. In the United States, on the other hand,
a combination of different selection tools are used. College applications
include the SAT or ACT (an exam, to be sure, though an optional one
for many colleges today) but also essays and an assessment of extracurricular activities and student background. As in other exclusively

exam-based systems, unless China's students attend an international school or study abroad, exams are the only way they may be selected into any subsequent stage of education, from elementary school admission to college admission. It is for that reason that we refer to China's education system as an exam system: yes, there are a lot of exams, but there are *only* exams. Exams are the only route through which selection occurs.

While China is not the only country that uses an exam system as the foundation of its education system, it is likely one of—if not the most—extreme examples of such a system. In some ways, this is only fitting: China invented the original exam over 1,300 years ago. And for the individual, it seems that China's uniquely exam-oriented education system delivers economic results at least on par with those of other systems. Take, for example, returns to education—as is the case in the rest of the world, there is an average return of 40 percent to a four-year college education. Moreover, an elite college education offers an additional 40 percent higher return, not to mention access to hidden benefits associated with life at the top of China's social hierarchy. In other words, China's system does deliver its graduates with an income higher than those who didn't make their way through the system. But how effectively does China's exam system actually educate its students?

THE PRE-COLLEGE YEARS

When most people consider the value of an education system, they often point in the direction of "human capital"—the skills, knowledge, and experience that an individual possesses.[1] This is because many education systems typically serve as a platform through which students can, at the most basic level, learn something. That "something" can help them succeed long after they graduate by being put to good use on the labor market. As such, one of the best ways to understand more about any education system is to gauge whether its students are actually learning. We began by gathering information on whether China's students are learning through the exam system prior to college, or more specifically, prior to the most consequential exam of their educational career: the gaokao.

One often-used international metric for analyzing how much students learn prior to college are the results of an exam that 600,000 fifteen-year-old students take around the world: the Program for International Student Assessment (PISA). PISA is a worldwide study designed by the Organisation for Economic Co-operation and Development (OECD) intended to evaluate global education systems by measuring fifteen-year-olds' performance across mathematics, science, and reading. On their website, the OECD explains that "PISA test questions don't gauge memorization of facts but demand that students draw on real-world problem-solving skills and knowledge." Such a mandate suggests that PISA prioritizes critical thinking over rote memorization. Critics of China's education system often identify rote memorization as a defining characteristic of that system.

As it turns out, China's fifteen-year-olds tested exceptionally well on the PISA exam. In the most recent round of PISA tests conducted in 2018, China ranked first in all three subjects, with a score of 555 in reading, 591 in math, and 590 in science, relative to the global average scores of 487, 489, and 489, respectively. Singapore, the next highest-scoring nation, had scores of 549 in reading, 569 in math, and 551 in science, while the US scored lower at 505 in reading, 478 in math, and 502 in science.[2] In other words, China's students outscored students in other developing and developed countries alike, including the US, Japan, and all participating European countries. These results suggest that China's education system is equipping students with human capital—its students are excelling on a test designed to measure exactly that, albeit using metrics that touch on a relatively narrow aspect of the broad definition that is human capital. While China has been criticized for manipulating their results on the grounds that the government only allows students in high-scoring metropolitan schools to sit for the exams, their results are still nonetheless remarkable, if not representative of the entire country.

Another research group spearheaded by the education scholar Prashant Loyalka set out to test whether China's dominance on the PISA scores persisted through college. In their groundbreaking study, our colleagues collected internationally standardized assessment data on critical thinking and STEM skills (skills in science, technology, engineering, and mathematics) from nationally representative samples of tens of thousands of computer science and electrical engineering undergraduates in China, India, and Russia, countries that collectively produce about half the STEM graduates in the world. They also benchmarked these skills against the critical thinking skills of US STEM students. Much like the findings from the PISA tests, their results indicated that first-year students in China exhibited comparable levels of critical thinking skills to their counterparts in the US, and both scored higher on these measures than first-year students in India and Russia. Similarly, first-years in China displayed significantly more advanced STEM skills in mathematics and physics than those in both India and Russia.[3]

These studies collectively suggest that, prior to college, an exam system is a well-oiled machine, designed with the express purpose of equipping its students with human capital. This alone marks China's exam system as unique—indeed, it seems particularly adept at facilitating its students' learning. And perhaps equally as important, China's exam system is allowing its students to learn enough in their elementary, middle, and high school classrooms to perform better than their biggest economic rival, the US, and even more broadly, better than most students in the rest of the world.

THE COLLEGE YEARS

Once students take the most consequential exam of their academic careers, does the exam system continue to facilitate such remarkable results? Because the gaokao is a milestone, it seemed only natural to measure students' skill acquisition around the time they sat for the gaokao and a few years after the fact. As such, Loyalka and his team continued to survey students' skills through the course of their college years. What they found came as a surprise: relative to their baseline results taken during a student's first year of college, China's students showed virtually no improvements in their critical thinking skills after two years of college. Not only that, but during their final two years, they began to exhibit declining capabilities. By contrast, students in the US made significant strides in critical thinking during their college years. As a result, despite similar scores at the beginning of college, students in China scored much lower by their fourth year than their fourth-year counterparts in the US. The results reveal similar patterns for math and physics skills. After two years, China's advantage over Russia and India in math and physics skills narrows substantially: while students in India and Russia experience gains, especially in math, students in China make negligible to negative progress—in other words, they're either stagnating or actively losing skills in college. These results held across both elite and non-elite colleges.

These findings should come as a surprise. Prior to college, China's exam system leaves students performing better than students anywhere else in the world. What is happening to students that leaves them at a disadvantage after four more years of education, education that is usually designed to build on the foundation laid during the first twelve years? To get a clearer sense of what students are learning during those four years, Hongbin and his team analyzed data from the China College Student Survey (CCSS), collected annually while Hongbin was working at Tsinghua University from 2010 to 2015. This entailed randomly selecting 100 colleges from a list of all 2,300 colleges in China. The selection was split up according to five geographical regions and, importantly, represented all the tiers of colleges. To carry out the surveys, Hongbin and his research team selected two to three survey administrators from each college. These administrators were typically responsible for registering students, teaching, or managing student affairs. To control the quality of the survey, the research team held several days of training sessions in Beijing for all survey administrators. Once the administrators were appropriately trained, they returned to their college and selected a random sample of students. They then gathered all these students in one location and asked them to individually and anonymously fill in their questionnaires. The completed questionnaires were then coded and mailed back to Beijing for data entry and cleaning to guarantee consistency and quality.

Survey data revealed that during their college years, China's students spent about twenty-four hours per week attending classes and twelve hours outside of class per week studying.[4] Contrast this with the study that found that China's high school students spent twenty-seven hours studying per week after finishing their in-school hours, which alone occupy at least forty-five hours of their week.[5] These numbers indicate China's college students spend roughly half as much time in class and half as much time studying as they did prior to attending college, which accords with the measurable decline in their skills.

All things considered, China's exam system seems less adept at facilitating students' learning in college. That said, Loyalka's work relies on two very specific measures of skills, and thus can't be generalized across all skills a student might pick up in college. For instance, college students in computer science likely learn programming skills beyond what they learned in high school that aren't captured by Loyalka's study. It is also the case that Loyalka's work represents the *average* student, who is unlikely to be motivated by an additional exam: the graduate school exam. With such a high influx of college graduates on the labor market, the value of a college degree is no longer what it used to be, driving more and more students to pursue another degree beyond their undergraduate one. If students didn't gain admission to an elite undergraduate university, they often attempt to gain admission to the graduate school of an elite university to "make up" for the lower-rank institution where they obtained their first degree. For these students, studying in college, keeping their GPA high, and learning enough to perform well on the increasingly competitive graduate school entrance exam is of paramount importance given the increasingly stiff competition for pursuing a graduate degree.

It's also important to point out that the skills measured by conventional skill tests are just one part of human capital. An individual's life experience and the associated knowledge they pick up along the way should not be discounted. Ruixue's experience alone can tell us this much. Though she might not have learned much by way of measurable skills in college, if she *didn't* go to college, she would almost certainly be working at the factory closest to her village. College exposed Ruixue to countless new experiences that expanded her worldview and led her down a new and exciting path. For her, such exposure may have been more important than all the courses she took in college combined. Like Ruixue, so many students across China are stuck in the classroom for the first eighteen years of their life preparing for the gaokao. And then? College grants them the freedom to explore life outside of the classroom with a pool of like-minded individuals. These experiences are the intangible, unmeasurable components of human capital that contribute to the future productivity of China's college students.

Nonetheless, there exists striking—though not conclusive—evidence indicating a weakness in China's college education system. It seems likely that under different circumstances, or even a different system altogether, that China's students could be learning so much more in college than they do now. These findings are consistent with the perception of the general public. Indeed, those who are able often choose to educate their children in China for their pre-college years but send them abroad for college. College is far from a useless enterprise for China's students, however. Just getting to college means that one has successfully passed the gaokao, which is a remarkable feat given the stiff competition across the country. The gaokao alone ensures that vast swaths of the country have higher levels of human capital than much of the world. And once China's students do make it to college, there's likely an array of benefits that they can reap from those four years. Economists simply haven't figured out a way to measure them.

EXAMINING THE EXAM SYSTEM

At this point, it's helpful to offer a brief recap to better contextualize these findings in light of China's exam system. Across elite and non-elite colleges, Loyalka's study indicates the weakness of China's college education system in facilitating its students' learning on one narrow aspect of human capital captured by skills measured by exams. And yet, both non-elite and elite college graduates continue to be rewarded by their employers down the line with higher incomes than their counterparts who graduated from high school. So the question is this—what are college graduates being rewarded for, if not primarily for the measurable skills they learn during college, and how does the exam system play into this?

What Hongbin and Ruixue found to be uniquely important to a student's reward on the labor market has everything to do with China's exam system. Because college admission is based almost exclusively on a student's gaokao score, the university that a student attends thus serves as a signal about one key fact: her ability to succeed as an exam taker within China's exam system. At every juncture in her educational career, her exam score had to serve as a signal strong enough to be selected into the next phase of education. If she succeeded in doing so, she would proceed onward. If she failed, however, she was either downgraded to a lower lane—a less prestigious elementary school, middle school, or high school—or eliminated from the system altogether. Because the education system is fundamentally grounded in exams, the gaokao is a culmination of every single test that she took up until that point. And like her, every other person who has passed through China's education system knows this. They understand just how challenging the exams are, and just how hard it is to achieve a winning score. For this reason, the gaokao is one of the strongest and most widely accepted signals of a student's ability that exists in China today, and the only metric considered when students are selected into any stage of education. In sum, the exam score associated with admission to a given college is a signal of one's ability—the higher a gaokao score, the higher the tier, and, in turn, the higher perceived ability.[6] Consider this in contrast with graduation from colleges elsewhere in the world. If a student graduates from college and says so on his resume, it's a signal of his ability in part because there is an underlying assumption that he really learned something during college. This assumption is supported by studies like Loyalka's that find that students in Russia, India, and the US make significant strides in their learning during college. But in China, that rate of learning is reduced, at least in terms of skills that economists can measure. Under China's exam system, the returns are due to the signal students send about their gaokao score.

In this light, recall how China's exam system resembles a tournament. Though the starting line of the tournament creeps ever earlier with each passing year, data suggest that for those students unmotivated by yet another exam, such as the graduate school exam, the finish line is as concrete as ever. Once students have taken the gaokao, they've crossed that finish line. This is a fact that most colleges recognize: it is widely understood that the college education system has a "strict entry, easy out" policy (严进宽出). While entrance exam competition is fierce, graduation is almost promised once enrolled. Some even estimate that China has one of the lowest college dropout rates in the world. In 2011, the Beijing-based Mycos Institute estimated China's college dropout rate at 3 percent, while the Ministry of Education gave an even lower figure, 0.75 percent.[7] With this in mind, it makes sense that learning stagnates in college in China (or at least the type of learning that can be measured by an exam). The gaokao marks the final push in the tournament for many students. And yet, exams are not unique to China. So many countries, the US included, use exams to select students for subsequent stages of education. So, how unique is China's exam system in this respect?

To answer this question, we will revisit economists' estimates of the returns to education. Recall that along with most other developed countries in the world, one additional year of college education increases labor income by about 10 percent in China. But even more than the return itself, economists are interested in parsing through the 10 percent to understand the following: what proportion of the return is due to their human capital and what proportion of the return is due to the system selecting students particularly adept at sitting for China's exams? This is a difficult question to answer.

Returns to education are measured using one's income. But comparing the incomes of two strangers—one who went to college and one who didn't go to college—would not give the true economic returns of each year of schooling. Though the learning that occurs in each year of schooling is likely among the most significant, there are countless other factors that could drive differences between two strangers' income, like family background, intelligence as measured by IQ, or even the neighborhood where one grew up. To circumvent this problem, Hongbin and his colleague Junsen Zhang used data they collected on 914 pairs of twins in five cities across China.[8] In both natural and social sciences, identical twins' participation in studies is an invaluable natural experiment: they allow researchers to isolate one variable by controlling for a variation in circumstances.[9] In Hongbin and Junsen's case, the twins data allowed them to isolate how much each additional year of schooling affects income, because the family background, genes (similar IQ), and childhood environment of a pair of identical twins is as close to alike as possible.

What they found suggests that in China, schooling plays a relatively small part in driving differences in the twins' income. More specifically, of the 10 percent return to each year of schooling, at most 3 percent could be attributed to education (that is, their learning/human capital and social network accumulated from their years in the system). The remaining 7 percent can be attributed to the education system's ability to select individuals with naturally high abilities or more advantageous family background. A family that had more advantageous social connections, for example, or one that emphasized hard work and high achievement would fall into this category. Here's what this looks like in practice. As twins, Bao and Betty have the same ability and family background. Bao attends college, graduates, and makes 140 yuan per month, or 40 percent higher than the baseline high school graduate's income of 100 yuan—this is the 40 percent return that comes with four years of college education in China. Betty, however, did not go to college, but still makes 128 yuan a month. So why does Betty make 128 yuan a month, even if she didn't go to college?

According to Hongbin and Junsen's findings, the fact that Bao was selected into the education system suggests Bao and Betty have higher abilities and a more advantageous family background. Because Betty shares these characteristics, even though she is not selected, she still earns 28 percent more money than those from families without a relation selected by the system. From this, you can see that in China, rather than building its students' human capital in college, the education system serves as a mechanism to select individuals with high ability or a more advantageous family background, who are then sorted into tiers based on their exam score.

This stands in contrast with other education systems. Let's look at the same family in the US. There, if Bao still attended college—any college, not an elite college—she would still make 140. But Betty, who still did not attend college, only makes 100—the same as the baseline. This means that Bao's return can primarily be attributed to what she learned during school (her human capital) and the connections she made during college. In other words, this research indicates that in the US, selecting students into a college based on their ability or family background and connections accounts for little of the total return to education, compared with China's two-thirds. Hongbin and Junsen also compared China to a few other countries, such as Australia and the UK, and found that overall, across these countries, education serves more to build a student's human capital and develop their social network independent of their family connections than it serves to signal their ability prior to the education itself.

As we've discussed, Ruixue and Hongbin also measured the return to another layer of the hierarchy: the economic returns offered by China's elite colleges.[10] They did so by comparing two sets of students: one set who scored just at the cutoff point for an elite college, and the other set who scored one point below the cutoff for an elite college. (The latter group, because they scored below the cutoff, have almost no chance of getting into these elite colleges.) By comparing these two groups, Ruixue and Hongbin largely ensured that observable differences in the economic return had little to do with students' ability: a difference of one point above or below the cutoff may boil down to a mid-exam hiccup, not the fact that they are less-skilled students. It was through this study that Ruixue and Hongbin effectively established that those going to an elite college had a return of 40 percent—the difference that was made by scoring one additional point at that critical cutoff. For comparison, it's worth noting that some research suggests that there is little return to elite colleges in the United States.[11] However, because the US lacks a standardized measure of college admission like the gaokao, economists are challenged to isolate the return to elite college education alone. Instead, factors like family background, social networks, natural ability, and actual learning are conflated, obscuring the true return.

This analysis further suggests that a large chunk of the high returns to elite college education could be due to the signaling effect. Employers are more likely to go to elite colleges for campus recruiting because there is seemingly a better chance of finding higher-ability students. Scoring just one point above the cutoff is what provides a student with this opportunity.

Scoring just one point above can also grant students access to a social club or network, which is important for their success on the job market. Because it's largely random to score either one point above or below the cutoff, the students around the cutoff point have on average similar family backgrounds. However, other than the lucky few around the cutoff, most students who get into elite colleges actually score much higher than the cutoff. On average, these higher-scoring students have a more advantageous socioeconomic background and parents who themselves attended college and belong to the CCP. As such, it's likely that the return associated with an elite college education is in part due to the social network formed throughout those college years.

As a prototype for an exam system and its associated trends, China exhibits unique characteristics relative to those countries whose education systems aren't grounded in exams. While education systems in countries like Australia, the US, and the UK focus more on building their students' human capital, China's education system instead serves primarily to select students of high ability or advantageous family background into the subsequent stage of education. Their status within the education system—at a top tier university—thus becomes a signal of their ability (and family background).

THE GAOKAO'S ENDURING LEGACY

The signal associated with one's gaokao score is a strong one. For better or for worse, gaokao scores follows students for decades after they take the exam. Attending one of China's colleges, and in particular, the 100 or so elite colleges, can increase a student's monthly wage significantly. Not only that, but a student's income at their first job predicts with a high degree of accuracy their income for years to come. If students start their career with a lower income, they end their career with a lower income. Attending an elite college affects your economic bracket for the rest of your life, not to mention the additional benefits associated with the change in status. And remember—all this rests on one exam that most students take when they are just eighteen years old. Though elite education is sought after across the world, its role as a selection mechanism—one that effectively sorts individuals into tiers based on their exam score—is unique. Instead of primarily serving to build human capital and develop a student's social network, as is the case in countries like the US and Australia, elite education is instead a signal of ability as proxied by a gaokao score. And that signal follows students for the rest of their lives.

No wonder we've borne witness to a phenomenon known as "first-degree anxiety." As professors, we've found that students from China who are studying at first-class universities in the US still lament over their first degree—or rather, their lack of an "elite" first degree. They've come to understand that even if they return to China with a master's or PhD degree from a prestigious university in the US, their first degree will continue to haunt them.

Over the course of a decade at Tsinghua University in China, Hongbin was responsible for recruiting junior faculty and overseeing graduate student admissions. In his experience, all junior faculty candidates were recruited from overseas university PhD programs. One important pattern he noticed in the hiring practices had to do with the undergraduate degree that candidates obtained while in China. Almost every faculty member he hired from overseas had obtained their first degree from China's top three colleges: Tsinghua, Peking, and Fudan University.

Though the eliteness of undergraduate degrees for graduate admissions are no less important, the irony is that relatively few applicants were from the top three elite schools themselves. Consider this in contrast with prestigious graduate schools in the US: a relatively high proportion of applicants to Harvard Law, for example, would likely hail from elite universities themselves. But in China, the students graduating from lower-level elite universities comprise the bulk of those applying to Tsinghua, as they want to have their second degree from one of the most elite universities in China in order to further advance in the hierarchy. They also preferred a masters degree over a PhD degree, as it was the most efficient route to putting that elite degree on their resume. Meanwhile, the students who already had undergraduate degrees from Tsinghua didn't need the advanced degree (also) from Tsinghua, as their undergraduate degree alone carried enough weight. If they chose to get their PhD, they typically opted to go abroad.

To further drive home the importance of undergraduate degrees, when Ruixue looked at LinkedIn data to understand the inflow of China's graduates to the US, she and her team found vast swaths of profiles missing information on their undergraduate institution—but not when that institution was an elite one. They conjectured that if they didn't obtain an elite degree, Chinese professionals were far less likely to list their first degree on their personal page, instead opting to highlight the "best" degree in their educational career. Such findings are in line with preferences of employers in China—only recently did China's government outlaw hiring based on students' first degrees, though they never formally audit any instances of "unfair" hiring practices. While it used to be the case that job descriptions explicitly stated that only students who attended elite universities should apply to the job, it's clear now based on who gets the jobs that an elite first degree is still the expectation, even if students go on to complete remarkable work after receiving their non-elite college diploma. Imagine if so much of your life, including your career, rested on a test you took right after high school.

Even as adults, we find our first degree continues to pop up in unexpected ways. Neither Hongbin nor Ruixue graduated from Peking, Tsinghua, or Fudan—the most elite of elite universities in China. While getting his PhD from Stanford, Hongbin met his wife. One of the first questions she asked him was where he went to college. When Hongbin told her he had attended China Agricultural University—a university ranked in the top thirty but not Peking, Tsinghua, or Fudan—his wife, the highest gaokao scorer in her province, scoffed. How did they both end up at Stanford? Ruixue has had similar experiences when speaking at universities around the world. If anyone familiar with China's education system introduces her, they emphasize her "atypical" route. In other words, she also didn't attend Peking, Tsinghua, or Fudan University. The funny thing about these examples is that both Hongbin's wife and those introducing Ruixue are making perfectly rational assumptions: in China, it's unlikely that you climb the hierarchy without attending an elite college, and even more unlikely that you end up at the very top without attending the best of the elite colleges. Their paths to elite universities in the US are extremely atypical given that they did not attend the most elite of universities in China—neither Ruixue or Hongbin believe they have met more than a handful of other scholars with paths similar to their own. That's how strong a signal one's gaokao score is. Indeed, the exam system continues to influence students' lives—ours included—decades after the exams themselves end. While our experiences have made us aware of the exam system's impact and have helped us recognize that many capable young Chinese miss out on elite education due to factors beyond their ability, we, too, can acknowledge our occasional susceptibility to these deep-rooted hierarchical views. When undergraduates from the elite three universities apply to work with us, we find ourselves taking a closer look at their applications than at those of students applying from our own alma maters, even though our alma maters are also part of the elite tier. In China, there is always another hierarchy.

Taking a step back, however, it's clear that such a system also creates inefficiencies for society writ large. Selecting students based on their gaokao score centers around the assumption that the gaokao score is a reasonable measure of ability. This narrow definition of ability effectively discounts other potentially important metrics of success. A student whose skill set isn't naturally suited to exam taking is, in many ways, relegated to the lower tiers of China's hierarchy at age eighteen. But such students have something valuable to contribute to society, even if that contribution doesn't exist within the parameters of traditional success.

With all this in mind, it's critical to remember the following: under China's tournament-like exam system, the behavior and trends we've borne witness to as researchers are rational. In isolation, though certain aspects of the system might seem strange, it all clicks into place when examined through the lens of an exam system. With employers rewarding only the highest of gaokao scores, it makes sense that families obsess over excelling on China's exams. And given just how strong and persistent that gaokao signal is, our PhD students who plan to return to China without an elite undergraduate degree *should* be worried—it's simply the reality of the exam system's power. If you're a student with one of the highest scores, you're set for life: you're rewarded year after year for an exam you took when you were eighteen years old. But for those students who aren't able to score in the top 5 percent, this system is a costly one. In many societies around the world, individuals have the opportunity to change their life outcomes well after they turn eighteen. But in China, many doors just close.

Now you have seen how and why countless families are so rationally invested in the tournament's outcome. We will turn next to analyzing who is behind the system's design as a centralized hierarchical tournament. Though the system does indeed work in favor of a select set of families, it serves nobody more than those drawing up the rules.

PART II

STATE

4

Political Logic

○ ○ ○

"The heroes of the empire are all in my pocket."

—Tang Taizong

"天下英雄，尽入吾彀中矣."   —唐太宗

July 2021 in China's capital—breaking a sweat was inevitable. Sweltering temperatures coupled with crippling humidity created conditions closer to that of a sauna than a city. Escaping the heat, Beijing's twenty million citizens would often seek refuge in their air-conditioned homes and cars or duck into a nearby storefront. No one chose to go outside—not unless there was a good reason.

Normally packed with tourists braving the heat, Xicheng District is at the heart of China's capital, encompassing many of China's most famous tourist sites. Infamous for the 1989 protests, Tiananmen Square, a vast, concrete expanse, is at the district's center. Built relatively recently, in 1651, it is the entrance to the Forbidden City, home to the emperors of China's historical dynasties. Since China opened its borders to the world in the 1970s, tourists from around the world have waited their turn to walk the city's halls. Not two blocks away stands Zhongnanhai, an ancient garden that now houses the headquarters of top CCP personnel. With thousands of years of rich history, there isn't much the streets of Beijing haven't borne witness to.

The summer of 2021, however, was anything but normal. In the wake of the COVID-19 global pandemic, traces of harsh regulations seeking to squash any remnants of the virus lingered on. The travel ban stood firmly in place—hardly anyone could come and go without an official stamp of approval, nearly impossible to obtain. Sites that were normally crowded with camera-laden tourists stood largely empty. While China's capital may seldom be called quiet, the heart of Beijing looked quite unlike summers past.

And yet—fireworks exploded, parades trundled through otherwise quiet streets, and songs like "Without the Communist Party, There Would Be No New China" echoed throughout the city, all standing in contrast to an otherwise quiet summer. The CCP was throwing itself a party—a celebration of one hundred years of prosperous leadership. Online censors and police had been working overtime to ensure there were no disturbances to the CCP's big celebrations. While law enforcement officials are normally a common sight in Beijing, especially in Xicheng District, patrols were out in full force that summer. Beijing's biggest attraction was no longer the city's ancient history but the ongoing celebration. For the month of July, everyone was on their best behavior.

Everyone, that is, except for several hundred parents. Despite Beijing's oppressive heat, they rallied together outside of the city's Education Commission building under the shadow of Pingan Street's Yuyou Alley—aptly translated as "youth education alley." Not two blocks away stood Beijing No. 4 High School, one of China's most elite high schools. Parents surely took note: many CCP leaders graduated from there.

These parents, without a doubt, knew three things. One—they were not supposed to be protesting in China. Two—they were not supposed to be protesting in the capital of China, in the heart of Beijing, near Tiananmen Square, and three—they were not supposed to be protesting in the capital of China, in the heart of Beijing, near Tiananmen Square, during the CCP's biggest celebration of the last one hundred years.

Scattered protests over the last few years have marked parents' discontent with government attempts to forge a more equitable education system. Recorded at a protest in 2016, Mrs. Zhang, an impassioned mother, voiced her frustration. "How can we send our kids to this kind of school? We fought and worked so hard and put down millions to buy an apartment to earn a decent life in Beijing. And now our kids will have to go to this kind of school?"[1] In 2016, Mrs. Zhang protested pilot testing of a policy that would rework the foundations of elementary school enrollment. In 2021, parents in Beijing protested the same policy in Youth Education Alley. This policy would shift the housing school district policy to a lottery system, giving families who would otherwise be unable to buy a multi-million-dollar home in the corresponding school district an opportunity to attend an elite school. And as you now know, though elementary school enrollment may at first glance seem trivial, it is one of the initial steps in setting a child up for success in China's education tournament.[2]

Because of the explicitly hierarchical structure of Beijing's schools, every parent is tasked with setting their child out on the right foot. Even though the overall quality of education in Beijing is high relative to the rest of the country, parents still fight to ensure that their children can attend the most elite schools among all the elite schools in Beijing. Doing so will give their child an advantage, one that might allow them to beat out their peers on the gaokao over a decade later. A finite set of seats at the best of the best schools for a fiercely competitive student population has made it particularly challenging for parents to succeed in sending their child to the school of their choice. And if a school can't support the number of enrolled students, families with older house ownership rights receive enrollment priority, and any remaining students are reallocated to nearby schools. Competition is stiff, and preparation starts early. Parents like Mrs. Zhang are well aware of this fact.

China's parents have been in a tough spot. Nonetheless, the Beijing parents had navigated within the system to achieve their ultimate goal: winning their child a seat in a school that would set them up for success on the gaokao. Parents had bought exorbitantly priced apartments in Beijing and, in some cases, jumped through legal hoops to secure the necessary hukou rights. These efforts were supposed to guarantee their child's school success. But then the government chose to change the system. Seemingly overnight, their efforts went completely to waste.

Parents' anger was not unfounded: the new lottery system would indeed nullify their efforts and investment. According to the new policy, parents who acquired ownership rights after July 31, 2020, would have to participate in a lottery. The lottery included not only schools and students corresponding to a house's neighborhood, but also students and schools in nearby school districts. Subjected to the whims of policymakers, parents' already slim odds of enrolling their child in a prestigious school had shrunk. This pushed many over the edge.

Dripping with sweat only exacerbated by their face masks, the crowd of parents ballooned from ten to fifty to a hundred, as Beijing once again bore witness to its citizens' anger. Quickly surrounded by watchful policemen—some in uniform, some in plain clothes—the crowd yelled back and forth with officials who sought to disperse the fervent crowd. A few active parents were identified as leaders and taken into police custody. "Free them, free them!" Chants boomed through the crowd.

In China, such protests are rare and often dangerous. Parents who choose to gather in protest could lose their jobs. Their social credit score could be permanently docked. In the most extreme cases, they could be thrown in jail. The bottom line, however, is this: despite the abundance of risk, these parents still took to the street, hoping against hope that the policymakers might take heed of their pleas. While there is no way of knowing with certainty what happened next, it's clear that when faced with the power of the CCP, these parents had little choice but to back down. At least they went down fighting, making their voices heard, all to give their child hope for succeeding within China's great tournament. Or would their actions cause difficulties for their children?

While such uprisings are rare in modern-day China, these parents are neither the first nor the last to voice their discontent with China's education system. At some of the most critical junctures in China's history, protests related to the education system are more the norm than they are the exception. Even so, where so many institutions crumbled when faced with the pressure of the masses, it is China's education system that rulers continue to return to, time and time again. What can explain its longevity?

We believe that China's education has stood the test of time because it is one of the most cleverly designed institutions in China's history, designed and wielded by the state as a powerful political tool, century after century. As both cleverly designed and politically useful as the education system is, however, it can also prove challenging to change. Policymakers who dealt with the fallout of the protest in Xicheng District know this fact all too well.

CHINA'S EDUCATION SYSTEM AS A POLITICAL TOOL

The most clever feature at the heart of China's education system is this: it has created a perceived channel for social mobility.[3] Societies with higher levels of social mobility tend to be more stable, as people are motivated to work to access a channel through which they can affect positive change in their lives.[4] Consider this on a smaller scale: an individual is far more likely to stay at and positively contribute to an organization if they feel they have the opportunity to move up at that organization. It is the opportunity for mobility that motivates people to continue working, and working hard, within the existing system. In the same way, the education system provides China's people with hope for upward mobility and, in turn, stability across the empire. When the emperor of the Sui dynasty first founded the civil service exam—among the first iterations of a formal "education" system—around 600 AD, the system lacked much of the ingenuity that characterizes today's system.[5] Nonetheless, the exam still provided a channel through which people could change their lives, albeit in a more limited sense, as the exam's official charge was to recruit bureaucrats from the non-elite. Standing in contrast to the previous system under which officials usually came from the existing aristocratic families, the imperial exams created a newly accessible channel for social mobility.

Accessing this channel is straightforward. A high test score is a ticket to advancement. This is a noteworthy design feature. Because the exam system provides everyone with a seemingly equal opportunity at changing their future, the responsibility to take advantage of such an opportunity falls on the individual. For this reason, if the individual fails to take advantage of the opportunity—if they cannot, for example, score high enough on the exam—the responsibility falls on their shoulders. In our experience, the common—and often false—perception remains in China today that if someone did not earn the score they hoped for, it is their fault. They weren't smart enough or hard-working enough to succeed. It's not that the rules place roadblocks in the individual's path, but instead that the individual didn't do enough to seize the opportunity. Individual failure is not viewed as systemic inequality, even though in many cases that is the logical explanation.

At the time of its inception, China's imperial exam structure was unique. Consider what you know about Europe's monarchies—how many rags-to-riches stories come to mind under a system like that? Many researchers have speculated about what, exactly, triggered the mass expansion of China's unique system. One of the leading theories was prompted by the history of a rebel named Huang Chao.[6] Huang Chao took the imperial exam in its existing, albeit limited form and failed repeatedly, thereafter resolving to overthrow the emperor and take the empire for himself. Although he eventually failed, he did succeed in eliminating many of his political rivals—the aristocrats. After Huang Chao's rebellion was quashed, the emperor realized he no longer had enough aristocrats in his court to effectively manage different regions of his vast empire, as so many of them had been killed by

Huang Chao. He also realized that the aristocrats were no longer around to oppose a system that was likely to replace the seat of power that they had inherited through the generations. As a result, he was free to seek out a new channel to attract talent from his vast empire to replace the hole that the rebel Huang Chao had carved out in his aristocracy. While the exam system had existed in a limited form, it was at this point—around 1,000 AD during the Song dynasty—that the imperial examination system began to gain some traction.

Regardless of whether that theory truly explains why the education system began to get a foothold within the empire, it brings up an interesting point. As a group, it was the aristocrats who were least likely to be pleased with the exam system. Both the emperor and the commoners benefited from the system: the emperor gained favor from the commoners for the appearance of openness, and a select few among the commoners were able to take advantage of that opportunity and change their fate altogether. Meanwhile, the exam system only served to delegitimize the existing aristocracy: it was apparent to all that they didn't have to take an exam to earn their position.

This brings us to another clever design feature of the exam system: whoever rules over it gains a pool of loyal and highly competent elite.[7] In most absolute monarchies, the aristocrats don't necessarily owe their power to the king or the emperor. Instead, power is inherited generationally. Under the imperial examination system, however, the newfound bureaucratic elite—those who had risen to power by exam success—did, in fact, owe their power to the ruler, as it was the ruler who benevolently bestowed such an opportunity upon them. And though the children of these newfound elite inherited some form of social capital, their status diminished with each generation unless they, too, passed the exam. Not only that, but because the new bureaucrats passed the exam based on their ability to perform on a test designed to select the next generation of bureaucrats, it was a more competent group of individuals who were helping the emperor rule his kingdom. Thanks to this new pool of loyal and highly capable bureaucrats, the ruler's seat would be more secure. If the ruler is less likely to be over-thrown by his elites *and* his elites are particularly competent, there exists a stable bureaucracy and thus a more stable society. In this way the exam system continues to foster both loyalty and stability, a fact that is borne out by data.

To show this empirically, Ruixue and her colleagues compared the probability of a ruler's overthrow across two systems: the European monarchies and China's dynasties. More specifically, they wanted to understand whether the exam system affected stability in China, and how the levels of stability compare to a system under which the elite *didn't* owe their power to the ruler. One way to measure stability is to examine the risk for a ruler to be deposed, a constant threat for any ruler. Ruixue and her colleagues assembled systematic data on this risk historically for both Europe and China, which entails calculating the probability of a rulers' deposition every year based on his "outcome"—staying in power, a natural death, or deposition.[8] As they expected, after the inception of the exam system, the yearly deposition risk declined from 2.3 percent between 500 and 700 AD to 0.2 percent between 700 and 1700 AD. In contrast, this risk was more than twice as high at 0.48 percent between 700–1700 AD for European rulers.[9]

But can the government still reliably count on today's education system to foster stability amid its pool of loyal and highly competent students? Over the past forty years, China's labor market has undergone significant reforms, leading to a shift in employment from the government sector to the private sector. Prior to these reforms, the majority of urban workers were employed by the state: the factory community of Hongbin's youth is just one example of this. But by 2021, the private sector accounted for roughly 64 percent of urban workers.[10] With China's economy and labor market becoming increasingly privatized, have China's students—especially the highest-scoring ones—changed their preference for working for the state? The question remained unanswered due to the lack of appropriate data.

Hongbin became curious about this question and decided to use CCSS data to answer it. In addition to collecting information on the variables mentioned in the last chapter, they also directly asked students to report their preferred employer using the following questions: "What type of work do you aspire to?" and "What type of work does your best job offer belong to?"

Their results may come as a surprise. While the exam system isn't a direct channel to the government in the same way that it was during the imperial dynasty, the students' preferences remain largely the same: 64 percent of college graduates still indicated that their top employment preference was the government. The probability of a student wanting to join the state sector didn't vary much with the eliteness of the college or college GPA. Even Hongbin was surprised when seeing this data—after China's economic liberalization and reforms, China's college graduates still prefer working for the state. He also found that attending an elite university boosts the odds of a student successfully securing a job with the state by 33 percent. In other words, China's education system still fosters a sense of loyalty to the government among the majority of its students, and the students who score the highest are still most likely to join the next generation of bureaucrats.[11]

While research credits this loyal pool of highly competent elite for fostering a more stable reign, the advent of the quota system only cemented the role of the education system as a bulwark of stability far beyond the ruler's elite circle. The oversight of the imperial examination system continued to pass from ruler to ruler, but one dynasty's rulers ran into a bit of a snag. The commoners who sought to rise through the hierarchy by way of the exam system came to believe that too many successful candidates hailed from China's southernmost regions, prompting anger and accusations of corruption. While the commoners were correct that there were more candidates from the South, it wasn't because there was corruption. Rather, the southerners were simply more prepared. Nonetheless, from a political perspective, discontented commoners were understandably viewed unfavorably by the emperor. It's generally important to have a balanced spread of power. If too many candidates are coming from one area, that area and those people might gain too much power. The problem was deftly handled with the invention of the quota system. As of 1425, under the new system, 40 percent of successful candidates would come from the north and 60 percent from the south, even if the southerners were still testing better than the northerners. Today, the quota allocation system is significantly more detailed than just north and south. Now, quotas are allocated across China's provinces. Recall that major metropolises like Beijing and Shanghai are designated as their own provinces with their own individual quotas, while politically sensitive regions, like Xinjiang, also garner significantly higher quotas than regions that are considered less politically sensitive. By allocating seats across the country, the quota system continues to attract talent from China's grassroots while simultaneously facilitating a balanced and stable spread of power.

Another particularly clever component of the quota system—and thus, the education system—is that it keeps families busy competing with one another. As we've mentioned, because seats are allocated regionally, the quota system ensures that everybody will know somebody or know of somebody who succeeded within the exam system. But because scores are assessed relative to others coming from the same regional quota, it also ensures that individuals are *competing* against people that they know—not against people from the South, nor against people from the next province, but against their neighbors. Even the tests vary by province to ensure that students can't directly compare their scores with students from other provinces. As a result, students like Ruixue didn't see students like Nan Nan as competitors. They came from different provinces, and thus their scores were not compared. These two factors—acknowledgment of merit and quotas—foster hope, but also the necessity to compete. It seems far more feasible to beat your neighbor than millions of nameless individuals from the south, but it also means that in all likelihood, only one of you will succeed. It's either you or your neighbor. And if you're a parent trying to give your child the best chance of success, the most logical path forward would not be to seek alternative paths through which your child might succeed, but to ensure your child's success within the existing education system. The system ensures parents' buy-in, year after year, which further bolsters societal stability: families are busily competing against each other to succeed within the tournament. These elements serve no one better than they do the ruler.

Last but not least, the ruler's monopoly over the contents of the education system ensures that students are taught to respect authority from the moment they set foot in the classroom. Historically, state-designated Confucian texts were used to prepare for examinations. Today, two publishing houses write most of the textbooks found on bookshelves throughout schools in China. These presses are entirely controlled by the government. Even the few private schools are required to teach some of the content espoused in these books. And while the government shuttered the tutoring industry overnight to alleviate the expenses on families' shoulders, it may have also been the case that they wanted education to be controlled and managed by the state, not the market.

Nonetheless, while China's curriculum is largely controlled by the central government, there's no guarantee that students will internalize whatever it is that they're learning. To test whether school curricula affects students' political attitudes and beliefs, researchers analyzed the impact of a high school politics curriculum intended to shape students' ideology introduced by the CCP between 2004 and 2010. The researchers found that China's students—at least the two thousand undergraduate students surveyed at one elite university—did indeed internalize much of the curriculum designed by the government. Following institution of the new curriculum, students trusted government officials more, viewed them as more civic-minded, and believed bribery was less prevalent. Students also viewed China as more democratic, influenced by a curriculum touting the merits of a "socialist democracy," though they were skeptical of unconstrained free markets and democracy.[12]

Hongbin and his team took this one step further by investigating the impact of the curriculum on students' political participation and career choices. What they found only confirmed what the previous researchers found: students' exposure to the new curriculum increased the likelihood of joining the CCP in college by 7 percent and enhanced the chance of securing state-sector jobs after graduation by 11 percent. Not only that, but the new curriculum redirected students' human capital investments toward skills deemed more valuable in the state sector.[13] While this feature of the education system—content control and ideological influence—is by no means unique to China, and indeed, is a hallmark of dictatorships through the ages, it is no less effective at bolstering stability and loyalty among those within the system.

Such changes to the curriculum may also have something to do with the rise of nationalism over the last decade.[14] Across social media platforms, netizens have begun to refer to China's youngest as the "Little Pink" (小粉红). The rise of nationalistic rhetoric in and out of the classroom is planting the seed of nationalism early, giving rise to a generation of so-called "pink" students who are well-suited to one day swell into a powerful sea of nationalistic "red" citizens who are loyal followers of the CCP. This phrase has seeped out of social media and is now commonplace across China.

CHANGES—AND ANGER—THROUGH THE AGES

While we've spent a significant chunk of our word count explaining why the education system is a particularly powerful political tool, it's equally as important to understand what gives rise to incidents of unrest, like that in Xicheng District. At first glance, such protests may suggest a weakness in the system. But by exploring other historical moments of unrest, it may in fact suggest just the opposite.

Perhaps one of the most notable instances of upheaval throughout the long history of China's education system was the imperial

examinations' abolition by the Qing dynasty in 1905. China was enduring what would later be known as the "century of humiliation" (1839–
1949), during which China experienced invasion and subjugation by
the West and Japan. The exam was considered by many intellectuals to
be one of the root causes of China's failings. They believed the exam
sought out men who were obedient to their elders and able to recite the
classics rather than those with political ability or technical knowledge
of modern topics like science and engineering.[15] After its abolition, the
dynasty attempted to modernize China by switching to a Western-style
education system. But for those who had invested so much time,
money, and effort into the older exam system, government resources
aimed at providing an alternative to the exam were simply intolerable.
The new system favored the existing elite even more than the old system. In other words, family background mattered more than education. For the mere commoner, this meant that there wasn't a clear path
to elite status, which also meant that the core mandate of the education
system was no more.

Consider the time that would-be elites spent studying for the
imperial exam. Those hopefuls had spent a significant portion of
their lives memorizing huge swaths of text. To understand those per-
sonally affected by the abolition of the exam, Ruixue and her colleague Ying Bai turned to newspaper reports and individual diaries
from 1905. On September 18, Zhu Zhisan, a member of the gentry
in Hubei province nestled along the Yangtze River, recorded in his
diary that many exam hopefuls had cried after they received word of
the exam's abolition. In early October, Liu Dapeng, another member
of the gentry in a relatively isolated village in Shanxi province,
remarked on the abolition in his diary several times. He soon learned
from his friend in the provincial capital that many students had
joined recently established organizations and was worried that "disasters and calamities will arise from them." Using Liu Dapeng's diary
entries, another researcher depicted the shock of the abolition to a
typical village:

> Liu woke up a few days [after the abolition] "with a heart like ashes" as
> he realized that his hopes for an official career had now completely
> vanished. When the sun came up he went out into the village street
> and found that everyone he met was talking about the end of the
> examinations. He talked with them about what a disaster it would be
> for the country, especially since no one knew what the graduates of the
> modern schools would be like. Together they wondered about what
> other changes there would be in the next few years. People realized
> that the ending of the examination system would transform channels
> for social mobility and that many other changes would inevitably
> follow.[16]

Imagine if you were in their shoes. You, too, might wake up "with a heart like ashes." For those with years—decades, even—of vested interest in the imperial examination, the abrupt change in their prospects was intolerable. So intolerable that many historians have conjectured that it was the abolition of the exam system that partially contributed to the eventual fall of the Qing dynasty.

Ruixue and Ying decided to gather the data to test this theory. To do so, they studied the quota system, as they knew the quota system created regional variation in expectations. They then analyzed the composition of revolutionary groups who led the charge against the Qing dynasty to understand whether more revolutionary participants came from regions with higher quotas relative to the population size. If the abolition had contributed to the fall of the Qing dynasty, it would be the case that regions with higher exam quotas—regions where more men were likely to become elite by way of passing the exam—were associated with a higher probability of revolutionary participation following abolition of the exam.

They found that those historians were correct. Instead of channeling their energy into passing the exam, those tear-stricken would-be elites turned their worry, anger, and disappointment into revolution. They wanted change, and an opportunity to control their future. Their data

proved that as Liu Dapeng predicted, those "recently established organizations" gave rise to "disasters and calamities" for the Qing dynasty:
regions with higher quotas were associated with a higher probability of
revolutionary participation after the exam was abolished. Just a few
short years later, in 1911, successful revolutionary activity overthrew the
Qing dynasty.

We can learn a few things from the abolition of the imperial exams.
For one, the abolition was an attempt to solve some major problems
underlying the system: the content was not meeting the needs of the
time. While other countries were teaching science and engineering to
advance their economies, China was still focused on classical texts.[17]
While inarguably important, this would be the equivalent of today's
most prestigious universities offering only a classics degree. Something
did need to change. But what the Qing dynasty's leadership did not
realize in their attempt to solve this issue was how important a channel
of social mobility was to the masses, and how devastating a unilateral
abolition of exams would be. The abolition reflected the poorly executed
will of the leadership, not the desire of the people. Slow change rather
than abolition of an institution that Chinese society had collectively
invested in would have been prudent. Instead, abolition mobilized revolutionary sentiment among hopeful gentry members, contributing to
the fall of the Qing dynasty.

Years later, Chairman Mao fell into a similar trap, though he was not
the one who ultimately had to bear the consequences. While the Qing
dynasty had one problem to solve—they felt the exam content was not
meeting the needs of the moment—Mao had another he wanted to
solve—he sought to shatter society's existing hierarchy and form a new
one of his own. In other words, Mao wanted a revolution.[18] Among the
best ways to get rid of the hierarchy in China was to abolish the exam,
as it was and remains one of the main mechanisms creating and maintaining the hierarchy. To create a new hierarchy, one that he could
mold to his liking, Mao created a new education system. The new
system involved sending over 22 million urban "educated" youth to the

countryside to learn from the rural peasants. What he saw as the corrupt bourgeois ideology of the education system would be all but obliterated, and the sent-down youth's spirits would be cleansed of the old education system's failures. Mao was successful in his endeavor to dismantle the hierarchy: he all but guaranteed that these youth would never get a formal education.[19] Even after he passed away and the Cultural Revolution became but a memory, it still hampered the sent-down youth's prospects of employment. Hongbin and his colleague Lingsheng Meng found that before the Cultural Revolution, 1.5 percent of the Chinese people attended college. But among the sent-down youth, only 0.5 percent received a college education after the Cultural Revolution ended. They were also less likely to be employed at age fifty, during China's reform period.[20]

After Mao's death, China witnessed another bout of large-scale protests. Unsurprisingly, those who had been sent to the countryside for re-education under Mao, who had endured years of poverty and displacement, demanded to return to their homes. Those same youth stood alongside millions of others in their demand for the restoration of a formal education system. Millions around China had missed their chance of getting an education during the Cultural Revolution, and thus, the opportunity to access a better life. With Mao's death marking the end of an era characterized by complete upheaval, pressure was mounting on the government to restore a sense of normalcy. Tens of thousands of petition letters from all around the country arrived in Beijing, demanding restoration of the education system and the gaokao, which was seen as providing new opportunities for employment. Professors around the country began openly attacking Mao's so-called education system.[21] Deng Xiaoping himself even concluded that Tsinghua University, China's most elite, ought really to be called "Tsinghua Elementary School" because those admitted students under Mao's recommendation system were quite literally at the level of elementary school students, having only ever been "educated" by their experience in the countryside.[22] Indeed, without an education system providing a channel for social mobility, China's millions of youth lacked any opportunity for advancement. Naturally, leaders returned to a tried-and-true method to ensure both stability and loyalty: the exam system. Restoring the gaokao served as the perfect pressure release valve to placate unrest. It also made Deng extremely popular.

Mao's actions represent another example of a new leader tweaking the education system in a way that reflected his own priorities. Instead of taking issue with the system's content, Mao took issue with the system's maintenance of China's social hierarchy. But whereas the Qing dynasty doubled down and refused to reinstate a channel for social mobility, Deng reneged on Mao's promise, recognizing the power the education system exerted over the masses and reinstating the gaokao. Along with it, he reinstated China's hierarchy.

Instead of introducing an entirely new system, today's leadership prioritizes equality. Although the government has instituted relatively significant changes over the last few years—tweaking the quota system, eliminating the housing districts, and abolishing the tutoring industry— our experience has made us think that these changes are really only the tip of the iceberg of what could have been and what may be coming. In 2013, Hongbin was tasked by education authorities to reform China's gaokao system. The goal was to introduce a series of tests that would roughly resemble advanced placement (AP) exams in the United States, which would ideally mitigate student stress: individual AP tests could be taken several times throughout high school, instead of the one all-important exam scheduled only for one day.

For several years, Hongbin designed, adapted, and perfected this new set of exams, writing the first series of textbooks that might be used to study AP Economics. As an experiment, he even taught thirty high school students selected from the top three high schools in the country. He also spent several summers training high school teachers from all over China how to teach for AP Economics. But suddenly the tests were scrapped. Hongbin never received much of an explanation, but he understood the following: China's people have relied on one test for their whole lives. They trust the gaokao. Reforming the gaokao is the equivalent of reforming the entire education system. Given how past reforms were received by the public, Hongbin realized that reforming the gaokao might cause protests unlike any that modern-day China has seen. He also knew that changing the exam might cause equity issues. While he trained high school teachers from all over China, none of them were from rural areas. Instead, it was the teachers from elite urban high schools who were prioritized to teach the exams. Yet again, rural students would fall behind. And while urbanites are, in many ways, the aristocracy of today, rural populations still comprise a little over half of China's population. Equity aside, putting them at any further disadvantage could be risky.

Hongbin's reforms were not the only initiative put on hold as the government moved forward in their vision of realizing "Common Prosperity" in education for all. Like the protests that unfolded on the steps of the Xicheng Education Building in 2021, most civil unrest has received little coverage, quickly hushed by state media. In an earlier attempt to implement a more equitable education system, however, the Ministry of Education in 2016 had expanded college quota seats for students from poorer provinces. Elite colleges were expected to allocate 6.5 percent of their seats to these students.[23] Infuriated with what they saw as an unjust policy, parents in over twenty cities around China took to the streets to advocate for their children's access to college education. The scale and vitriol fueling protests seemed to take government officials by surprise, so much so that they backed down, abandoning the changes altogether. Similarly, China's government has also tacitly walked back their all-out abolition of the tutoring industry: though monolithic tutoring enterprises like New Oriental are still prohibited by law from offering their services, recent anecdotal evidence suggests that the government is no longer enforcing their anti-tutoring policy when it exists on a smaller scale.[24] In calling off their sweeping reforms, China's policymakers seem to be recognizing the following: China's education system is a tournament. Whenever you change the rules of a tournament, there will inevitably be losers. The successful implementation of a policy seems to hinge on how many of those who are losing out will protest. China's people rarely protest—unless it involves their children's education, which is widely viewed as one of the few routes through which they can change their life outcomes.

Taken together, the abolition of the imperial examination system, Mao's drastically reinvented education system, and the equity-minded administration of today can be viewed in a similar light. With new leadership comes new policy priorities, and new policy priorities often bring change to China's education system. But because China's education system is a tournament, any change of the rules means that at least someone loses. The bigger the change, the more people lose. An abolition of the system means that most everyone who had invested in the system loses. The system's strength—and the rulers' propensity to return to it, time and time again—lies in the tremendous investment of China's masses. In this light, consider how the abolition of the imperial examination system contributed to the fall of the Qing dynasty. As a political tool, the education system is a powerful one. But considering how much vested interest there is in the system, leaders of all stripes must carefully weigh the repercussions of whatever change they intend to make to the education system. Otherwise, they may face a protest on a scale larger than that in Xicheng District, larger than they are able to contain.

A SYSTEM ENGINEERED FOR GOVERNANCE

The education system is one of the most powerful political tools that the government has at its disposal. Together, the many clever design features of China's exam system bolster the ruler's power and secure buy-in from the masses year after year by serving the ruler—in today's day and age, the CCP—as a powerful political tool. Rulers must simply tread carefully when shaping the system to reflect their own political priorities in order to ensure a careful balance of winners and losers. Historically, throwing such caution to the wind has triggered revolutionary sentiment.

The exam system has survived for over a thousand years because it's such a cleverly designed system. Above all else, it provides the crucial channel for social mobility that fosters hope, stability, and loyalty among the masses, particularly the elite. There are, however, several other elements of the system that only further cement its role in ensuring social stability:

1. Scoring well on the exam is the only criterion for advancement— the higher the score, the better the outcome.
2. The responsibility to take advantage of such an opportunity falls on the individual because of the simplicity of the system's design. As a result, when people lose, they accept the fault as their own.
3. The exam recruits talented individuals to serve in the government.
4. The new elites owe their power to the ruler.
5. The quota system ensures a balance of power by recruiting individuals from different regions.
6. The quota system keeps families busy competing with each other. Because the stakes are so high, they are unlikely to pursue opportunities outside of the system.
7. The government has a monopoly on the system's content and effectively controls it to promote ideology consistent with their political priorities.

All of these features bring us to the following conclusion: China's education system is a highly centralized, political one—it is the state who writes the rules of China's largest tournament, and in doing so, sets up the tournament so it is the government who will continue to come out on top. And while China's so-called "ruler" has evolved from an emperor to a chairman to a general secretary, China's leadership only continues to reap the political benefits offered by the system. Indeed, the goal of China's education system remains a political one: to develop the next batch of competent officials loyal to the central core of the CCP. The hierarchical nature of the system continues to rank students based on one metric—their score on a test—and only the highest-scoring students join the ranks of the government. College graduates indicate that their number one job preference is a government job, and it is the highest-scoring students who are more likely to realize this preference. In this way, China's education system—the centralized hierarchical tournament—does effectively meet its goal, serving the very institution that designed it: the central government.

5

Centralization
and the
Rise of STEM

o   o   o

"With a good grasp of mathematics, physics, and chemistry, you can travel the world without fear."

"学好数理化，走遍天下都不怕。"

—Chinese proverb

In 2023, for the first time since the pandemic, Ruixue returned to China. That year, she and her former classmates gathered around a table piled high with Hunan cuisine for what was typically an annual reunion. Not that the food mattered, though—Ruixue was there to get a better sense of China's education system from those who were living within it. In China, rapid change is a constant. As a result, perspectives from individuals within the system often diverge from those of external observers. Ruixue's former classmates, many of whom also majored in economics, went on to become professors in the field and were now teaching at some of Beijing's most elite universities. It was the insights of these former classmates that Ruixue was particularly eager to hear.

July is always a busy time for professors in China, and also a challenging time for the professors who work in the economics departments at China's most elite universities. About one month after China's students finish taking the gaokao in June, they learn their scores. It is around that time, in early July, that professors, especially those who work at China's most elite universities, are charged with recruiting the highest-scoring students from the far-reaching corners of each and every province of China.

That year happened to be the first year that professors were once again sent across the country to conduct their annual recruiting ritual since China's officials announced the end of the pandemic in December of 2022. The professors noticed that some things had changed. In the years prior to the pandemic, professors in economics departments generally faced few challenges in successfully recruiting the highest-scoring candidates to their departments. Students had seemed more interested in STEM fields than they had been in the early 2000s, but after the pandemic, the uptick in interest increased. When the professors asked students why they wanted to specialize in STEM fields, many of the students expressed variations of the same intent: they wanted to better serve their country. While the professors knew that students wanted to pursue majors that would offer prestigious employment after college, they hadn't often heard such a sentiment expressed about the STEM fields.

Economics, science, technology, engineering, and mathematics had always been popular fields in China, but now economics was slipping further and further behind the STEM fields as the demand among the highest-scoring students for an economics degree was no longer what it once was. This year, professors had to face it head on, in person, as they tried and failed to draw the highest-scoring students to their departments.

"Our golden age is behind us." Ruixue's colleagues lamented the fall of their field's popularity. Their departments were no longer as desirable as they once were. Unlike days past, they no longer had their pick of China's top test-takers, which they felt was apparent in the declining quality of their students. Indeed, within the professors' departments, they had noticed that their students' average gaokao

score had fallen. Much to their chagrin, the best and brightest were lost to their colleagues—now more aptly viewed as competitors—in the STEM fields. Down the line, their diminishing status may have implications for the benefits they enjoy as professors. For now, they simply lamented what they saw as a decline in the quality of their students.

I, Ruixue, empathized with my colleagues. Both Hongbin and I have noticed a similar decline in students' interest in our fields in the United States. When Hongbin received his PhD from Stanford in the early 2000s, both the economics department and computer science department graduated about 170 students every year. In 2023, just over twenty years later, that number for economics has dipped to 100 students, with the smallest class of 69 students graduating in 2018. That same year, the computer science department graduated 320 students, over four times that of the economics department.[1] Without a doubt, these trends indicate that the United States, too, is witnessing a growing interest in STEM fields, especially computer science. The scale of these trends, however, is incomparable. In the US, the number of STEM students doubled between 2009 and 2021, increasing by roughly 300,000 students. But in China, while the size of the graduating pool of STEM students also nearly doubled, it marked an increase of about 2.5 million students. In other words, the size of China's STEM student pool is over eight times that of the US's.[2] This outsized pool of STEM talent in China has even given rise to damaging stereotypes that suggest that Chinese students, and even more broadly, Asian American students, have some sort of innate gift for the STEM subjects.

Though there are certainly parallels in students' rising interest in STEM in both the United States and China, we've noticed that the driving force behind the demise of the golden age of economics in China is not the same market-driven one as in the United States. Like most changes that come to pass within the education system in China, there is one institution responsible: China's central government.

The centralized nature of China's education system allows the government to drive the system to serve its agenda, political and otherwise, albeit with care. Since China opened to the rest of the world, many would argue that its agenda—in particular, its economic agenda—has been quite effective. After all, China is actively competing against the United States for the title of the world's largest economy. When deftly orchestrated, China's education system can be an incredibly strong one. But how do they go about doing so?

Centrally controlling an institution that stretches across one of the world's largest and most populous countries, one that touches millions of lives each year, is no easy task. It is impossible for central leadership to be in every school at all times. Instead, the government can dictate big-picture policies: they set the agenda from start to finish, designing the many procedures and exams necessary to keep the system running according to plan. To ensure proper follow-through on their well-laid plans, however, the central government must exercise control over two major components of the system: its people and its resources. Doing so, and doing so well, is still no easy task.

We'll start with the people. In China, anyone who works for the education system, from a kindergarten teacher to the dean at an elite university in Beijing, is part of the state sector. At every level of the government, there is an institution, the Personnel Quota Office, in charge of implementing the quota regulations within the state sector. These regulations specify the number of positions and personnel of a certain rank that can be allocated within any of the institutions under the state sector's umbrella. Quotas are enforced by the Personnel Quota Offices at each level of government. For example, if a high school in Jilin wants to have five more teachers in their school system, the school needs to apply to the local education department. The local education department then applies to the local Personnel Quota Office as well as the local Personnel Office and the local Public Finance Department, because the school needs both the five quotas as well as the allocation of state funding to support five new teachers. This fact alone is crucial to understanding centralized control of the system. Because these positions are all part of the state sector, it is the central government that dictates how many positions are available within each part of the system.[3] They can decide to create a position. They can also decide to eliminate a position. In this context, consider the hidden benefits that allow public-sector employees to address three of the largest expenses for most of China's families: education, healthcare, and housing. It only makes sense that the central government decides how many people get access to such benefits. Too many and the hidden benefits would flow too freely. Too few might foster the dangerous perception that too much power is concentrated in the hands of a select few.

In addition to deciding how many positions are available within the education system, the central government also dictates the power and hierarchy associated with administrative university positions. Administrative university positions are part of the CCP bureaucratic ranking system, and the power associated with each rank is dependent on the tier of the university. The highest-ranked universities in China, including Peking University, Tsinghua University, and Fudan University, have power equivalent to the position of a vice minister. This means that both the university CCP secretary and president—the two highest positions in a university—have power equal to that of vice ministers. Meanwhile, deans at these elite universities are at the level of a director or county mayor. Consider this in contrast with the United States: What if the dean of Harvard Business School held state-sanctioned political power? These rankings are in place to ensure that individuals in positions of power within the education system can enjoy all the benefits associated with similarly ranked positions within the government. While officials at the most elite, highest-tier universities technically have the most power, the president at a third-tier university would also have a ranking, albeit much lower, just like all administrative university positions.[4]

Note that high school, middle school, and elementary school administrative positions do not have official ranks. This, too, is indicative of the hierarchy: much like in the United States, university positions are often viewed as relatively more prestigious—they are closer to the government, after all—and thus positions below them in the hierarchy do not warrant the hidden benefits associated with official rankings in the CCP. However, data show that higher-ranked positions within any institution in China, from elementary school to elite colleges, are unquestionably more desirable. This stands in contrast to the United States, where administrative positions in academia are usually among the least desirable posts that one can hold. In China, each step in the hierarchy brings with it more hidden benefits and more resources.[5] In high-ranking universities and other prestigious state-sector positions, such benefits are explicitly bestowed by the central government.

In addition to controlling the people charged with running the system, the central government also controls the money flowing into the higher education system. While the government has made efforts to diversify its funding sources (*entirely* funding all aspects of the education system would be a tremendous drain on resources), the vast majority—67.6 percent, as of 2016—still comes from government funds. However, such funds are not distributed equally across all of China's universities. Elite universities at the top of China's hierarchy often receive priority in funding, as do the fields within the elite universities that are considered particularly important.[6]

By exercising control over the people and the money flowing into the institutions that the people control, China's central government effectively manages the education system. Yet so much of what we've touched on occurs within higher education, especially elite higher education: the university faculty and administrative positions, the students attending the universities, and the money flowing into them. This leads us to reiterate a nontrivial caveat. Because China's education system is truly massive, it would be inaccurate to say the central government is itself reaching into the furthest corners of China's education system. Beijing, as we said, is *not* in every classroom around the country. In fact, while the system is centralized in its major decision-making, it is relatively decentralized in its implementation. Think about it this way: if China's education system is a symphony orchestra, the central government is the conductor. The conductor must rely on the various musicians to follow through with their instructions. In this case, the musicians are all of China's local governments.[7]

While local governments own and fund most non-elite universities and all pre-tertiary institutions, namely elementary, middle, and high schools, they are still subject to centralized control. At every level of the system, there is a Department of Education, and each department reports up the food chain. If they do not follow the central policies, the officials at any level could be removed or, in extreme cases, put in jail. Meanwhile, if they implement the policies particularly well, they are more likely to be promoted. It is through this hierarchical incentive structure that the central government is able to wield control effectively, even from Beijing. In other words, China's central government controls the system by controlling the personnel and providing pointed policy direction, while it is the local government who are in charge of implementing the policies and coming up with much of the funding to do so.[8]

And despite the fact that the system is logistically decentralized— the local governments are responsible for day-to-day implementation and follow through—remember that the entire pre-college education system has one purpose: to prepare students to excel on the gaokao. The gaokao is the final movement in the symphony leading up to college. If the first movements deviate in any way from the central plan, then the students under that local government's control will fail, which only spells trouble for the local government. Indeed, the gaokao is arguably the most centrally controlled component of the whole education system.

THE RISE OF STEM

Centralized control over the education system grants China's government a monopoly over one of the resources at the heart of every country's development: its human capital. Around the world, countries have long recognized that human capital, the collective value of a population's skills, knowledge, and experience, bolsters labor productivity that drives innovation and long-term economic growth.[9] Education is the number one way to raise a country's human capital. While it is reasonably possible for most governments to control the quantity of human capital by educating greater numbers of its population, China's education system is unique in that it also controls the *type* of human capital available.

Driven by decades of aggressive expansion, China produces roughly one in every five of the world's college graduates today. After taking China's helm in 1978, Deng Xiaoping decided to drastically change the scale and scope of China's education system. He envisioned a system that was accessible to the masses. He also envisioned a system that would equip students with the skills necessary to succeed on the labor market and propel China's economy forward. He ensured this by returning to the curriculum taught before the Cultural Revolution, one that prioritized the sciences over Maoist political thought.[10] With the central government behind him, he successfully spearheaded an era often referred to as the "massification" of China's higher education system.[11] In 1976, only about 1 percent of eighteen- to twenty-four-year-old students were enrolled in college. By 2021, however, an astounding 57 percent of eighteen- to twenty-four-year-old students were enrolled in China's universities. Compare this to the United States, where the overall college enrollment rate for eighteen- to twenty-four-year-old students was 38 percent.[12] Though today's students may not be learning as much as they *could* be learning in college, recall that gaining admission to college alone requires mastery of the gaokao. China's students thus rank best in the world on standardized measures of skill

assessment. With the central government's control over China's policies, its people, and its resources, China was able to expand its higher
education system at an unprecedented pace. In this regard, controlling
the education system has allowed the central government to control the
quantity of its human capital. It's no coincidence that at the same time,
China has experienced an unprecedented period of economic growth.

While the quantity of China's human capital was the first step in
catalyzing China's remarkable decades of economic growth, the type
and composition of China's human capital is equally, if not more,
important. In order to compete with the United States for the title of
world's largest economy, China would need to secure sufficient human
capital. As we've established, China's massive education expansion over
the last several decades has accomplished just that. The next step would
be to supercharge specific fields that are responsible for driving economic growth.

When China joined the World Trade Organization (WTO) and
needed guidance in navigating complex economic territory, the government allocated a bounty of resources and higher quotas to elite universities, especially those that specialized in economics. The government
takes similar measures today, enlarging the quota for STEM majors
and directing funding for these fields toward some of the best universities. Even within a single university, the economics department is
losing seats to STEM departments. This redirection is exactly what
Ruixue's colleagues, the economics professors, find so disheartening.
The central government can also open entirely new universities that
specialize in fields prioritized by the government. In 2015, for example,
China's Ministry of Education launched microelectronics schools at
Peking University and Tsinghua University, among twenty-four others,
to train engineers in integrated circuit design, manufacturing, packag-
ing, and testing, as well as integrated circuit equipment and materials
at the undergraduate, masters, and doctoral levels.[13] By training engineers in fields that are critical to US-China competition, these programs are responsible for attracting the human capital foundational to

sustainable growth in the industry, long past when students graduate. And even if they don't attract as many students as their counterparts in the West, large numbers of Chinese students will end up in STEM fields following their graduation because these new universities and majors exist. Employed in industries poised to compete, they will continue to serve the government's purposes.

Yet, opening the doors to entirely new university programs and increasing the quotas and funding only affects the supply side of the equation. In other words, these measures can help to increase the sheer *number* of students graduating from these universities in these fields. What these measures can't necessarily influence, however, is the demand side of the equation. The government hasn't explicitly forced any of the country's highest-scoring students to major in STEM fields. Nonetheless, Ruixue's colleagues have reported that the highest-scoring students state they want to study STEM to better serve their country. When Hongbin graduated from college in the 1990s, the government could create incentives to encourage the highest-scoring students to study in desired fields by guaranteeing them positions in the state sector. Today, the government has moved away from explicitly guaranteeing postgraduate employment. Instead, the government leans heavily on its state media. Because state-controlled news outlets and social media accounts are among the most widely consumed media sources in China, the government can count on its citizens to receive the explicit message that STEM majors are worth investing in, as well as an implicit message: students in these fields will receive government support and, more important, a job after graduation.[14]

Such messaging also travels fast by word of mouth—education is a hot topic in any household—and visibly manifests in the career prospects of China's families. Take Hongbin's family, for example. He has two nephews who are five years apart in age. Following in his uncle's footsteps, the older nephew chose to study economics, thinking his decision wise. Five years later, his younger cousin opted for computer science. Now, even though they both scored well on the gaokao and earned degrees from two elite universities, only one nephew has job prospects in the sectors of his choosing. Unsurprisingly, it is the nephew who majored in computer science, trusting that the government would have his back. Indeed they did. It is anecdotes like this that are hard to miss these days in China—study STEM, and you will be rewarded.

All considered, it's no wonder that the highest-scoring students reported to Ruixue's colleagues that they wanted to study STEM to better serve their country. This epitomizes another of the strengths of China's system—they can rapidly influence not only the supply of students but student's demand for opportunities to study in these emerging fields. By publicly shifting its priorities toward STEM, the government nudges its highest-scoring students toward fields that will help the country achieve economic superiority. By directing their highest-quality students into one field, the central government is expecting that these students will become industry leaders in cutting-edge fields. And by investing in these industries in parallel, the government effectively creates a university-to-industry pipeline. It's precisely for this reason that Hongbin, Ruixue, and many of their former classmates majored in economics and went on to become economics professors when the major was popular: the government all but told them to do so. Now, however, the central government is shifting its policy priorities to STEM universities in the hope that these fields will be responsible for driving economic growth and innovation down the line. In contrast, while the United States might be hoping that some of its brightest people are heading into those fields, the government lacks a mechanism that can so explicitly direct the supply and demand of its most talented according to a set agenda.

In addition to these measures on the student side, the government has also begun to offer incentives to facilitate university faculty's research in these fields. Those who publish high-quality research in a particularly desirable discipline—say, microchips—earn cash prizes from the government. But cash prizes aren't just handed out to any publication pertaining to microchips. Academic journals are ranked based on how "impactful" the journal is, or how many citations an article can get. The highest-ranking journals are usually those that receive the most citations, which would confer a higher-impact ranking. Given the emphasis placed on rankings and hierarchy in China, it follows that only publications in the highest-ranking globally recognized journals come with the highest of cash prizes.

If a professor not only produced globally recognized, high-quality research, but also produced a high volume of research, there is another set of prizes available—promotion, and in turn, funding. Publications in high-tier journals are a prerequisite for any promotion. Without fulfilling the quota necessary to advance in a given field, it is nearly impossible to receive a promotion. Without a promotion, it's much harder to receive funding. The central government closely monitors researchers and their publications to reward them for findings that will promote growth in the most desirable fields.

THE FALL OF THE SOCIAL SCIENCES

Equally as important as what the government promotes, however, is what the government chooses to criticize. Though students across China recognize that STEM fields are gaining more traction than ever before thanks to explicit government support, China's leadership has maintained a relatively stable relationship with the hard sciences over the last several decades. The epigraph at the beginning of this chapter says as much: there is no need to fear if you study STEM fields. Since Deng Xiaoping and his administration initiated China's sweeping economic reforms, it was well understood that the hard sciences were to play a significant role in shaping the future of the nation. Even before that, the imperial exams were abolished partly because critics felt that there wasn't enough of a focus on the hard sciences, which, in their opinion, contributed to China's lack of development. In an ideologically sensitive country like China, such constancy can be attributed to the relatively straightforward nature of the hard sciences; indeed, math rarely threatens the views of the regime. On the flip side of this stability, however, is the government's relatively volatile relationship with the social sciences.

It's possible to map the ideological trajectory of the government by looking solely at its relationship with the social sciences. As both a student and professor, Hongbin experienced firsthand the evolution of economics in China. Until the early 1990s, the only school of thought taught in China was known as "political economy," which applied Marxist theory to the Chinese context across all aspects of the field of economics. This is the economics that dominated Hongbin's classrooms in both high school and college. He still remembers the four main tenets well: 1) capital and capitalists are morally wrong—they exploit labor; 2) only labor can create value, not capital; 3) the market is inefficient because prices fluctuate wildly and cannot reflect the real value of the labor that contributed to creating a given product; and 4) capitalism, or the market economy, is just a transitory stage on the long road to Communism.

In the early 1990s, however, leadership began to give more leeway to universities. Recognizing that the expansion of their economy might require information from the West, central leadership began allowing its university faculty to teach a more Americanized version of economics known as "Western Economics," albeit in a limited fashion. It was around this time that Hongbin, a university student, opted to take a rare Western economics class taught by a young professor who had just returned from a one-year visit to Israel. The name and course description made it clear that while China could learn from the West, those lessons would not be absorbed without a healthy dose of skepticism. Throughout that semester, Hongbin and his classmates used a photocopied English textbook written by Paul Samuelson, one of the first Americans to win the Nobel Memorial Prize in Economic Sciences.[15] They could only read it in a highly restricted section of the library.

While the professor didn't seem to have the best grasp on what "Western Economics" really meant, Hongbin found the concepts as fascinating as they were shocking. Indeed, Western Economics wasn't as much a different branch of economics as it was the complete opposite of the Marxist economics with which Hongbin was so familiar. A market-based economy that is actually good? And efficient? Capital can create value—not just labor? These concepts were entirely antithetical to everything he'd learned up to that point. But to Hongbin, they intuitively made sense. What shocked Hongbin the most, however, was the absence of who he thought to be the greatest economist ever known to man: Karl Marx. For the first time in Hongbin's life, he frequented the library every day. He wanted to know what Samuelson had to say.

Years later, when Hongbin eventually returned to China to teach at Tsinghua University, in 2006, the Marxist economic theory of his early years had been totally upended. Economics has officially become westernized. Marxism was merely required as a politics class in the economics department; all newly recruited professors had received their PhDs from North America or Western Europe; and most dramatically, the school required most undergraduate classes to be offered in English. For over a decade, Hongbin taught western-style economics in English at Tsinghua. At the same time, most top economics departments transitioned to an American-style tenure system, and young faculty were required to publish in the top economics journals in English to be promoted. It was this era that Ruixue's colleagues dubbed "the golden age."

Having returned to China in recent years, Hongbin has watched the trend lines reversing. The central government is requesting that China's professors write their own version of economics textbooks in Chinese (certainly not in English). New content must emphasize Chinese characteristics: all the examples in the book need to revolve around China, all the while emphasizing the Marxist theory that Hongbin learned as a youth. Many economics departments once again count Chinese economics journals as top journals for promotion cases, even though they are widely known to be of lower quality than their English-language counterparts. The line between politics and economics is growing increasingly blurry.

Even usage of the English language—which, to leadership, serves as a symbolic representation of "the West"—has traveled a tumultuous path. During China's reform and opening period, many were exposed to the West for the first time, sparking an English language-learning fever across the nation. English became associated with success on the job market.[16] In response to the fervor, thousands of English tutoring companies sprang up, including New Oriental, Crazy English, and VIPKid, to name a few. But the factor driving most to learn English was likely this: English is a section on the gaokao. In recent years, however, central government action limiting English instruction has triggered an increasingly heated debate about the existence of English on the gaokao, and even about teaching English in elementary, middle, and high school classrooms across China. Collectively, such controversies can be more broadly understood as a reflection of China's ideological move away from Western influence. In the coming years, if the trend continues, it's likely that English will fall off the gaokao altogether.

Recent changes on the gaokao similarly reflect the ideological agenda of the CCP. Today, students are still tasked with picking one of two tracks to pursue on the gaokao—natural sciences, the government's preferred track, or the social sciences. From when Hongbin and Ruixue took the gaokao until quite recently, both tracks had to sit for a politics portion on the gaokao. Now, only one track needs to: the social sciences track. Such a shift only reiterates implicit government sentiment. From their perspective, STEM students pose little ideological threat to the regime. Social science students, on the other hand, do. As such, they are required to memorize and regurgitate political theory that bolsters the ideological superiority of the CCP.

It's clear that the government's attitude toward fields other than the hard sciences is relatively volatile, reflecting the political and ideological trends of China's leadership. During a period of reform, the social sciences were open to new ideas, ones that were born far from China's borders. Leadership prioritized economics, believing that educating its students in the field would facilitate growth that paralleled Western trajectories. Today, this couldn't be further from the truth. Indeed, one need only analyze the trajectory of the social sciences and the content taught in China's classrooms to get a better sense of China's ideological and political priorities.

• • •

China's government effectively controls the people running China's education system, the money flowing into the system, and both the quantity and type of human capital through a well-implemented and particularly convincing incentive structure. Using lots of carrots—study STEM and you'll get employed—and sticks—study social sciences, and you may be left high and dry—the government is able to use the education system to serve its needs. Over the past few decades, it has deftly crafted policies to guide the education system to serve its agenda. Researchers now produce more publications in cutting-edge fields, and China's best and brightest heed messaging to pursue degrees and employment in these same fields.

There are also key differences in the level of centralized control of education between the United States and China. In both, local governments are responsible for the day-to-day operations of their respective education systems. Local officials in charge of local education systems are elected and held accountable by their local constituents. But in China, local officials are held accountable only by their bosses in the central government. This means that across China, each local system follows the same set of instructions set forth by their boss. Meanwhile, in the United States, each state's local government makes its own decisions on their state's public education system, usually according to the values of their constituents—even one state's textbook can look different from another's. Even if the US federal government wanted full control over education, the decentralized nature of the system would make such a task nearly impossible.

Not only that, but the speed and scale of trends is a unique benefit of a centralized system. While the US government may also look to recruit more talented individuals into strategic fields like STEM, their hands-off approach means that leadership must wait for the market to react. In China, there is no such delay—they can act immediately and without hesitation. And with a population four times larger than that of the United States, the number of individuals affected by government action in China relative to the US is incomparable.

There's no question that China's government is a force to be reckoned with: it has many tools at its disposal to mobilize China's families one way or the other and wields them effectively to best serve its political and economic agenda. Though such tools are only as effective as China's families are receptive, the trend lines would suggest that China's families are indeed quite receptive, internalizing and acting upon messaging delivered by China's government. It's no wonder that the epigraph at the beginning of this chapter—"With a good grasp of mathematics, physics, and chemistry, you can travel the world without fear"—has gained such traction among China's families. Together, the public's perceptions and the government's actions strengthen one another, serving as an effective feedback loop that allows both parties to achieve their respective goals. It's not that China's students excel at STEM because they have an innate gift for STEM education, as the stereotype might suggest. Rather, it is the central government's firm direction and families' willingness to buy into the system that sways so many toward pursuing a STEM education.

6

Education and Global Power

o o o

"Science and technology are the primary productive forces."

—Deng Xiaoping

"科学技术是第一生产力。"

—邓小平

Over the course of its long and winding history, China's ever-changing factions have tweaked, abolished, and reestablished the exam system, serving to mirror both society's relative turmoil or stability as well as the ruler's agenda. At the outset, the exam system's priority was to assist the ruler in comfortably holding their power. Today, that remains as true as ever. And yet, now more than at any other point in China's—or the world's—history, political stability is deeply dependent on another factor: economic growth. It is for that very reason that today's education system reflects another reality of today's society: the deeply interconnected nature of China's politics and economy. One need only examine the government's emphasis on STEM and the relative decline of the social sciences to understand that the CCP hopes to leverage the system to serve its economic interests. But what, exactly, has been the role of the education system in shaping China's economic power?[1]

EDUCATION AND CHINA'S GDP

Since China's leaders initiated sweeping economic reforms in 1978, China's GDP per capita has increased at a rate of about 10 percent annually. This is the fastest rate of growth that any large country has sustained continuously. If you'll recall, it was over this same period that an increasingly large share of China's labor force also became educated. For starters, the average years of schooling for adults aged twenty-five or above rose from 4.0 in 1980 to 8.8 in 2014. Meanwhile, from 1977 to 2021, the number of newly admitted college students in China increased by thirty-seven times, from 273,000 to 10 million. And while the total employment in China increased by only 6 percent, from 739 million in 2000 to 784 million in 2020, the share of college-educated workers in the labor force more than quadrupled, from 6 percent to 28 percent.[2] The parallel expansions of China's GDP and college-educated work-force led us to wonder just how much education was responsible for fueling China's expansion over that period.

To go about answering this question, it is necessary to understand the factors responsible for driving GDP—the total production of a given country over the course of a year—at such an unprecedented rate. At the most basic level, GDP is equal to the number of workers multiplied by the productivity of each worker. China's dramatic growth can thus be broken down into a growth in the size of the working-age labor force and improvements in labor productivity. Labor productivity itself can also be further broken down into different strands: human capital and the more efficient usage of that human capital. As demonstrated by the statistics above, human capital improved by leaps and bounds over the past forty years. In parallel, China's labor also moved to more efficient sectors: from forced agriculture to manufacturing, and away from the state to the private sector.

Next, to ascertain how changes in these factors affected China's economic development, Hongbin and his team compared the relationship between education and GDP in China to the relationship between education and GDP in other countries, like Japan and the US, between 1980 and 2014.[3] Unsurprisingly, he and his team found that in all of these countries, when a country's average education level increased, so too did its GDP.[4] While many factors contribute to a country's production, Hongbin and his team found that there exists a very clear relationship between education and GDP: as much as 74 percent of the variation in GDP across countries can be explained by the variation in the average years of schooling in a country. This relationship exemplifies one simple truth: in most any country, education and GDP go hand in hand. It is this fact that gave Hongbin the ability to predict the GDP of an "average country" in the world based on that country's average level of education.

Yet, when China began its reform process in the 1980s, it was not an "average country" in two key respects. For one, the lingering effects of the Cultural Revolution meant that levels of human capital in China were relatively low—the average years of schooling among adults was only four years, which meant that China's people could barely read and write. Such low levels of education also meant that China's GDP per capita was low, at only about $600 a year. Not only were China's people not particularly well-educated, China did not fully utilize the human capital that it *had*. Hongbin's analysis shows that if China had fully utilized its human capital in 1980 as an "average country" would have, its income level would have been ten times higher, at roughly $6,000 a year. In other words, the potential productivity of China's human capital was only 10 percent utilized. Hongbin and his team attributed this to the fact that China's economy was being operated as a planned economy, one that was largely cut off from the rest of the world, which resulted in a less efficient and thus less productive workforce.

As China's reforms continued to unfold and its departure from isolationism facilitated an era of increased foreign investment and export opportunities, China began to move steadily toward the global average. By 2014, after just three decades of practically nonstop reforms, China had nearly reached the global average: the role of education in contributing to China's GDP is similar to the role that education plays in both the US and Japan. Moreover, China's steady improvement in the level of education in the past four decades also means that China is moving closer to the United States in its level of education and GDP.

Going one step further, Hongbin and his team broke down these changes to determine how much the improvement in human capital was responsible for shaping China's trajectory. In doing so, they found that one-third of these changes were driven by a rise in human capital, while two-thirds were due to China more efficiently using that human capital.[5]

This decomposition is revealing in two key dimensions. Firstly, it confirms that education has been a significant contributor to economic growth, accounting for roughly one-third of China's 10 percent annual GDP growth during the period—an impressive figure, given that long-term US GDP growth has averaged about 3 percent per year over the past century. China's leap from an average of four years of schooling to producing one-fifth of the world's college graduates underscores how essential its expansion of human capital has been in driving economic transformation. Secondly, the findings highlight that having an educated workforce alone is insufficient. In fact, two-thirds of China's growth can be attributed to reforms and policies that enabled the effective utilization of its human capital. This emphasizes that economic progress depends not only on education but also on policies that unlock the potential of a skilled labor force.

What's important to remember is this: sustainable growth hinges on a country's ability to fully leverage the potential of its human capital. Consider the Cultural Revolution for a stark contrast—during that period, China's most educated individuals were pushed to the margins of society, assigned to manual labor in the countryside rather than contributing to economic growth. A major issue in the 1960s and 1970s was the high unemployment rate among educated urban youth, which was among the reasons Mao sent 20 million urban youth to the countryside.[6] Compounding the problem, centrally controlled wages were detached from education or productivity levels, offering little incentive for workers to excel or innovate. As a result, China's human capital was severely underutilized during that time. However, with the post-reform era, educated individuals began to receive recognition and rewards for their productivity, both through higher wages and elevated social status. This shift encouraged them to join more productive factories and industries, where they were surrounded by similarly capable workers, further enhancing output. These changes underscore how China's reforms allowed for a more effective application of its expanding human capital, turning it into a key driver of the country's rapid economic growth.

Ironically, history seems to be repeating itself. China's economy has experienced a significant slowdown over the past decade, especially since the COVID-19 pandemic. Occurring alongside economic stagnation, youth unemployment has surged to concerning levels. Nonetheless, unemployment is far less grim than that of the 1960s and 1970s during the Cultural Revolution. Yet, at the same time, China's human capital has reached an all-time high, with over 10 million students graduating from college each year. This paradox raises two critical questions: Why isn't the educated workforce driving economic growth? And are Chinese students becoming over-educated?

It is important to recognize that merely increasing the number of college graduates is not enough to ensure sustainable growth. Human capital, though vital, accounts for only a fraction of economic development. Recall that even at its peak, it contributed to just one-third of China's rapid growth. More crucial to long-term success are market-friendly policies and stable geopolitical conditions—both of which are currently under fire.

Nonetheless, the commitment to education expansion reveals in part the economic agenda of China's leaders. Since Deng Xiaoping came to power in the late 1970s, it has been clear that he and subsequent leaders not only have understood the power of human capital in contributing to economic growth but have acted on that knowledge, aggressively seeking to improve China's level of education throughout the whole country. They have effectively reshaped the economy so that it can utilize the potential of its human capital. Taken together, it's clear to us that China's government does know that educating its people is the key to raising its economic power. That's why they have embarked on one of the most extraordinary education expansions that the world has ever seen. And yet, regulatory crackdowns on the platform economy, the tutoring industry, and the property sector, combined with the draconian zero-COVID policies and fiscal struggles at the local level, have stifled economic dynamism in the short term. Adding to the pressure are trade tensions with developed nations and restrictions on technology exports to China, which are likely to exacerbate economic challenges further. The current landscape highlights the need for smarter policy reforms that can better harness the potential of China's highly educated workforce and reignite economic growth.

EDUCATION AND TECHNOLOGY

Driving forward GDP is likely high on the priority list of most any leader around the world. And though it is an abstract and oftentimes unwieldy concept, it serves as a key indicator of far less abstract concepts, like higher employment and higher income, among other factors that contribute to a higher overall standard of living. Another equally important and, perhaps, equally abstract factor is this: technology. Put simply, technology is anything that helps society produce things better, faster, or cheaper. While two countries might funnel the same amount of resources into completing the same project, one country might be more productive than the next. This advantage—the ability to produce more with the same amount of resources—can often be attributed to technology. From the advent of knitting needles long ago to the modern complexity of artificial intelligence or quantum computing, technology has been a driving force of rapid change.

While GDP often serves as an indicator of the health of a country's economy and its standard of living, it also allows countries to compare their relative economic power and assess the next frontier of competition. So, too, does technology. Take, for example, the Cold War: both the US and USSR poured money into their technological capabilities, from nuclear weapons to the space race, to assert their ideological superiority and military strength. Today, technology—specifically, indigenous technological innovation—fuels competition between the US and China. Consider the US-China chip war. Chips are at the crux of the modern economy, lighting up both the devices that we rely on daily and emerging technologies critical to national security and military capabilities. To prevent China from gaining an edge in chip production, the US passed a slew of sanctions designed to cripple China's production of such technology. And yet, as the summer of 2023 drew to a close, one of China's biggest tech firms, Huawei, released a new phone. In that phone was technology that caught the United States flat-footed: the technology behind the chip powering the phone was far more advanced than the United States believed that China was capable of producing, calling into question the efficacy of the sanctions. Just over a year later, the Chinese company DeepSeek released an AI model that was believed to be both more efficient and cost-effective than existing models. The model's debut underscored China's ability to produce a higher quality output with less advanced inputs, making global headlines and causing shockwaves to ripple through stock markets in the process. Though some doubt remains regarding the true costs and exact models of chip that DeepSeek employed, the fact that it is an open-source tool adds to its authenticity. Such situations collectively indicate the speed with which China's government can respond when necessary.

By throwing money and well-educated workers at the target industry, China's centralized system is able to cultivate the resources necessary to counteract external pressures at a speed far greater than a typical market economy would allow. Indeed, from the Cold War to the US-China tensions of today, it is a country's technological capabilities, sometimes even more than a country's GDP, that is the focal point for geopolitical competition. Nonetheless, while critical to competition in and of itself, technology also has implications for GDP: new technology often boosts productivity, and productivity in turn boosts GDP. Much like education drives GDP, education, too, has supported China's ability to effectively drive technological advances.

Worth mentioning here is one event that has allowed China to compete as well as it does today: China's accession to the WTO in 2001. This event allowed China to integrate into the trend toward globalization and global value chains. Such circumstances collectively served as fodder for a budding manufacturing sector. Shortly after its WTO accession, China became known as the "factory of the world," a title it earned for producing a wide range of cheap goods like textiles, apparel, toys, furniture, and machinery. In recent years, however, China has increasingly moved into more competitive and high-tech manufacturing markets, aiming to export more technologically advanced goods like broadcasting equipment, computers, integrated circuits, electric vehicles, and even modern services like TikTok and DeepSeek.[7]

Economists have shown that the rise of education often leads to the rise of technology.[8] Is this also true in China? Xiao Ma, an economist and former student of Ruixue's, studied the role of college expansion in this technological upgrading of China's economy.[9] By measuring a firm's exposure to college expansion by the growth in the local number of college-educated workers, he found that firms exposed to a larger pool of college graduates experienced an increase in exports and domestic sales. These same firms also increased their investment in research and development (R&D), which is often associated with innovation. His study highlighted how college expansion and trade fed off one another. By developing a hypothetical model under which college expansion did not occur, he established that without college expansion, R&D would increase, but by 72 percent less. Without trade, R&D would also increase, but by 31 percent less. In other words, college expansion and China's openness to trade facilitated by the WTO worked in parallel to upgrade China's economy. Such findings certainly suggest that China's education system and the human capital it has delivered has been a crucial component of upgrading China's technological capabilities over the last several decades.

At face value, Xiao Ma's findings might suggest that China, with all its newfound human capital, is capable of independently innovating and upgrading its technological capabilities, as R&D is a common proxy for innovation. But before jumping to that conclusion, it's worth noting a couple of key facts. Measuring innovation is incredibly challenging—some might even argue impossible. While researchers have come up with several proxies for innovation, including R&D investment and invention patent applications, every measure has its flaws. As China underwent its technological upgrading, it may have been the case that China's new pool of human capital helped upgrade technological capabilities not through innovating themselves, but by learning from the international ecosystem that was suddenly at their fingertips. While education can certainly help individuals innovate, it can also give them the tools to mimic technology effectively. After all, how well can you read a highly technical manual written in a foreign language without ever having gone to school?

One method through which China has learned from the international ecosystem is by importing foreign technology. To do so, China pushed through policies that made foreign access to its market conditional on technology transfer to domestic firms. Put simply, China told foreign firms that if they wanted to do business, they had to give their technological know-how to China's firms. This practice rose sixfold between 2002 and 2012, with 85 percent of the increase occurring in industries key to China's advancement.[10] Such a practice has led one researcher to dub China the "re-innovation nation," in turn feeding the claims of others who criticize China's ability to truly innovate. Instead of innovating cutting-edge technology, it has been suggested that China may have utilized its human capital to *reproduce* cutting-edge technology. Importing and copying technology is not unique to

China—such a practice dates back to the days when countries first started to industrialize. And yet, it certainly escalated US-China tensions and strategic competition.

The use of these technology transfer policies is not to undermine the progress that China has made in its own right. As we know, one of the most tried-and-true methods to bolster domestic innovation is to produce the best scientists. The best scientists in turn produce top-notch research, which can be applied for practical purposes in China's industries. China's education system is uniquely positioned to produce the best scientists. This fact is one that China's government recognizes: indeed, by directing its most capable students to study STEM in college, China hopes that it can increase its country's scientific productivity and guarantee a future of domestically innovated technology. So has it succeeded?

As of 2019, among the top 1 percent of the world's most-cited publications, China's authors occupy the largest share by a wide margin.[11] Meanwhile, among the top fifteen universities responsible for producing the highest quality publications in 2022, China's universities filled nine of the fifteen spots, several of which surpassed Harvard University, Stanford University, and the Massachusetts Institute of Technology.[12] While many of China's leading scholars were likely influenced by Western education through earning secondary degrees abroad, China's education system seems capable of producing researchers who produce some of the worlds' best work, which bodes well for its ability to innovate independently.

On *measurable* publication outcomes, it is indisputable that China has been performing remarkably well. Yet, like measuring innovation, measuring publication quality is a challenging business. Though citations often serve as a conventional proxy for the quality of a publication, they are just that—a proxy, which means that there are inevitably flaws in its true ability to capture quality. It's also the case that citations can easily be artificially inflated. While a publication could be cited often because it's a new, cutting-edge paper that will bring China closer to the frontier of innovation, it is also possible that authors and their friends cite each other's papers to boost everyone's citation count. Only time will tell whether such research will drive domestic technological innovation.

THE FUTURE OF CHINA'S EDUCATION SYSTEM

The astounding expansion of China's education system has unquestionably contributed to China's dominance as one of the world's largest economies, playing an outsized role in driving GDP growth and upgrading China's technological capabilities. But such growth has not occurred in isolation. Decades of reforming, opening up, and learning from its peers has given China the tools to arrive where it is today.

And yet, where China is today is fundamentally uncertain. China's leadership has announced its intent to usher in a new era, wherein China's goal is no longer that of Deng Xiaoping's era—to hide and bide—but rather to lead a reconfigured global order. China's education system has been vital to reaching this turning point. But now, China is moving closer to the stage of development that requires indigenous innovation. Soon, China must produce its own new, cutting-edge technology to drive growth and remain competitive instead of importing and dissecting foreign technology. The United States and other Western countries have increasingly sought to decouple from China, particularly in the field of technology. It's clear that China both *wants* and *needs* to shift its course. To achieve its domestically driven innovation goals while simultaneously adapting to an increasingly hostile foreign environment, China needs a new mandate for its education system: to foster a pool of human capital that is capable of independently driving GDP growth and cultivating domestic innovation.

The education system may face some challenges in doing so. If you'll recall, we've described China's education system as "centralized," "hierarchical," and as a "tournament." While these characteristics may have benefited China in its rise, they may now serve as obstacles in China's path to leading a new global order.

For one, rapid shifts in political priorities by the central government can suddenly render entire segments of the college-educated population relatively obsolete. Take Hongbin's nephew's economics degree, for example. As he planned for college, he believed that it would be wise to major in economics. But just five years later, the government was giving priority to engineering majors over economics majors. Despite the central government's best efforts, it's nearly impossible to plan a system from start to finish. The future holds countless unforeseeable circumstances that will affect the government's policy agenda. On a new path, China can no longer allocate its resources by following the roadmap charted by other countries. These realities may cause the government to misallocate its resources. And as you'll recall, a major component of successful GDP growth is efficiently using one's resources. Can China's centralized education system peer into the future and allocate its human capital for efficient productivity to ensure GDP growth for years to come? And can it aptly predict where it needs to funnel its resources to achieve both short- and long-term goals?

Another issue pertains to the hierarchical nature of China's education system. As was mentioned earlier, Hongbin and his colleagues found that on average, 64 percent of China's college graduates indicate that their top preference for postgraduate employment is the state sector. Because of the hierarchical nature of China's society, it's only natural that a majority of students would want to join the sector at the top of the hierarchy—the state sector. It shouldn't come as a surprise that it's the elite college graduates who are rewarded by the central government with employment in the state sector: if you'll recall, for students at elite colleges, there was a significantly higher likelihood of receiving job offers from state-owned enterprises and a significantly lower likelihood of working in private enterprises. It's important to acknowledge that this is not inherently a pro or a con of China's system—talented individuals occupying key positions in the state sector undoubtedly benefits China's political and economic systems. But so many of China's most talented seeking employment in the state sector may ultimately result in a brain drain on the private sector. Not only that, but past research has firmly established that the private sector operates far more efficiently than its publicly owned counterpart, which doesn't bode well for economic growth.

The prevailing preference for work in the state sector also has implications for innovation in China. Indeed, in countries around the world, frontier innovation often occurs in the private sector. China is no exception—consider the success of innovative private businesses like Shein, Tencent, Alibaba, Unitree Robotics, DeepSeek and Byte Dance. However, with China's college graduates indicating that their top preference for postgraduate employment is the state sector, can the private sector attract enough human capital to cradle the innovation for which it is so well known? Because entrepreneurship and innovation are closely intertwined—entrepreneurs often drive and capitalize on innovation that occurs in the private sector—Ruixue, Hongbin, and their colleagues decided to explore whether and how these employment preferences affect entrepreneurship in China. By linking college admission data for 1.8 million students with firm registration records in China, they found that within a college, individuals with higher gaokao scores—a proxy for "talent" in this context—are less likely to create firms. When they do, however, their firms are more successful than those of their lower-score counterparts.[13] These findings suggest that the people most likely to become successful trailblazers in their field, potentially starting the next unicorn tech company, are those who are most likely to join the state sector. And why wouldn't they? With the fall of many influential private businesses, it's clear that no one in the private sector, not even the sector's most successful, are above the government—the government is at the top of China's hierarchy. Though the education system may be capable of fostering the human capital necessary to drive technological innovation, the hierarchical nature of China's society makes it less clear whether the government can incentivize young graduates to enter private industries that will be tasked with pushing forward China's position as a technological leader.

The factors discussed above are likely to drive big-picture trends in GDP and technological innovation. But by zooming in a bit, one can understand further how the centralized hierarchical tournament that is China's education system might affect those same outcomes on an individual level. One of the most typical critiques of China's education system is that it cannot successfully foster the talent of intelligent but anomalous individuals who we'll henceforth refer to as "China's Einsteins." From the first moment that China's students enter the classroom—and likely even before then, thanks to early exam prep—the goal of the system is clear: to enable students to achieve the highest possible scores on each exam. Exam successes are not hidden but very clearly publicized: students are sorted into classrooms based on their exam scores, and those with the highest scores receive the most attention from teachers. Teachers are encouraged to produce top-scoring students in order to eventually receive a promotion themselves. With such black-and-white metrics for what it means to be "smart" and "successful," there is very little reward for outside-the-box thinking. There is also a very well-defined archetype of a smart student: one who asks the fewest questions but scores the highest on exams. But perhaps it is the case that some top-ranked students are ill-suited to such a system, more inclined toward discussion-based classrooms and those that encourage intellectual curiosity. With such a unidimensional idea of success, China's Einsteins may underperform in the face of such rigidity.

Regardless of whether they are well-suited for the system, China's Einsteins would still need to take exam after exam until they are faced with the final metric of success—the gaokao. It is that exam that decides so much of their future. But what if China's Einsteins weren't meant to study economics or engineering? What if they were more talented or interested in physics or other fields, but checked the box they knew the government would have wanted them to pick, the one that they would be most conventionally rewarded for choosing? Having been so conditioned by China's definition of success—climbing the hierarchy by winning the tournament—their choice to study engineering would indeed be the rational one. And yet, on an individual level, we see how such a system may create the potential for further misallocation of resources. China's Einsteins may not even test into elite colleges, in part because they may not score well in the non-STEM fields. After all, the gaokao is a composite score, which would discount any individual incredible aptitude. Einstein himself, who took the entrance exam for the Swiss Federal Institute of Technology, failed the language and history sections. When China's Einsteins fail sections of the gaokao, they may fail to access an elite college's resources, so critical to fostering success. Indeed, when the government sets clear metrics for success, it may ultimately be directing its human capital in the wrong ways. And while this hasn't hurt China to the extent that it has prevented progress, now more than ever, the government needs to do more. It needs to foster a welcoming environment for China's Einsteins, both to produce breakthroughs that will keep China at the technological frontier and to drive efficient growth. It's less than clear whether the current model is capable of doing so.

Let's suppose some of China's Einsteins did well enough on the gaokao to gain admission to an elite college and eventually join the field of academia. Those same black-and-white metrics of success may prevent them from realizing their full potential. Unlike in most conventional research settings, publication incentives in China are not purely for scientific progress. Consider how the hierarchy plays into publications. By compiling a dataset that included the publications and biographical information of the deans of major research schools, departments, and institutions of economics over the course of two decades, Ruixue and her colleagues found that even though they had a significantly higher administrative workload, deans produced 37 percent more publications after their promotion than before they were promoted to dean.[14] This increase can be attributed to the dean's control of resources: scholars catered to their dean by becoming the dean's co-authors, even though such publications often fell outside the dean's area of expertise. Such findings support the claims of two leading scientists working in China, Yigong Shi and Yi Rao, who published an article in *Science* in which they stated: "to obtain major grants in China, it is an open secret that doing good research is not as important as schmoozing with powerful bureaucrats and their favorite experts."[15] Interestingly, Yigong Shi held the posts of dean and vice president at Tsinghua University, and later became president of Westlake University, a new Chinese university focused on STEM. Yi Rao, too, was a dean at Peking University. Knowing the realities of the system, China's academics have to play the tournament to their advantage and take on the positions that they know will be necessary to achieve their goals. But without playing that game themselves, China's Einsteins' ability to meaningfully contribute to scientific research may be dampened by the reality of China's system. Instead of pursuing subjects they are passionate about and skilled at, they may simply cater to what the dean hopes to publish. The rigidity of the system prevents those Chinese Einsteins from achievement in their preferred fields. Such rigidity may inhibit innovation generally—how many Chinese Einsteins is the system stifling?

. . .

So many of China's successes today revolve around its investment in and rapid expansion of the education system. It is the demanding nature of China's precollege years that equips the government with human capital beyond that of any other country in the world. With policies that effectively utilize this human capital, China has been able to harness its people's potential, propelling GDP growth at unprecedented rates for several decades.

On a more individual level, China's education system is a training ground for success outside of the exam system. China's hierarchy is no less rigid, even with a diploma in hand, and it is the tournament-like nature of China's education system that sets its students up for success within the hierarchy far beyond their graduation date. Up until now, such a system has facilitated China's economic success. But now that China's goals are fundamentally shifting, it may be the case that its education system, too, must fundamentally shift to create the circumstances necessary for technology and innovation, particularly in the age of AI. But the centralized, hierarchical nature of the system that has been so effective in propelling growth may hamper it from fostering scientists responsible for such cutting-edge technological innovation.

Nonetheless, even without a college education as intensive as those in years prior, China's students still emerge from the education system with the skills necessary to produce so many of the outcomes that we've discussed here. Now imagine if the four years during college were as rigorous as the many leading up to them. The system is already effective. But perhaps it could—and will—be so much more so.

PART III

SOCIETY

7

Values and Institutions

o   o   o

"Without the gaokao, how could you compete with the second generation of the rich?"

—Slogan used to motivate students

U p to now, we have discussed how individuals and the government have interacted with one another over time to shape China's education system and its social hierarchy. But without dissecting society and its accompanying institutions, we'd be missing a critical piece of the puzzle. Three forces—individual, government, and society—collectively shape today's education system, and even more broadly, the China we know today. To begin to understand society's role, we need to explore what it is that China's society values. Clearly, it is at least in part the country's meritocratic education system, which has served as a cornerstone of China's society by sorting people into different levels of the hierarchy for over a thousand years.

Though we have alluded to the importance of meritocracy to China's education system, we have yet to examine it at length. Meritocracy is the notion that individuals can advance in society through their own merit. Full of promise and hope, meritocratic sentiments have quietly seeped into various corners of global societies. In the United States, meritocracy has been reimagined as the American Dream, the idea that individuals who pull themselves up by their bootstraps can grab the equality of opportunity supposedly available to all Americans. With a little hard work and savvy, nothing is out of reach. In China, the education system seems to convey a similar message. Hope for a better future by way of a meritocratic system is one of the fundamental tenets driving families to compete for their student's chance at accessing one of China's elite institutions, and in turn, a better life.

And yet, meritocracy was never intended to support such lofty ideals. The term was coined by Michael Young in a satirical book published in 1958 known as *The Rise of Meritocracy*.[1] In his writing, Young constructs a dystopian society stratified by "merit" and "intelligence" to critique England's former tripartite system of education, which sorted students into educational tiers based on an exam that they sat for as children. Sound familiar? Recognizing that the term meritocracy had since shed many of its negative connotations and instead had been co-opted to support narratives like the American Dream, Young continued to criticize the ideals set forth by such a system in an essay he wrote in *The Guardian* in 2001: "It is good sense to appoint individual people to jobs on their merit. It is the opposite when those who are judged to have merit of a particular kind harden into a new social class without room in it for others."[2] Many have joined Young's camp criticizing meritocracy in recent years, but for different reasons—instead of serving as a remedy for inequality, critics would argue that it serves as a justification for inequality.[3] In their eyes, a true meritocracy is more myth than reality given the unequal socioeconomic realities and limited social mobility that persist across global societies. In the United States, these beliefs have given rise to highly controversial policies like affirmative action.

As such critiques might suggest, any meritocratic system is inherently a hierarchical one: if merit is the basis for hierarchical advancement, then a hierarchy must exist. But all societies are hierarchical in some way—humans have yet to produce a perfectly equal society—and not all societies emphasize meritocratic systems as the basis for societal advancement in the way that the United States and China have come to. In more theoretical literature, social scientists have identified two additional channels through which the individual can obtain status in society: connections and luck.[4] On the most extreme end of the spectrum, a society based on connections would be characterized by succession—wealth is passed from generation to generation with few alternatives. On the other hand, luck at its most extreme would result in citizens' random assignment to different levels of the hierarchy. In reality, there is no perfect example of any of the three channels, as most societies emphasize a mixture of all three in determining who gets to the top of social hierarchy and why.

In China, this hierarchy is clear and well-defined, with political elites sitting comfortably in the upper tier. How to advance within the hierarchy is equally as clear. Historically, it was the imperial examination system that would funnel candidates directly into the top of the hierarchy as government officials. Today, it is the gaokao that serves the same purpose. And in both of these systems, merit determines whether candidates are worthy of advancement. But per Young's criticism, the "merit" component of meritocracy is a particularly subjective term— what is "merit of a particular kind?" While merit is defined as the quality of being particularly good or worthy, determining what is good and worthy once again boils down to what a society values. Which leads us to our point of departure: what does China's society really value? And, more broadly, what can we learn about China's society from examining the interplay between China's education system and its value system?[5]

WHAT DO CHINESE PEOPLE VALUE?

To begin understanding what a society values, researchers often turn to what is known as the World Values Survey.[6] A detailed survey with close to three hundred questions, the World Values Survey collects data that allow researchers to analyze people's values, beliefs, and norms across countries and over time. The survey is conducted every five years, covering around 120 different societies and comprising close to 95 percent of the world population. China is one of those 120 societies. We explore the most recent round of survey data, conducted between 2017 and 2020.[7]

For starters, we decided to zero in on a question that prompted survey respondents to choose qualities they felt were important to instill in children at home. The listed values included the following: good manners, independence, hard work, a feeling of responsibility, imagination, tolerance and respect for other people, thrift, perseverance, religious faith, not being selfish, and obedience. Among the qualities that China's parents found most important was hard work: 71 percent of respondents valued teaching children the importance of hard work at home. While Americans similarly valued hard work at 68 percent, less than half of Canadians and EU respondents agreed. Respondents were also asked to indicate whether they agreed with the following statement: "Hard work doesn't generally bring success. Success is more a matter of luck and connections." American and Chinese respondents disagreed at nearly identical rates, while Canadians, Japanese, Korean, and EU respondents were much more likely to believe that it is luck and connections, not hard work, that results in success. Indeed, American and Chinese respondents seemed to agree not only on the value of hard work but also on its eventual payoff. Through this lens—and, perhaps, taking into account the various anecdotes you've read throughout this book—hard work may be what both societies deem "worthy," and thus may underpin meritocratic sentiments.[8]

This emphasis on hard work was where the similarities ended: both societies seemed to disagree on how exactly to balance work and play. When asked whether they value leisure time as very important, only 21 percent of Chinese respondents believed so. Among the US, EU, Canada, Japan, and Korea, China's score ranked the lowest. Similarly, when asked whether work should come first, even if it means less spare time, China ranked the highest, at 21 percent. Though they followed China next in the line up, the US trailed China by a significant margin at a measly 6 percent. Relative to the other countries in this group represented in the World Values Survey, it seems that China's respondents valued hard work above play, at rates that more than tripled the response of any other country listed above. While both the US and Chinese respondents believed in the value of hard work, Chinese respondents' commitment to their work appears far more extreme. This discrepancy might be explained by their belief that hard work is a duty toward society: nearly double (26 percent) the number of Chinese respondents strongly agreed with the sentiment that work is a duty toward society as did the Americans (14 percent).

Given their emphasis on the value of hard work, the lack of emphasis on leisure time, and the belief that work is one's duty to society, it makes sense that 20 percent of Chinese people strongly believe that without work, people would become lazy. Only 3 percent of Americans held the same belief. If analyzed through the lens of success and failure, if hard work—not luck or connections—is what leads to success, it follows that its opposite—laziness—would be a sign of failure.

In addition to the World Values Survey, another survey conducted by Martin Whyte more explicitly asks respondents questions about how they viewed success (wealth) and failure (poverty).[9] Whyte's survey compared nationally representative survey responses from 2004, 2008, and 2014 to track how respondents' answers changed as China's society became increasingly less equal. He then compared survey responses from China with those of other countries. Interestingly, his findings largely align with those of the World Values Survey.

In one question, respondents were asked how much lack of ability factored into why people were poor. Whyte explains that across all three surveys, Chinese surveys were "off the charts" relative to other countries: at nearly double the rate of other countries, 61–65 percent of China's respondents felt that lack of ability was a major factor in explaining why people remain poor. In the US, for example, only 35 percent of respondents agreed. Yet, when considering findings from the World Values

Survey indicating that China's respondents believed poverty begets laziness, such findings shouldn't come as much of a surprise. To China's respondents, it's not social inequality that drives poverty and failure. Instead, it is the fault of the individual: lack of ability and laziness underpin these realities. Though respondents from the US did agree to an extent, China's respondents were nonetheless more extreme in their belief.

On the flip side of that coin, Whyte asked respondents to explain why some people are rich. Roughly 70 percent of Chinese respondents emphasized the importance of talent and of ability. These rates were higher than that of any other country, though the United States followed closely behind at nearly 60 percent. Survey respondents were also asked how much hard work contributed to one's success. Much like in the World Values Survey, 61–68 percent of Chinese and 62 percent of US respondents believed that hard work was a significant factor behind one's wealth.

China's respondents' continued emphasis on hard work and talent across both the World Values Survey and Whyte's study builds a clearer picture of what traits its citizens view as meritorious. American respondents similarly believed in the value of hard work and talent, but Chinese respondents were often more extreme in their views. Instead of unequal socioeconomic structures or luck, the respondents in China were far more likely to attribute failure to laziness and lack of ability.

But are these values connected to the long-standing exam institutions? Using data that proxy the historical influence of exam institutions across Chinese counties, Ruixue and her colleague found evidence linking these institutions to enduring beliefs in meritocracy. Specifically, respondents from counties with a higher historical success rate of exam candidates are more likely to agree with the statement that success is primarily determined by effort. They are also less likely to believe that social networks are more important than ability in achieving success. This evidence highlights the long-term influence of the exam system on contemporary societal values.[10]

MERITOCRACY AND ITS INSTITUTIONAL FOUNDATIONS

Taking into account these data, let's return to the original discussion of meritocracy. As mentioned earlier, meritocracy is a particularly broad term: "merit" can mean different things to different societies depending on what their citizens value. As borne out by the data, the United States and China seem to have relatively parallel views regarding merit, which can roughly be equated to talent and hard work. Because societies often take great care to ensure that their education systems reflect the traits that their citizens value—the culture wars over curriculum content in the United States provide one such example—one might expect the US and China's system to resemble each other, at least to some extent. And yet, the two countries have chosen markedly different approaches to their respective systems.

The two systems experience a particularly sharp departure when higher education is considered. Higher education serves not only as a way to channel individuals into the hierarchy, but also as a hierarchy in and of itself. In the United States, success is owed to a variety of factors—ACT/SAT scores, GPA, extracurriculars, and letters of recommendation, to name a few. At Harvard University, for example, admission officers are tasked with developing a personality rating based on the myriad information applicants provide.[11] Such ratings are meant to treat applicants holistically and consider the breadth of their lived experience. Meanwhile, success in China boils down to a single factor—gaokao scores. Both countries' systems are designed with meritocratic values at their core, given that talent and hard work undeniably contribute to success across the considered metrics. So what's driving the difference?

For one, though both societies value talent, the metrics considered in higher-education admission suggest that the US and China might view talent differently. In China, merit is narrowly defined by one score, and that score is meant to measure two things: cognitive ability and hard work. This is likely why, in part, the score follows individuals long after they take the test—cognitive ability, or intelligence, is considered a useful indicator of ability for consideration by employers, and even more broadly, an indicator of likely success in society. As for hard work, the gaokao is a test that one must learn how to take. It is only through years of hard work and discipline that one can earn a competitive score. In the United States, though cognitive ability and hard work are factors in college admission—standardized testing and GPA are likely meant to measure exactly that—the many other criteria are similarly proxies for a more broadly defined version of talent. Perhaps community service is meant to stand in for empathy, while extracurricular activities are meant to proxy leadership ability. Such differences show up in the classroom as well: a model student in China sits quietly, asks few questions, and performs exceptionally well on the exam, while a model student in the US also performs well on exams but is encouraged to ask questions and actively engage with classmates. Simply put, the "talent" aspect of merit shakes out differently in each society.

But while talent might explain in part the differences between the two systems, it doesn't explain why China has so wholeheartedly settled on one single metric to quantify talent. In an exam system, it is the exams that ultimately determine one's success. This one metric provides a sense of transparency, of objectivity, of justice, for students and families fighting to come out on top. But they only value such transparency because of the realities of China's weak institutions beyond the pages of the exam. Our use of the word *institutions* here is intentionally broad: institutions can be cultural but also political (democracy versus autocracy) and legal (rule by law, whereby law is above politics, versus rule of law, whereby law is used as a political tool). At their core, however, the functions and limitations of institutions can be expressed by their relationship to power: where power can be constrained and where power can be abused. For example, the legal system can serve as a check on power, but it also can serve to reinforce existing power dynamics. "Weak" institutions are unable to protect the vulnerable from abuses of power.

It's not that China's people are idealists who only believe in the power of an exam to predict intelligence. Rather, China is a society known for connections and petty corruption—hence, the weakness of its institutions. This awareness is woven into the very fabric of China's language. The phrase "to each according to his contribution" is a tenet at the heart of socialism; it's taken to mean that everyone should receive a share of the wealth according to their labor. But the phrase has since been adapted to reflect a more cynical reality. In place of the word "contribution," Chinese people have substituted another word— "father." With this substitution, the phrase takes on a new meaning: instead of getting a share by proving their merit, everyone gets their share courtesy of their family connections. This popular turn of phrase indicates that people do realize that China is not a meritocracy—not fully, at least. Like everywhere, connections and corruption undoubtedly play a role in paving one's way through life.[12]

Past research, coupled with Hongbin's and Ruixue's experiences, has shown that leveraging one's connections for personal gain is more a cultural norm than it is an outlier in China. For example, Hongbin and his team found that students with higher household income or more elite parental backgrounds were more likely to receive job offers in the state sector. These are highly sought-after positions for students who have just graduated college.[13] The role of connections is particularly prominent when the CCP is involved. Meanwhile, those whose parents are government employees are more likely to become business owners.[14] On average, they are paid 15 percent more right out of college than those whose parents are not government employees.[15] Not only that, but entrepreneurs who are CCP members are more likely to obtain loans from banks or other state institutions and are afforded more leeway in the legal system.[16]

And yet, the power of connections is by no means unique to China. Hongbin and Ruixue will openly acknowledge that it is only through the help of the connections within our network that we have collectively landed in a position to be able to write this book together.

Importantly, however, connections are legal. Corruption is not. But in China, the line between connections and corruption is particularly murky. It is precisely because of how murky these waters are that the term *corruption* ought to be approached with nuance. Corruption is dishonest or fraudulent conduct by those who hold power. With this in mind, consider the following examples.

We'll start with the institution of education. Around the holidays, it is common practice to give *hongbao* to teachers. Hongbao are red envelopes filled with money, but in today's China, hongbao have come to represent many types of gift, like highly sought-after seasonal fruit or a gift card to China's version of Amazon. These gifts are not handed to the teachers in the classroom, but instead are sent over WeChat or to the teacher's house, where the teacher can open the gift in the privacy of their home. Such giving may be practiced with a tacit understanding—I'll pay you this small gift to continue educating my child to the best of your ability. On the flip side, if a family doesn't give their student's teacher a hongbao, might it be the case that the teacher no longer deems the student worthy of their attention? Alternatively, hongbao could be seen as a simple gesture of appreciation. Point being—who knows? In such a competitive atmosphere, recall that families will take any advantage they can get.[17]

Consider another example, recently discussed on Chinese social media. One vehicle rear-ended another in a small county. Both drivers immediately exited their vehicles and made some phone calls. Shortly thereafter, a group of family and friends began to make their own phone calls on behalf of their party. Some even arrived at the scene of the accident. When the traffic officer arrived, both groups attempted to influence his course of action based on their connections. It was the individual who was somehow most connected to the officer who was treated most favorably.

Finally, consider this last example, set in a medical institution. In China's hospitals, it is very common to give doctors some form of payment on the side for their treatment. In fact, it's highly unlikely for a doctor *not* to accept such gifts as compensation for their medical treatment. Unlike in the United States, Chinese doctors make a paltry amount of money by way of their salary. Instead, they make their money by accepting these gifts. As a result, if you don't pay the doctor and everyone else is paying the doctor, maybe the doctor won't treat your loved one with as much care, or maybe you won't get priority for the surgery that might save your loved one's life.[18]

These are examples of the murky waters of corruption in China. Within the institution of education, teachers are employees of the state and are in positions of power. Without clear guidance dictating what constitutes an acceptable holiday gift versus one that seeks favor, the line between seeking favor and conveying appreciation is a fine one. Meanwhile, in the legal institution, citizens cannot rely on an impartial legal system to seek recompense. Instead of hiring a lawyer, they are best served by tapping into their pool of connections to influence the eventual outcome. Finally, in the medical institution, doctors, too, are state employees who explicitly accept compensation for private gain. Across all three cases, it's important to note that many of these behaviors are fueled by an underlying fear that if one doesn't give a gift, call in connections, or accept under the table compensation, it may be the case that someone else will. It's like rushing to get off an airplane—if you don't rush into the aisle as soon as the plane lands and everyone around you does, you'll be last one off the plane, even if you'd rather everyone would just wait their turn. If you, too, don't do something to give yourself a competitive edge, you're at a disadvantage. This is no secret: in 2012, the CCP launched an incredibly public campaign aimed at cracking down on some of the more extreme cases of corruption in China. Later, in 2023, government officials directed their anticorruption efforts at the field of medicine.[19] Very quickly they realized that if they were to continue their crackdown, there would be no doctors left to practice medicine in China. They seemingly abandoned the cause shortly thereafter.[20]

Across all these cases, it is the strength of connections and the prevalence of corruption that make the institutions themselves weak, unable to protect the vulnerable from abuses of power. The United States, too, has its fair share of corruption. Yet, in democratic political systems like the US's, power—particularly, political power—is checked far more often than it is in autocracies. Consider the corruption cases of high-profile congressional politicians like Robert Menendez or George Santos. Both cases appeared for weeks—months, even—in national headlines, precisely because corruption at that scale and scope is relatively unusual, and when spotted is considered newsworthy. In China, however, it's an assumption that many officials at the highest levels are engaged in corruption, at least to some extent. As a result, under an increasingly autocratic political system like China's, citizens are acutely aware of the potential for members at the top of the hierarchy to abuse their state-sanctioned power. Those at the bottom of the hierarchy may not even have connections to leverage for personal gain, let alone engage in all out corruption. So how can the average citizen ever compete?

In China, the answer to this question boils down to scores—scores of all kinds, though gaokao scores are the most important of them all. Thanks to their transparency and objectivity, scores have become the best tool that Chinese people have to fight against the inevitable corruption and abuse of connections they encounter within existing institutions. Through this lens, it is China's education system that allows average citizens to even the playing field. A single metric—the gaokao—minimizes the avenues through which corruption can occur and heightens the sense of transparency. Like any tournament, the rules of the test are clear and well-defined, while the scores themselves are public and the grading process is double-blind. The scoring system serves as a relatively simple check on power. Every generation, every family, every student: short of leaving the system entirely for international educational opportunities, there are few exceptions. Recall the importance of this opportunity from earlier discussions around social mobility—indeed, sometimes all families need is hope that they, too, can ascend the social hierarchy. This is an explicitly advertised benefit of the gaokao system. As the epigraph to this chapter asks, without the gaokao, how could you compete with the second generation of the rich?[21]

Taking all of this into account, we've come to believe that the lack of transparency and prevalent corruption within China's institutions strengthens Chinese belief in a meritocratic education system. Instead of having a check on power tied up within the institutions themselves, it is the education system that has itself become a powerful tool to check these imbalances of power and reward those who are most meritorious. China's exam system is so powerful precisely because China's people trust this objective score to quantify their merit, particularly when there are so few opportunities to do so objectively elsewhere in society.

It's also important to note that without an education system that rewards China's most hardworking and talented individuals, its institutions likely wouldn't thrive, as they do today. In a relatively corrupt environment, a meritocratic system helps ensure that high-ability individuals—not just those with connections—are selected for key roles. This system reinforces the legitimacy of these institutions, as officials who scored highest on the gaokao, a widely trusted measure of merit, are seen as deserving of their positions. Moreover, these officials are likely more capable governors than those who might have been chosen solely for their connections.

Though as an indicator of hard work and talent the gaokao may be the optimal choice, China does recognize the value in other characteristics in its students. Take, for example, the honorary title of "well-rounded student" (三好学生). As a young student, Ruixue was presented each year with the title. These students were supposed to be well-rounded in three respects: they were of sound moral character, they were athletic, and they were good exam takers. Students who held this honorary title were held up as models for what a good student "should" be. Yet, Ruixue always found the awards a bit ironic—they certainly hadn't tested her morality or athleticism, and seldom do so across rural China. Even though these other values were important, she knew her future success depended on one metric alone—her score on the gaokao.

Merit is also used as a measure in consideration of financial aid for China's college students. Hongbin looked at how aid is distributed among China's college students to understand who garnered support from the system. Was preference given to those from lower socioeconomic backgrounds, or to those considered meritorious? The financial aid system covers just under half of all college students in China, with aid averaging 2,547 yuan per student in 2010, or roughly half of the annual tuition of 5,000 yuan during that year. There are technically two types of financial aid: need-based scholarships and merit-based scholarships. However, Hongbin and his team found that instead of being directed to those who most needed it financially, the scholarships were most often given to students with "merit": more than half of poor students who needed it could not access need-based aid, and 64 percent of the need-based aid beneficiaries were not actually the neediest students but those who had the highest GPAs or gaokao score.[22]

Though China's education system might aim to promote other values—for example, morality, athleticism, and equity—success continues to boil down to merit in the face of its weak institutions. In China, a clear, measurable score in the form of the gaokao has become one of the few indicators of success that people have come to trust. They are loath to stray from it.

THE FAR-REACHING IMPLICATIONS OF FAILURE

If success is a high score on the gaokao, the flip side of this equation is how China views failure. More than in any other country, in China, failure is considered the opposite of success—a lack of merit. Unsurprisingly, this is also a defining feature of China's education system. Students are forced to shoulder the burden of their failure on the gaokao for decades after they take the exam, operating under the assumption that they are less deserving or less capable of succeeding within society because they were unable to prove their merit on society's most widely accepted platform. Our data indicate that they often face a lowered socioeconomic status and social discrimination for poor scores, even if their failure could be attributed to invisible structural inequalities holding them back. How might Chinese views on failure manifest in other aspects of society?

As China has become an increasingly wealthy country, income inequality has skyrocketed. Today, levels of inequality surpass much of Europe and more closely resemble the US. The share of China's national income earned by the top 10 percent of the population has increased from 27 percent in 1978 to 41 percent in 2015, while the share earned by the bottom 50 percent (a group that includes 536 million adults) has dropped from 27 to 15 percent. Not only that, but wealth is more concentrated than income: the top 10 percent holds approximately 67 percent of China's wealth compared with 41 percent for income. Even more staggering, the top .001 percent owns 5.8 percent of China's total wealth, which is roughly equivalent to that of the bottom 50 percent.[23] Given that China is governed by the CCP and thus operates under a communist political system, one might expect there to be popular support for greater equality in income distribution.

A typical government response to address inequality might involve using taxes as an instrument for redistribution. In Whyte's survey, however, individuals were asked to respond to the following statement: "in order to meet everyone's needs, there should be redistribution from the rich to the poor." Across all three surveyed years, Chinese respondents were relatively unsupportive of such politics, and in the most recent year support was at its lowest: 25 percent. By examining such attitudes through the lens of their values, however, this might make a bit more sense. If Chinese people attribute failure to a lack of hard work, lack of innate talent, and laziness, it thus follows that the poor are blamed for their failure, much like poor scores are punished under China's education system. If their impoverished status is their fault, no amount of redistribution would address the root cause. The tyranny of meritocracy, indeed.

Using multiple sources of survey data, Hongbin and his colleagues show that China's government, likely recognizing the low appetite for redistribution among its population, used redistribution sparingly as a means to address inequality.[24] From 1998 to 2018, the income growth rates of income after taxes and government transfers for most of the population did not significantly differ from the growth rates of income before taxes and government transfers. This difference becomes noticeable only for those in the bottom 20 percent of earners or in the top 20 percent of earners, though the overall disparity was relatively small at less than one percentage point per year. And when compared to other countries, their research revealed that redistribution resulted in a reduction of the top 10 percent income share by only 4 percent in China, relative to 25 percent in France and 19 percent in the US. Meanwhile, redistribution led to an increase in the bottom 50 percent income share by 6 percent in China, relative to 52 percent in France and 53 percent in the US. Such findings underscore the fact that China's government has chosen not to leverage redistribution as a tool to address rising inequality nearly to the same extent as a country like France, or even the US.

At the same time, however, rising inequality is a natural byproduct of the fact that China's economy has experienced remarkable growth. Recall that though China was relatively equal in the 1970s after the Cultural Revolution, people were equally poor: poverty was rampant and quality of life was dismal. As such, though inequality has skyrocketed, so, too, has the average citizen's quality of life. In many ways, China's booming economy serves as evidence of the strength of China's value system. With hard work and talent, the country has emerged as one of the world's leading economies. In order to continue on their trajectory, it is only natural to assume that it is hard work and talent that will propel China's economy into the future.

Though hard work and talent have by no means flagged among China's population, its economic trend lines have. Though it was unlikely that China would be able to sustain the rapid rate of GDP growth characteristic of the last four decades, the slowdown nonetheless threatens the stability of the regime as citizens begin to face newfound hardship and express discontent that goes hand-in-hand with economic distress. One such expression of discontent is known as the *tang ping* movement. The tang ping movement, or "lying flat," gained steam on social media platforms over the last several years and serves as a rejection of social pressure to overwork and overachieve. Some citizens are beginning to believe that no matter how hard they work or how talented they may be, they may nonetheless struggle to find employment and to embody conventional definitions of success.[25]

Neither has rising inequality nor the accompanying social discontent in China gone unnoticed by China's government. The Chinese government launched a campaign known as "Common Prosperity," which seeks to reduce inequality. Yet, China's leadership took pains to emphasize that their policies would not lead China down a path of redistribution nor egalitarianism. Instead of instituting a tax—one that would resemble redistributive policies that garner relatively little public support—China's leadership took a different tack, instead announcing that they expected China's most wealthy to begin donating large amounts of their wealth.[26]

With citizens increasingly skeptical about their ability to advance in society and the government's unrealized tactics of reducing inequality, might it be the case that China's citizens begin to view failure differently? Might their values begin to shift to reflect the changing tides of China's economy?[27] While change is certainly possible, existing research indicates that values and beliefs are relatively static. It would likely take a unique set of circumstances to shift values to the extent that existing institutions would see reform.

. . .

China's education system reflects many of the values at the core of China's society. This deep value of and faith in China's meritocratic system, one built on the foundations of hard work and intelligence, have persisted for well over a thousand years. But despite the parallels borne out by the survey data between the value systems of US and Chinese citizens, China has taken a fundamentally different approach to developing its system. We suggest that the exams at the heart of China's culture are necessary in the face of weak institutions influenced by connections and corruption. Together, these forces ultimately drive citizens to buy into a single-score system to ensure the transparency and objectivity they are unable to find elsewhere. And yet, in recent years, rising inequality has come to threaten the understanding that hard work alone can drive success and that failure is truly the fault of the individual.

In the next few chapters, we'll begin to explore just how much China's education system and the values that it cultivates have come to shape institutions both across and beyond China's society.

8

A Mirror of Society

o   o   o

"At the edges of the land, all are the emperor's subjects."
                                         —The Book of Songs

"普天之下，莫非王土．"   —《诗经》

From the outside looking in, analyzing any country's education system is one of the best crash courses in understanding a society and what it values. But as an individual experiencing the system firsthand, it is also one of the first places to learn how to exist in society—what sort of behaviors are rewarded, and what sort of behaviors are punished. While students in China learn the myriad facts and figures central to success on the gaokao while passing through the education system, they are also learning how best to compete within a centralized hierarchical tournament. Note, here, our use of the word *a* instead of *the*. A centralized hierarchical tournament with clear, measurable, and merit-based indicators is a feature of society writ large, not just the education system. And it is China's education system that prepares students to successfully engage with the tournament-style model that they are bound to encounter throughout their lives as citizens in China's society.

Before we dive into an explanation of the many tournaments across China's society, it's crucial that we establish causation—or rather, a lack thereof. It is not that China's education system conceived these other centralized hierarchical tournaments. Instead, the education system reflects China's obsession with tournaments and is simply the first such tournament that students will encounter. By teaching its pupils how to thrive within a centralized hierarchical tournament, the education system also reinforces the existence of the tournament model beyond the four walls of any classroom. They are two sides of the same coin—the education system is just the first of many tournaments that students encounter, both reflecting and reinforcing this model across China's society.

THE POLITICAL TOURNAMENT

Mirroring China's education system, China's political system also features a clear and well-defined centralized hierarchy. If you'll recall, the centralized and hierarchical characteristics of the education system are themselves a product of the political system. In its earliest manifestation, China's education system—then, the imperial exam system—was explicitly designed by the central government—then, the emperor and his closest circle—to select men of promising talent to serve in the level of government designated by the level of exam he passed. Only after the exam was abolished in 1905 did the two systems separate. The centralized and hierarchical nature of today's education system echoes its previous structure as a two-in-one system.

Though China's political system remains as hierarchical as in days past, its administrative structure has evolved over the years. At the top of today's political hierarchy sits China's central government. Immediately below it are the provincial governments. As of today, mainland China has thirty-one provincial "units"—four centrally administered cities (Beijing, Shanghai, Tianjin, and Chongqing), twenty-two provinces, and five autonomous regions. Each province is then split into prefectures. On the rural side of China, each prefecture includes a number of counties, which are further divided into townships. On the urban side of the equation, each prefecture includes districts, which are then divided into sub-districts. There exists a government at each level of this structure—the central government, the provincial government, the prefectural government, and so on down the pyramid. Intuitively, the closer a position is to the central government, the more powerful it is. On top of that, the more prestigious the position associated with control over that area is, the more prosperous or economically valuable the region becomes. Note here that the central government sits in the nation's capital, Beijing, which is not only a political center but also an economic center. This logic also applies to provincial capitals. Standing in contrast with US state capitals, China's provincial capitals are typically the most developed city in a province, underscoring the fact that the political hierarchy shapes China's urban landscape.

China's political system is as centralized as it is hierarchical. Apart from the central government, there is an explicit regional assignment for each level of the hierarchy. This is by design—there is no region outside of the central government's jurisdiction, which means that leaders at this level are technically responsible for it all, if they choose to intervene. Again, much like the education system, power of all kinds is centralized at the top of the hierarchy—the "big decisions" about anything and everything are made by the central government. Leaders below them in the hierarchy are expected to follow through on the plan.

Though both the education system and the political system share these features, the main metric for scoring the tournament under the education system—the gaokao—is not a useful tool in the political system. In democratic societies with a popular vote, the success of a politician is largely determined by the support of constituents. If voted back into office for a second term, it's assumed that the politician was relatively successful. But China, as an autocratic political system, does not rely on a voting mechanism to evaluate the performance of its bureaucrats. Nor can it rely on the imperial exam to sort promising candidates into the political hierarchy. So how are bureaucrats evaluated and ranked relative to one another in the political tournament?

Before the CCP initiated its sweeping economic reforms in 1978, a bureaucrat's performance was based on one measure: political conformity. Although political conformity remains important—particularly so in recent years—several newer criteria for performance evaluation have been introduced into the evaluation process. However, what has remained unclear is whether the newly introduced indicators will truly replace political conformity as the most important performance measure, and if so, to what extent. It was Hongbin and his fellow PhD student, Li-An Zhou, who first began to hypothesize that GDP growth rates were being used as a critical metric for bureaucratic performance evaluation.[1] If their hypothesis were true, the central government would promote bureaucrats who were best able to grow the GDP of the area that they were responsible for. Hongbin and Li-An decided to test this by examining provincial leaders' performance as measured by GDP growth throughout their time in office. Outside of the black box that is the central government—positions that essentially mean that the leaders "won" the tournament—provincial leaders are the most important local officials who are responsible for the largest portions of China's economy.[2] After painstakingly digitizing thousands of pages of documents on CCP personnel that the pair dug up from dusty books in the basement of Stanford's Hoover Tower, they produced the first-ever digital dataset about China's top politicians, including 254 provincial leaders who served in twenty-eight Chinese provincial units from 1979 to 1995.

In support of this tournament-style hypothesis, Hongbin and Li-An found that GDP growth rate did indeed impact the probability of promotion or termination, and by no small amount. Throughout the course of their study, the average provincial GDP growth rate was exactly 10 percent per year. However, the growth rate varied significantly, from -16 percent to 30 percent, indicating that some provincial leaders performed far better than their peers in the tournament. Their performance did not go unnoticed. If, for example, the provincial GDP growth rate increased by 8 percentage points, from 10 percent to 18 percent, then the chance of promotion for a provincial official would increase by 50 percent, and the chance of their termination would decrease by 37 percent.[3] Note that the average probability of promotion is small, at 7.5 percent, which makes the impact of GDP performance that much more significant. Hongbin and Li-An's study proved that an official's ability to deliver on their province's GDP is a clear indicator for their odds within China's political tournament, effectively replacing political conformity as the primary measure of success.

What makes this even more competitive is that evaluations are determined based on two factors: your performance relative to other provincial leaders *and* your performance relative to your predecessor. The latter factor equalizes the playing field for those in provinces that have a naturally slower growth rate. Consider, for example, two leaders in the US. One in charge of New York, a state with one of the most dynamic economies, would likely have an easier time driving growth than one in charge of Vermont, a state with one of the smallest econo-mies. Even though his performance will still be compared to the official in New York, the official in Vermont is not going to be penalized for the economic circumstances of his region because his GDP score will be evaluated relative to the person who held his position immediately prior.[4] Nor can the New York leader simply rely on the naturally robust economy in his region—he must expand the economy at a faster rate relative to the leader prior *and* relative to each provincial leader across the country. By simply swapping out gaokao scores for GDP in their performance evaluations, the central government kept the tournament at the heart of the imperial examination system alive and well.

Hongbin and Li-An's work in the 1990s highlights that using GDP growth rate as a key performance indicator for officials mirrors the gaokao scoring system in several ways. First, it aligns with the central government's priorities by emphasizing measurable outcomes that reflect economic performance and selecting officials based on a form of meritocracy. Just as gaokao scores foster competition among students, GDP-based evaluations drive competition among local officials, motivating them to pursue growth—a dynamic that often benefits the broader economy. Second, it is straightforward to understand and implement given that a GDP growth rate is just a single number, much like an exam score. Third, GDP growth rates enable transparent comparisons across regions and over time, ensuring consistency in evaluations. Fourth, the metric is relatively objective. Although some officials may attempt to manipulate GDP data, such actions carry significant risks. Inflated figures increase tax obligations to the central government, creating financial burdens, while sustained inflation of growth numbers would lead to unsustainable exponential increases. Not to mention that manipulating data is a serious offense under the CCP, with severe consequences.[5] Lastly, officials are bound to the system, with limited external career options and, in many cases, no opportunity to exit the hierarchy, making their performance within the structure even more critical.

In so many words, these findings support the idea that though China's political system is not a democracy, it *is* a centralized hierarchical tournament with meritocratic elements. It is centralized: big-picture decision-making power, particularly regarding the country's direction and promotions of the country's next most powerful leaders, is in the hands of the central government. It is hierarchical: there is a clear pyramid that officials are tasked with climbing. And it is a tournament: officials are made to compete against one another on the basis of their merit, as proxied by their ability to grow China's economy. By relying on a structure that prioritizes merit-based promotion determined by a simple numerical indicator, the central government can ensure that economic competence is rewarded, paralleling previous efforts that rewarded ability as measured by imperial exam score.

Nonetheless, we imagine that many observers of China are bound to ask—what about connections? And they are right to do so: we'd be remiss to ignore their prevalence in Chinese politics. In their original study, Hongbin and Li-An further showed that having connections to leaders in the central government increased the probability of promotion by 45 percent and decreased the probability of termination by 47 percent. Building on their work, Ruixue and her colleagues later showed that though connections are also powerful indicators of success, they are only powerful in the presence of merit. Using the resumés of CCP officials, Ruixue and her colleagues measured connections between provincial leaders and top CCP officials in the central government based on whether they used to work in the same branch of the Party or the government at the same time. Like Hongbin and Li-An, they measured performance using the GDP growth of the province that each provincial leader ruled over. What they found suggests that connections are powerful advantages in promotion, but only if an official also exhibited a strong GDP performance. Even if they were well-connected, weakly performing provincial leaders were unlikely to be promoted. In other words, connections help leaders advance, but only if they perform well—the bottom line is still their GDP performance.[6] Their findings suggest that meritocracy and connections can in some (limited) cases complement one another to produce mutually beneficial outcomes—the officials are rewarded for their connections, and the region benefits from the official's parallel dedication to economic growth. But in other cases that we'll soon discuss, it's likely that the two substitute for one another, resulting in scenarios where connections dominate merit. In those cases, the region's prosperity almost inevitably dwindles. Such instances provide another data point supporting the pitfalls of autocratic leadership, often rooted solely in the power of connections.

And yet, things are changing. The relationship between meritocracy, connections, and success within the political system tends to evolve along with the changing tides of leadership. This is particularly so under autocratic political systems, as autocrats tend to wield outsized power over their country. While China's Deng Xiaoping era marked the beginning of a period emphasizing meritocratic selection in parallel with relatively autocratic rule, the central government's actions in recent years suggest regression toward trends reminiscent of the pre-Deng era. In 2013, acknowledging for the first time a relationship between economic growth and individual promotion, China's central government stated that they hoped to "improve the assessment and evaluation system for local government achievements by *correcting the bias of judging achievements solely based on the speed of economic growth.*"[7] Later, Ruixue found that as of the 19th Party Congress in 2017, the relationship between GDP growth and promotion has altogether disappeared, while connections to top leaders remain an important predictor for political promotion. Consider such findings in light of China's recent economic downturn—without a reward for economic growth, local officials may be squandering their resources in favor of cultivating connections, which they would ultimately be rewarded for over facilitating economic progress.[8]

Though China's political system and China's education system govern very different aspects of its society, these two institutions share the same foundation, both centralized hierarchical tournaments with meritocratic characteristics. Nonetheless, China's education system has been in place for over a thousand years. The CCP? Just around one hundred. Without such a longstanding and well-respected institution like China's exam system, the volatility of the political tournament is noticeably more pronounced. And as is the case with any observed volatility in China's education system, volatility in the political system results from changing priorities within the central government.

THE ACADEMIC TOURNAMENT

Given how central both the political system and education system are in China's society—as a citizen of China, it would be nearly impossible to forgo some form of interaction with either of the two—it follows that the structure of a meritocratic centralized hierarchical tournament might be mimicked elsewhere. And indeed, beyond these two exists yet another system that shares the same foundation: academia. China's academia is unique in that it straddles multiple lines. Though it is a public institution that often overlaps the education system itself, one might think it lacks an obvious metric by which success can be measured. But as we'll discuss shortly, this is far from the case.

In earlier chapters, we've touched on aspects of the hierarchical and centralized nature of the world of academia. As a refresher, recall that as a public institution, positions at universities are part of the government and thus fall under the umbrella of the CCP bureaucratic ranking system. Those at more prestigious universities are always the universities at the top of the hierarchy, which itself is explicitly dictated by the central government and is a critical determinant of the amount of resources that any university will receive. However, for those familiar with academia in different countries, like the United States, it would be fair to say that though they aren't necessarily centralized, such systems *are* extremely hierarchical. *U.S. News and World Report* famously ranks academic institutions each year, and the same schools invariably end up at the top of the ranking each year. Not only that, but academia is notorious for a highly competitive atmosphere fraught with rigidity in its hierarchical promotion structures. However, China's academia exhibits characteristics of the centralized hierarchical tournament that sets it apart in the worldwide field of academia.

We'll start with the features that make academia in China particularly hierarchical. Both in and out of China, academics vie for what is known as tenure—a position that guarantees them a permanent role in their department. Earning tenure in China is equally important and likely as competitive (if not more so) than earning tenure in universities elsewhere. In the United States, after professors earn tenure, the subsequent promotion would be to full professorship, though this is usually more of a formality if the academic is reasonably active in research. While this is also the next step for tenured associate professors in China, it is by no means automatic, as there are usually far fewer positions available for full professors courtesy of the quota system, which we'll discuss below.

Earning tenure is likely one of the most pivotal points in most academics' careers. And yet, even if academics in China do earn tenure and then become full professors—a steep climb—these are simply among the first few steps in ascending the academic hierarchy. After doing so, academics in China are then tasked with earning various accolades, titles, or scholarships associated with specific metrics (usually publications or citations) to continue their ascent. These include the National Award for Talented Young Scientists, the Changjiang Scholarship, and the One Thousand Talent Program. Though these titles are some of the most prestigious owing to their affiliation with the central government, they don't even begin to skim the surface: there are hundreds such titles associated with specific provinces, programs, and universities. The ultimate goal for any academic, however, is to earn the title of "academician" (院士), which grants them membership to the Chinese Academy of Sciences or the Chinese Academy of Engineering.[9] Such a position is equivalent to a highly ranked CCP official (a vice minister), and represents the pinnacle of the academic hierarchy. Earning it necessitates a stellar publication and citation record coupled with a robust network of connections.[10] Few can accomplish such a feat, which makes the title a rare one: just a few hundred academics in China currently hold it and are usually in the golden years of their career. Universities themselves also pressure academics to earn these accolades, as the government ranks universities based in part on the point value associated with a particular accolade. The more professors with accolades, the higher the university's point value. The higher the university's point value, the higher the university's ranking. Like the academics, universities must accrue these points to climb the ranking, and in turn, earn funding. Though the hierarchical structure inherent to academia is by no means unique to China—indeed, academia is likely one of the more uniformly hierarchical institutions around the world—the seemingly endless number of steps beyond simply earning tenure does set China apart. In the United States, the endgame for most professors is tenure. But in China, another hierarchy exists within each institution, and another within each department, resembling a never-ending stack of Russian dolls.

This discussion brings us to another point, one that relates to both the centralized and tournament-style nature of academia. As we explained in Chapter 5, the Ministry of Education sets a quota specifying the number of positions and personnel of a certain rank available within each university. In practice, this means that the government decides how many tenure positions are available in each department at every university. In a particular academic school, for example, there's only one or two full professor quotas in a year but around fifty tenured associate professors vying for the position.[11] Much like for students taking the gaokao, the quota system is just another rule in the tournament: because the quota system ensures that there are always fewer positions available than there are candidates to fill them, if you don't win that seat, you effectively lose. Step after step in the hierarchy, academics in China are forced to compete with those around them for the same prize. Meanwhile, in the United States, any number of faculty in a given department can have tenure. Candidates competing for tenure are effectively competing against themselves, not against other people in their department for the same position. Unlike in China, it is not a zero sum game.

Another facet of this centralization has to do with what is known as personnel records. As part of the state sector, universities are tasked with collecting each of their employees' personnel records (档案), which contain information on the employee's life dating back to their primary school years, including details like criminal records, gaokao scores, and previous employment. In many ways, it would be akin to what the US government would review as part of a background check. To make any career moves (usually from one university to the next), the academic's original institution would need to release their personnel records to the institution that they'd like to move to. If a university is not receptive to the academic leaving their institution, they will post-pone releasing the records. Note that they usually aren't—why would any university let an academic go unless they were actively a drag on resources? And it's unlikely that such an academic would be getting an opportunity at another institution, anyhow. In some cases, they may never get around to it.[12] The quota system ensures that there are a finite number of positions available at each university, so a random open position that doesn't already have a number of people vying for it is highly unlikely. It's even more unlikely that there's a random position open long enough for an academic to successfully lobby their university to release their records.

And if that isn't enough, moving from one university to another disrupts the hidden benefits associated with their university position: newer faculty are almost automatically shunted to the bottom of the benefits system that rewards seniority. The job benefits associated with specific universities, including schooling for one's children, are often an important factor to consider as well. As a result, academics both have relatively few opportunities and are disincentivized to leave their current employer. Such circumstances ensure that they are forced to compete for opportunities within their home institutions. In contrast, in the United States, if a university makes an academic a competitive offer, it is entirely up to the academic to decide how to proceed. In sum, these factors essentially mean that there's no external job market for academics in China, and the job market that does exist is controlled by university leaders, who themselves are part of the central government.

Before diving into the metric that most effectively renders China's academia a tournament—and in many ways, serves as the characteristic that most differentiates it from other systems of academia—it's helpful to first provide some more information on evaluation under the tenure system. At the core of any academic institution is its faculty. Recruiting and retaining talented faculty is a crucial matter of business for any academic institution hoping to maintain or cultivate its reputation. Universities around the world—China included—have adopted the tenure system to help accomplish this task. For those unfamiliar, the US tenure system requires prospective tenured professors to log some number of years (usually six) as an assistant professor, which is more or less a trial period throughout which they're under observation by senior members of the faculty. During that trial period, assistant professors are tasked with publishing an array of papers designed to build up their resume and establish a good track record. They must also develop positive working relationships with members of their field. After those years are up, senior professors in the department evaluate their performance and decide whether to grant them tenure based on evaluation letters written by tenured professors at similar institutions as well as the candidate's record of papers. The tenured faculty in the candidate's prospective department then gather to vote on whether the candidate ought to receive tenure. A tenured position is so sought after and highly competitive across the field of academia because it guarantees a professor a permanent position.

The US tenure system relies on both subjective and objective measures—the number of articles published and journals' relative prestige, the number of citations each paper has accrued, as well as opinions of those in the candidate's academic community. But as we discussed in the last chapter, subjective measures are often caught in the tangled web of manipulation associated with corruption and connections throughout China's society. Though China took notes from this tenure system, they adopted a form of the system that more closely resembles those that we are all too familiar with—namely, a tournament-style structure.

Instead of evaluating professors who are up for tenure based on a series of more holistic factors, China's academia developed a hierarchical scoring system. To do so, they compiled a journal list ranking some of the most important academic journals and assigned each journal with a letter score: A+, A, A-, B+, B, B-. Any journal considered at a C level or below was excluded as insufficiently prestigious. For every field—economics, computer science, biotechnology, and so on—there exists a list of corresponding journals. These lists were first compiled in the 1990s in Hong Kong and have seldom changed since, given just how much they factor into career advancement.

To be even considered for tenure in economics, assistant professors in China are presented with a series of benchmarks that they are required to meet. For one, they must publish six papers or the equivalent of six papers that are published in journals deemed prestigious by the ranking system. At least three papers need to be published in A-level journals or above. The other three can be B+ journals or above. Assistant professors can also "substitute down"—a paper in one A+ journal is equivalent to two papers in A journals, and one paper in an A journal is equivalent to two papers in A- journals—but cannot "substitute up"—two papers in A- journals do not equal one paper in an A journal. They also need at least one of their six papers to be authored by them alone, without a co-author, and they must have received a competitive funding opportunity from the central government, namely the Natural Science Foundation or Social Science Foundation. If all these requirements are met, then an assistant professor is considered for promotion for tenure. But consideration does not equal success, owing to the highly constrained number of positions set by the quota and the number of academics competing for the position. The same rules follow as in the political tournament: one's score is compared with every other candidate vying for the same position within one's department. This system inevitably fosters a highly competitive atmosphere as each candidate races to publish adequately high-quality papers and achieve the department's highest score to beat out their colleagues for the next promotion. The prize is another step up the hierarchy.

Hongbin had firsthand experience with this system, both as a young PhD graduate on the hunt for a tenure-track position and as a full-fledged professor. In 2001, Hongbin was about to finish his PhD at Stanford and was considering employment at several of the universities in Hong Kong. But when he began the application process, he found that he couldn't even qualify for consideration at the Hong Kong

University of Science and Technology (HKUST) because he would not be able to publish his thesis in any of their A-list journals. Even at that time, he took issue with the journals on their economics department list. Many of the economists at HKUST who had collectively assembled the journal list were more theoretical or mathematical economists, while Hongbin himself was an empirical economist. The fact that the journals through which he would publish his thesis were internationally recognized ones in the field of economics carried no weight, merely because they were not on the department's list for recognized journals. Such a scenario begs the question—who decides what journals are fit for consideration? And more important, what if they're wrong?

Hongbin secured a job at a competing university, the Chinese University of Hong Kong (CUHK). There, two senior professors in the economics department happened to be empirical labor economists like Hongbin, and thus had developed a slightly different journal list that more closely aligned with the work Hongbin had published. But even at CUHK, he found himself at the heart of another controversy related to the journal ranking system. After he was hired at CUHK, he stayed for four years as an assistant professor, throughout which time he published a series of papers in highly ranked journals and subsequently secured a score high enough to earn a position as a full tenured professor. But many of his colleagues took issue with his promotion, believing that the journals he had published in were too easy, even though they were technically on the approved journal list. After a highly contentious and relatively rare voting process, the decision was made to downgrade one of the journals he had frequently published in—*The Journal of Development Economics*, a leading journal on the study of developing countries—from an A to an A-. Ten people voted to keep the journal on the list. Eleven voted to downgrade the journal. No matter how arbitrary it may seem, the quality of the journal list is of the utmost importance to Chinese academics: ultimately, that list and the associated scores are responsible for deciding their future within the tournament of academia.

The world of academia in China is in a class of its own. China's unique quota system designed by the central government coupled with the point-based evaluation system renders academia a tournament—if someone else wins, you lose. Not only that, but in China, the hierarchy is endless; unlike in the United States, tenure is just one of many steps to achievement for professors in the field. Lastly, there is no functioning job market for professors in China. Owing to the centralized system, they are effectively stuck at one university to play the tournament. Though it shares characteristics with academic institutions around the world, academia in China represents an extreme example of systems elsewhere across each metric of the centralized hierarchical tournament.

COSTS AND BENEFITS OF ALL-POWERFUL INDICATORS

We've now identified centralized hierarchical tournaments that exist throughout China's society, from education to academia to politics. Though these examples fit neatly into our outlined structure, it's important to recognize that variations of this structure are at the core of so many systems throughout China on a smaller scale. A career in the private sector, for example, would exhibit many of the characteristics we've discussed here. Though most companies might not be centralized at the national level, they likely exhibit a hierarchical work structure with clear, quantifiable targets for success set by the individuals at the top of companies' hierarchy. Even those who are unfamiliar with China's corporate culture may have heard tales of the punishing "996" work hours associated with employment at many of China's tech companies—9 a.m. to 9 p.m., six days a week—particularly so in recent years as China's work culture has butted heads with American work culture.[13] Considering that individuals are directly compared to one another for promotion, it would follow that if your immediate colleague somehow put in more hours, they would get the promotion.[14] This competitive atmosphere fostered by hierarchical tournaments is likely the bedrock of companies and institutions throughout China, if only you know where to look.

Even though tournaments may push China's people to extreme ends, such a structure has also been responsible for driving growth across China's society: people at every level of the hierarchy have strong incentives for achieving the targets set out by those senior to them. Officials are tasked with growing the economy, academics for producing vast quantities of research, and students for performing among the best in the world on standard measures of educational quality. And this isn't new—China's history can offer similar examples of clear and quantifiable indicators used to motivate those at every level of the hierarchy. During the Great Leap Forward, for example, Mao set clear targets for steel production. Likewise, throughout the era of the one-child policy, there was a clear target: one child, and one child only. As shown in recent research by Hongbin and his colleagues, to meet their goal, the central government introduced the one-vote veto policy, strictly prohibiting promotion of government officials who failed to meet the fertility target.[15] For better or for worse, success in China often boils down to some simple metrics.

But if we delve into the "for worse" end of that equation, it becomes clear that such strong incentives can produce unexpected distortions. As we've previously touched on, China's academics produce the most research in the world, though it may not be of the highest quality or particularly innovative. As long as it boosts their score under the ranking system, it will suffice. Meanwhile, politicians have undeniably been responsible for so much of the economic growth at the heart of China's rise, but at what cost? The broken window fallacy, a key concept in economics, highlights such distortions. If one were to accidentally break a window, turn around, and repair that window, the resources and production necessary to repair that window would contribute to overall GDP growth. But if the same individual broke that window again just for fun, even after repairing it once, the resources and production necessary to repair that window contribute to GDP *again*. This could happen endlessly, with the same result: GDP numbers would technically increase, but there would be no real value added to the economy. In most cases, such a cycle evolves into a drag on productivity, as those resources could likely have been utilized elsewhere more efficiently with significantly higher payoffs.

To see such distortions in practice, one need only look at China's extensive infrastructure investments by local governments: they artificially generate demand for infrastructure construction, then tear down roads, bridges, and buildings only a few years later, just to quickly turn around and rebuild them. Doing so does indeed boost GDP and likely improves the quality of the infrastructure, but is considered by many to be a waste of resources. As demand has peaked, construction giants that have long served to prop up the economy have (very publicly) come tumbling down, only to send painful shockwaves throughout the rest of the economy. Such practices have come at the cost of addressing other, equally important matters that either don't directly contribute to GDP growth or don't do so at the pace that local officials might need to secure their promotion, like instituting environmental regulations or addressing systemic inequality. Though some of these distortions are relatively harmless, others have and will continue to produce dangerous outcomes, ones that the leaders in the central government fail to predict ahead of time.[16]

One example of a particularly dangerous outcome comes to mind. At the onset of the COVID-19 crisis in the early months of 2020, the government tasked officials with following through on a policy that they had newly dubbed "zero-COVID." In doing so, the government effectively replaced their previously all-important indicator—GDP growth rate—with a now well-known metric: COVID cases. In a race to produce the best outcome, local officials aggressively clamped down on their regions to ensure limited transmission. At first, such measures were welcomed, and even declared innovative. China became a world leader, hailed as a nation that responded quickly and effectively to protect its citizens. But as the pandemic wore on, the central government failed to adapt, maintaining the correctness of their zero-COVID indicator. COVID prevention measures became increasingly draconian as officials sought new means through which they could make their score even lower. Only after the White Paper Protests—one of the most public and destabilizing events that the government has witnessed in recent memory—was the government receptive to abandoning their COVID indicator to adopt GDP once again as an important measure of success. But at that point, the harm had already been done.

Considering these examples of harmful distortions that stem from unidimensional indicators, it may be helpful to discuss what is known as Goodhart's law. The law states that when a measure becomes a target, it ceases to become a good measure. The cases provided above illustrate exactly that—there's a tremendous amount of manipulation, and subsequently, distortions, that are bound to occur, even if efforts to reach such targets are undertaken in good faith.[17] You can see this across all of China's centralized hierarchical tournaments, from the education system's exam, the political tournament's GDP indicator, and academia's journal-based scoring system to more painful instances like the zero-COVID measure and the one-child policy. Seldom do any policies set forth by the central government exist with a truly unidimensional goal. And yet, unidimensional indicators achieve exactly that—unidimensional outcomes—which ultimately sacrifice the other, equally important dimensions the government might have hoped to realize at the outset.

•   •   •

As this chapter draws to a close, it's worthwhile to circle back to where we began: the education system both influences and mirrors so many facets of China's society. Though education is neither the first nor the last centralized hierarchical tournament that China will witness, it is the first that any citizen will encounter. Indeed, by implicitly training its students in the doctrine of the merit-based centralized hierarchical tournament, China's citizens are well-equipped with the tools necessary to succeed beyond their years in the education system.

In an era of globalization, throughout which China has increasingly garnered power on the global stage, China's influence has expanded both visibly and invisibly. As a foundation of China's education system, and by extension, its society, it may be the case that the influence of the centralized hierarchical tournament is one such example of China's invisible influence. As helpful as it is to analyze China's society using this framework, we have found it equally as helpful to explore debates splashed across headlines in the United States through a similar framework. What happens when China's tournament goes international?

9

The Exam Empire Expands

∘ ∘ ∘

"More than happy, we are just relieved . . . [my wife] and I have focused on our sons' education for 16 years, starting with our [eldest son] in kindergarten. Now that [he] is at Johns Hopkins and [our younger son] is at Stanford, we can finally take a deep breath and relax. From now on, their education is their responsibility. [My wife] and I are done. Honestly, and not to sound morbid, but if I died tomorrow, I would die a happy man."

—A Chinese American parent's reflection on
educating his children in the US

Before former president Richard Nixon met with Chairman Mao in 1972, and in the few decades that followed, much of China's population remained in the dark: limited access to information outside of China and a general lack of mobility meant that the world didn't stretch far beyond one's own province, city, or even town. Though China's population was large, China was still, economically speaking, quite small. Owing to its isolation from the rest of the world, education—more specifically, China's obsession with education—remained confined within the country's borders.

Today, however, China is neither economically small nor closed. Over the course of the fifty years following the two leaders' historic meeting, China entered its "reform and opening up" era, characterized by unprecedented development and an embrace of globalization. In

2001, China acceded to the WTO, and in 2009, it surpassed the US and Germany to become the world's largest exporter.[1] The resulting shockwaves that rippled through local labor markets in the US are now known as the China shock.[2] Though China is perhaps best known for its manufacturing exports, another of China's exports is no less consequential: its talent. Owing to rising income and booming college expansion, China's citizens have leveraged the trend toward globalization to seek educational opportunities overseas. As the number one importer of China's talent, the US has witnessed a particularly large influx of Chinese students.[3] How has an influx of Chinese talent affected education systems beyond China itself?

To answer this question, we'll end this book much as we started it: with a personal look at how China's education system has shaped the arc of our lives, ultimately landing both of us here in the United States. Recall that after attending elementary, middle, and high school in China, we both went on to attend college in Beijing, the nation's capital. Like many to come after us, it was roughly at this point that our paths began to lead us far beyond China's borders.

· · ·

The year he graduated from college, Hongbin found himself with little to do over the summer. Although he, along with the twenty-nine other economics students in his year, had been promised a prestigious position at a state-owned bank in China, boredom and the Beijing heat prompted him to apply for a position as an enumerator for the fieldwork of an American doctoral student in economics named Albert Park.[4] Shortly thereafter, he landed the job. Despite having studied "economics" for the four years prior, Hongbin couldn't make heads or tails of the fifty-page survey he was meant to be administering. He peppered Albert with questions daily. At the end of the summer, Albert told Hongbin that if he really wanted to understand the survey and the fieldwork, Hongbin ought to apply to the university Albert himself was attending—Stanford. Though Hongbin had never heard of Stanford, he took the leap. He applied for the PhD program, was admitted, and in 1995, for the first time in his life, left China. The government wasn't pleased with this decision, however, and forced him to retroactively pay back the tuition for his undergraduate degree—after all, he didn't follow the path that they had paved for him—forcing him to scrape together sufficient funds from his family and friends to fund his overseas endeavors.

In 2007, just twelve years after Hongbin, Ruixue, too, inadvertently stumbled into her overseas PhD program. After her undergraduate degree, Ruixue went on to complete her master's degree at Peking University. Despite studying economics as an undergraduate, she ran into a dilemma similar to the one Hongbin faced: the content taught by newly minted overseas professors stood in stark contrast to what she had been exposed to in China. This new form of economics was extremely mathematical and wielded modern analytical tools, while her earlier studies had focused on discussing the ideas of Marxist writers who explored larger issues of class and inequality, issues that Ruixue found particularly compelling. Facing a crossroads after graduation—should she go on to pursue some form of economics, or pursue another one of her many interests?—Ruixue sought inspiration from the work of one of her favorite film directors, Ingmar Bergman, whose work she had seen and enjoyed with tutoring money she had earned. Bergman just so happened to be Swedish. After receiving her acceptance letter, she set off for a PhD program in economics at Stockholm University. Though she discovered that many Swedish people thought Bergman pretentious, her studies in economics yielded better results: it was in Stockholm that she discovered the field of political economy, which she thought of as a happy marriage of the two sides of economics she had previously explored.

Upon graduating from their respective doctoral programs, both Hongbin and Ruixue chose to pursue a career in academia. Years passed, over the course of which they collectively taught thousands of students across Hong Kong, China, Europe, and the United States.

Like each education system, each university and group of students brought with them their own unique characteristics. Nonetheless, their experience as students and teachers in China's education system continued to follow them wherever they went. About ten years ago, Ruixue and Hongbin crossed paths for the first time when she invited him to speak at the University of California, San Diego. Upon discussing their shared interest in exploring China's education system through an empirical lens, they have since embarked on several research projects. In doing so, they discovered that the most important features of China's education system can be summarized simply as a centralized hierarchical tournament. And now, as more and more Chinese students follow their path in pursuing education overseas, they are beginning to see how the system is leaving its mark around the world.

FOLLOWING THE EXAM EMPIRE: FROM CHINA TO THE UNITED STATES

As you now know, Ruixue and Hongbin's path overseas and eventually to the United States was by no means straightforward or planned. Ever since Nixon's fateful meeting with Mao in 1972 launched China into an era of renewed formal diplomatic relations with the United States, Chinese students have begun to seek education in the US. But in the late 1980s and early 1990s, it was less common for students like Hongbin and Ruixue to pursue education abroad, which can be attributed to China's relative isolation. Hongbin had never even heard of Stanford at the time of his application. The very first cohort in the 1980s was only about two thousand students. Along with other cohorts throughout the 1980s and 1990s, these students did not come in pursuit of an undergraduate degree as many do today, but rather sought a graduate degree or joined an exchange program. This was in part because Chinese students couldn't yet afford to acquire an undergraduate degree. Because American universities provided full scholarships for graduate degrees, Chinese students who didn't necessarily hail from an advantageous socioeconomic background were increasingly able to access overseas study opportunities.

Two factors contributed to changes in these initial trends. Along with globalization came a remarkable rise in China's income across all tiers of the income distribution—the average adult experienced an annual income growth rate of 7.9 percent between 1988 and 2018.[5] In parallel, college expansion caused the supply of college graduates to increase at least twenty-five-fold from 1999 to 2011. Analysis shows that college expansion was a major factor contributing to the increase in Chinese students studying in the US, accounting for approximately 20 percent of the inflow of students pursuing graduate education in the United States.[6] Over time, higher education became not only a norm but an expectation for vast swaths of China's population, and one that they now had the funds to invest in. By 2019, the number of Chinese students studying in the United States was 134 times that of 1980, amounting to a 13.4 percent annual increase.

With increased income, more students are now coming to the US for undergraduate education and high school than for graduate studies. In 2019, when Chinese students studying in the US reached its peak, a total of 400,000 Chinese students came to the US, a majority of whom came in pursuit of undergraduate (150,000 students) versus graduate degrees (130,000 students). Some 23,000 students even attended private high school in 2019.[7] Today, it would be more unusual for households in China to be unfamiliar with some of the most well-known American universities. An entire industry is devoted to aiding Chinese students throughout their overseas admission process, though usually for a hefty price. Most of these students state that the pursuit of excellence in education drives their overseas endeavor, though some undoubtedly hope to avoid the grueling trials of the gaokao.[8]

It's important to note that these numbers are likely undercounts of the true extent of the exchange between the two systems, as they capture only the individuals who obtained a student F-1 visa for the explicit purpose of studying in the United States. Those who have a non-Chinese passport (for example, those who were born in the US but grew up in China and later returned to the US), as well as those who have visa types that are not student visas, are not captured by our data. When Hongbin came to the US as a visiting scholar, for example, he held a J-1 visa for individuals approved to participate in work- and study-based visitor exchange programs. Like Hongbin, many researchers, scholars, and post-docs in the United States are on non-student visas.

As both countries' education systems produced an ever-growing supply of intertwined human capital, the two countries also began to gravitate toward one another as collaborative partners. China is now the US's top collaborator. In life sciences, for example, co-authored publications between the two countries account for 7 to 8 percent of all publications in the US.[9] Chinese talent has also benefited American enterprises. Ruixue examined innovation in biotechnology, a rapidly evolving field of discovery and innovation that the United States has long dominated. She found that as many as three-fourths of biotechnology-related patents filed by ethnic Chinese inventors in the US from 1976 to 2019 were assigned to American companies. Meanwhile, only 8 percent were assigned to Chinese companies. In other words, American businesses have reaped the rewards of Chinese talent produced by the two countries' education systems.[10]

Though the United States also shares close ties with other countries' education systems, China's size has rendered the scale of the overlap incomparable. As a result, public educational institutions in the US have come to rely on Chinese capital as a major source of income. Consider the fact that international students pay on average three to four times more in tuition than in-state students at public universities in the US, and that Chinese students represent one-third of those international students.[11] This pool of money generated by Chinese students' investment has even allowed public universities in the US to boost their in-state enrollment and faculty recruitment. Public universities have even gone so far as to insure themselves against a lack of Chinese students: in 2017, the University of Illinois at Urbana-Champaign took out an insurance policy to cover the $60 million in tuition that Chinese students paid to the university, in case an unforeseen event precipitated a sudden drop in Chinese student enrollment.[12]

Beyond education, Chinese immigration to the US has remained high and rising. In 1980, the number of people immigrating from China to the US made up 3.14 percent of the total immigrant population. But from then until 2019, the number of immigrants from China to the US increased by approximately 546 percent, at which point Chinese immigrants represented 6.35 percent of the total immigrant population.[13] More than 60 percent of the US Chinese population was born in foreign countries, and first-generation immigrants constitute the majority of the US Chinese population. Today, Asian Americans represent the fastest growth rate of any major racial or ethnic group.[14] Roughly four million Americans identify as Chinese American.[15] From our own experience, we've found that education plays a significant role in many immigrants' decisions to come to the United States: in the housing searches of our Chinese friends in San Diego and San Francisco, school districts are among their top priorities.

PLAYING THE TOURNAMENT BEYOND CHINA'S BORDERS

China's education system—the centralized hierarchical tournament—is affecting American education and life. Along with their suitcases, Chinese immigrants have brought with them a set of norms and expectations rooted deeply in their time spent coming of age in China. One of these "norms" we have spent the better part of this book discussing is an understanding of the education system as a tournament, with an objective and clearly defined scoring system. The tournament's arrival in the United States has not gone unnoticed, sparking debates around what education should fundamentally look like.

In China, the obsession with elite schools is one that is rewarded. Positions at the top of the hierarchy are seldom achieved by those who do not attend an elite university, and those who do not score well on the gaokao cannot attend an elite university. As a result, families will do their very best to ensure that the gaokao is subject to neither the connections nor corruption that tend to govern other aspects of China's society in the face of relatively weak institutions. Not only that, but because elite universities are those that are most well-funded by the government, a student's tuition is often cheaper than it would be at a lower-tier school. As a meritocratic system that seemingly transcends the connections and corruption so typical of China's society, the education system provides families from every walk of life with a sense of hope, and with it, agency: they, too, can change their lives through accessing an elite education.

In the United States, society does not reward an elite education in the same way. Paths to socioeconomic success are far more diverse than in China. Though a degree from an elite university is often helpful to climbing the career ladder, lacking one by no means sends an individual to the bottom of the socioeconomic distribution. University admission in the United States employs a holistic applicant review process, of which standardized testing is just an increasingly small part. A student's success hinges not only on their ability to score well on an exam, but also on a variety of other credentials that a student can build throughout their years leading up to admission decisions. Last but not least, an elite degree is one of the most expensive across all universities: for some of the most elite, tuition and other fees can cost over $100,000 each year. In recent years, some have even suggested that the return to an elite college education does not offset the sky-high price tags that come with the degree.[16]

Even though elite education is not rewarded to anywhere near the same degree in the United States as it is in China, the obsession remains alive and well, as national and local-level court cases, coupled with our own experiences, have shown. But even before we discuss these, it's important to point out that for any immigrant, leaving one's home country means leaving behind a network of connections, as well as an intuitive understanding of cultural norms. This is perhaps even more true for immigrants from China. One Chinese netizen suggested that "climbing the vines" (爬藤)—a popular euphemism for attending any Ivy League institution—was one of the few ways to compensate for these disadvantages and to gain access to the upper echelons of American society.[17] Though they lack connections, Chinese immigrants nonetheless carry with them the belief—one that is absolutely true in their cultural context—of the importance of education to social mobility, which in turn strengthens the perceived importance of elite colleges, even in the United States.

We'll start with a court case that garnered a trove of media attention: the Harvard lawsuit.[18] In 2014, an organization called Students for Fair Admissions representing Asian American students sued Harvard University for its use of race as a key factor in their admissions process. As we have mentioned previously, Harvard uses the standard "holistic" approach in admission, rating applicants on a scale of one (the best) to six (the worst) across five categories: academic, extracurricular, athletic, personal, and overall. According to the plaintiff's analysis, however, Asian Americans were consistently receiving lower ratings on the personality score from admission officers (but not alumni interviewers). Across other measures, like SAT scores—arguably the most objective measures outlined in the holistic process—Asian Americans consistently outperformed their peers.

It's important to note that there's no homogenous "Asian American" view on education, including affirmative action, elite college, or meritocracy. Within the Asian American community, the Chinese American diaspora has itself been galvanized by such debates. Rather, among those who have been moved to take political action opposing affirmative action or other equity-based initiatives, we believe that the framework of China's centralized hierarchical tournament can shed light on some of the underlying rationale. In a similar vein, though the subject of these debates are high school and college students, it is, in many cases, their parents who are moved to action. From China to the United States, parents are doing their best to raise their children and facilitate their success. And yet, parenting styles are deeply rooted in a parent's own experience. In China, where long-term socioeconomic success is predicated on one's ability to obtain an elite degree, and admission into an elite university is predicated on academic achievement, it is only natural that a parent with this contextual background would strive for the same outcomes—entree into an elite university—for their own children. It is also the case that it is China's most elite—those at the top of China's hierarchy owing to their own academic achievement—who most frequently make their way to the United States, as highly skilled workers are far more likely to be able to obtain a visa. But in the US, where paths to socioeconomic success are more diverse, and academic achievement is one of many factors that contribute to long-term success, parents likely do not focus on academic achievement to the same extent that their Chinese counterparts do.

Returning to the original lawsuit against Harvard, it's clear that what the plaintiffs take issue with is the subjectivity of the holistic system. If they are outscoring other potential admitted students on the objective measures, it ought to follow that they would be more likely than their lower-scoring peers to gain admission to an elite university—after all, this is how it works in China. And yet, as perfect SAT and ACT scores prove insufficient for admission to elite institutions like Harvard time and time again, the sense that the system is fundamentally unfair continues to grow. This piece of evidence aligns with fears among Chinese families that so-called holistic scores are easily subject to manipulation. The framework that many Chinese parents had previously thrived in was one that, above all else, prioritized the attributes that they feel the holistic system lacks—transparency and objectivity. Without a clear and well-defined scoring system at the heart of an admission process, and even more broadly, an education system, failure can be chalked up not to the individual but to the system. Without the connections that they might have in China, Chinese parents seemingly lack other avenues through which they could positively influence their student's chance of acceptance. As such, the only natural course of action is to change the system.

Though the Harvard case is likely one of the most high-profile instances of the tournament's influence on US national politics, its presence is even more salient in local-level school districts. After all, college admission is the culmination of the twelve years of schooling leading up to those fateful admission decisions. And much like in China, Chinese families' preparation for admission to elite colleges starts long before students submit their college application. Having educated his children in both China and the US, Hongbin has first-hand experience with the conflict arising between the two systems. To date, Hongbin's daughter has attended seven and his son six different public and private pre-tertiary schools across Beijing, Hong Kong, and Palo Alto. For Hongbin, the problems began on his daughter's very first day of elementary school in China. This was due to the fact that Hongbin and his wife opted not to teach his daughter math or Chinese characters before she attended school as a first grader—a student's first year of real schooling, given that kindergarten more closely parallels daycare—in part because they believed it was too early, but also because his daughter didn't need to take a test to attend Tsinghua University Elementary School. If you'll recall, a perk of a Tsinghua professorship (a position at the top of the hierarchy) is that a professor's children don't need to sit for an exam to cinch a guaranteed spot at one of the best elementary schools in the country. Soon after his daughter started school at six years old, she returned home with a math test on which she had scored 69 out of 100. She needed Hongbin's signature. Not thinking too much about it, Hongbin signed the paper and handed it back to her.

A few days later, his daughter's teacher called Hongbin, asking if he had signed his daughter's math test. He said yes. Incredulous, the teacher proceeded: "You know she only got 69 points, right? Do you know that without her terrible score, the average would have been 98 points? Other parents would have come to us if their child had gotten this low score. What kind of parent are you?" To Hongbin, such a line of questioning was completely unfounded—his daughter had just started school. How could she possibly know all the content? The teacher shot back, "the average student starting school is supposed to be able to do addition, subtraction, multiplication, and division for numbers up to 100. They are supposed to know 2,500 Chinese characters. We don't have time for your daughter. Please find her a tutor and come to school one day to observe our class." As he was instructed, Hongbin followed his daughter to school the very next day and took a seat in the back row of the class. Before class even began, the teacher handed each student a test with 100 math questions on addition and subtraction. Each student had five minutes to complete the test. Nearly every one of them earned a 100.

This was Hongbin's first direct exposure to the tournament as a parent. So much had changed since Hongbin himself was a child. His earliest years were spent running around the maze of the factory, or better yet, huddled over a chess board. Though he, too, had to sit for countless exams, his unique timing as a student passing through the education system immediately after the Cultural Revolution made it so that he never truly experienced the education system as a competitive tournament in its entirety. In fact, the most formative years of his education took place in the United States, where he attended his PhD program. He took to China's social media, venting,

> I don't understand why our school forces children to memorize
> Chinese characters so early. At age 10, most Chinese probably know
> the same number of Chinese characters—the ones that we really use.
> Thirty years later, we still know those same Chinese characters. So why
> bother? And for math, kids shouldn't have to learn at such a young
> age. Math is a skill that most can pick up naturally later!

But already, at his daughter's first year in school, he had arrived at a crossroads—should he urge her to compete in the tournament? It seemed the only route he could take to ensure that she kept up with her classmates and to remain in her year. Was that really the only way forward? Though he resisted its pressure for as long as he could, avoiding teaching or tutoring his children and allowing them to approach academic work later and at their own pace, he eventually gave in, tutoring his daughter at home in Chinese characters for several months at a time to catch her up to the standards of those competing alongside her.

Nonetheless, Hongbin did not want his children to conform entirely to the tournament, nor the norms it so often fosters. As he learned as a student at Stanford, he encouraged them to ask questions—any kind of questions—and challenge their teachers and other adults in school or at home if they didn't understand or agree with what was said. But he faced pushback here, too—once, his daughter brought home a Chinese test on which she missed one question. Though she memorized the poem in its entirety, she failed to memorize the name of the author. He told her not to worry, as he thought it a boring question anyway—there are millions of modern poets. What he didn't anticipate was his daughter telling her friend what he had said. That friend then reported his comments to the teacher. The teacher was angry and summoned him to the classroom, chastising his behavior as a parent and his lack of respect for their curriculum. Indeed, the teachers, and even other family members, found the behavior that he encouraged to be extremely rude. Operating against societal expectations was a painful experience for everyone in his family.

Later Hongbin's work brought him to Palo Alto, where he was a prospective candidate for a faculty member at Stanford. It was then that his daughter, at that point a fifth grader, got her first glimpse of the United States. Hongbin enrolled her at the local public school in the Palo Alto Unified School District (PAUSD). Little did Hongbin know that PAUSD was at that time probably one of the best public-school districts in the entire country. His daughter thrived in the

American school system: the days were shorter, the holidays more frequent, the homework minimal, and the tests few and inconsequential (until high school, at least). The PAUSD community also emphasized extracurricular activities, meaning that his daughter spent far more time outside of the classroom than she had before.

A year passed without incident, at which point Stanford permanently hired Hongbin, and his daughter easily settled into the reality that she would not be returning to her school in China anytime soon. Shortly thereafter, however, he received an unusual phone call from his daughter's math teacher—according to him, Hongbin's daughter talked too much during class and was distracting her classmates. When he confronted his daughter about her behavior, she said she was bored. The math taught in sixth grade was math that she had learned as a third grader three years earlier in China. After jumping through some administrative hoops, Hongbin's daughter sat for several skip tests and passed two grades of math. To qualify for a summer program, she also had to sit for the SAT. As a seventh grader, she earned a 790/800 on the math section.

• • •

Though he did not realize it at the time, Hongbin had become just one of many parents who had unintentionally brought the tournament to PAUSD. By simply being a student in a top-tier public school in China, Hongbin's daughter was literally years ahead of her American counterparts. The reality of the differences between the two education systems was simply too large to bridge. That said, Hongbin's daughter's case is not representative of most families in the PAUSD school district who are familiar with the tournament-style education system. In his daughter's case, it was her years spent in China, an altogether separate education system, that gave rise to such differences. Instead, it is the strategies that these parents learned, either from their time in China or from their own parents: how to succeed within a tournament-style education system. As Natasha Warikoo pointed out in her work, *Race at the Top,* Ruixue and Hongbin similarly came to believe that these differences have led to issues that have impacted parents and students alike both in and out of the classroom.[19]

The tension Hongbin's daughter experienced in a US public school district can be viewed as a microcosm of a larger debate: what happens when expectations about education systems differ? And when strategies for achieving success within that system differ? Driven by an increase in Chinese immigration, of which Hongbin was on the early end, a rising number of Chinese students have matriculated to public schools in the Bay Area over the last two decades. Relative to the rest of the country, schools in the Bay Area have a high percentage of Asian students. In line with our sense that elite education is still a priority for many Asian families, data indicate that among schools that have a higher proportion of Asian students, there is a higher proportion who choose to apply to elite schools. To illustrate this point, we'll use the percentage of students at each school applying to the University of California, Los Angeles, one of the top public colleges in the country with an acceptance rate that routinely falls below 10 percent. In 2023, 35 percent of students at Palo Alto High School were Asian students; 55 percent of its students submitted an application to UCLA. Another school in Palo Alto, the Gunn High School, has 46 percent Asian students; 61 percent applied to UCLA. At the school that has the highest percent of Asian students at 88 percent—Mission San Jose in Fremont, California—78 percent of students applied to UCLA. In contrast, Mountain View High School has only 25 percent Asian students; 19 percent of its students applied to UCLA in 2023.[20] Though these Asian American students may not have attended school in China like Hongbin's daughter, many of their parents might have. And if the parents didn't, perhaps their parents' parents did. When parents with different experiences and different strategies for success are responsible for children in the same school district, a divide almost inevitably emerges.

On one side of this divide are parents whose strategies for success are formed by beliefs consistent with China's centralized hierarchical tournament: they want to rank students early on, using lanes for different students. In practice, this might involve one grade with three different lanes for one subject: an advanced lane, a standard lane, and a remedial lane. In their eyes, the determining factor for the ranking ought to be a standardized test, with clear and objective indicators. The rationale behind this is simple: students have different talents and interests, causing some to advance beyond their peers. These parents believe that it is inefficient for teaching and learners alike if students of vastly different levels are mixed into one classroom—some kids get bored, lose interest, and learn little in a class that they do not find challenging enough, while other students find it challenging to keep pace. Having lanes, or even allowing students to skip grades, would solve this problem. Underlying this, however, is the looming issue of college preparation: one's math level is an objective measure of a student's academic achievement. Without the differentiation that lanes offer, students with stronger backgrounds in a given subject wouldn't have the advantage of indicating such by using their advanced status as a proxy for their ability. Notice the underlying argument here—an objective measure of talent, as represented by one's academic achievement, drives parents to take a stance on one side of this debate. For them, a hierarchical ranking system based on one's scores provides a clear solution to this issue, allowing high-achieving students to stand at the front in the tournament as early as middle school.

But on the other side of this divide are those parents whose strategies for success were shaped by beliefs apart from China's centralized hierarchical tournament. It is these parents who believe that having lanes might hurt students by fostering a rat-race mentality, exerting undue pressure on children at too early an age. Kids who advance to a higher subject level might not be those who are genuinely interested in and passionate about the subject, but instead are those who are most worried about their college applications. Students thus learn the subject outside of school, normally by hiring a tutor. Those on this side of the divide are not wrong in making this assumption. Once, Hongbin's daughter's geometry teacher in Palo Alto asked the twenty students in her class—all of whom had skipped at least one grade—who had tutors at home. Only two students didn't raise their hand. This sort of example is exactly what parents on this side of the divide point to: lanes and skipping grades fosters a competitive and high-pressure environment for students, narrowing the definition of success to achievement on a select few subjects. Kids who are in the remedial lane may actually pick up on math at a perfectly normal speed. They're just lacking a tutor. Of course, there is also the issue of equity—those who cannot afford to hire tutors outside of school are at a disadvantage.

As you may know, many of these tensions circle around one subject in particular: math. In the PAUSD, the math hierarchy follows a simple trajectory.[21] In sixth grade, students take Pre-algebra (foundational math); in seventh grade, they take Pre-algebra (concepts in math); in eighth grade, Algebra 1; ninth, Geometry; tenth, Algebra 2; eleventh, Pre-calculus; twelfth, AP Calculus. But as it stands, there are also lanes in each grade—an advanced lane and a standard lane. For example, AP Calculus (designed at the national level by the College Board) has two levels: AP Calculus AB and AP Calculus BC. Students in the advanced math lane would take the BC class, as the class includes a broader scope of subjects and is generally considered to be more challenging.

In 2019, however, PAUSD began implementing what is now known as the "de-tracking" initiative, which has effectively put an end to the advanced versus standard math lanes for reasons of equity and student mental health. The initiative instead sets all students on track to begin geometry in ninth grade, sans lanes. Their efforts mirrored the San Francisco Unified School District's de-tracking initiative implemented five years earlier. Parents who lamented the extreme competitiveness in classes like math embraced the initiative. But unsurprisingly, parents who supported the tournament-style education were not pleased—without lanes, there was no clear rank that set their child apart. Meanwhile, students who wanted to forgo simply tracking into advanced math and skip a grade (or two) of math were met with similar barriers.

Over the last few years, parents have frequently raised the issue that PAUSD provides opaque grade-skip testing requirements: the district does not disclose the content of the skip tests, while students who have experience taking the test argue that random material apart from the curriculum they are attempting to test out of is featured on the test. Together, they argue that PAUSD purposefully makes the tests unreasonably challenging so that students cannot skip grades. Not only that, but PAUSD has eliminated multivariable calculus, the course immediately following AP Calculus BC from their curriculum, so that even if students do succeed in the notoriously challenging skip tests, they no longer have a course to take through PAUSD in the final years of high school.[22]

In 2021, a group of Palo Alto parents filed a lawsuit that took issue with PAUSD's math skip tests.[23] According to the lawsuit, the skip test has two parts: a standardized portion and a portion developed by PAUSD. But the second part, according to the parents, "is not calibrated, has highly variable results, includes material that is far beyond the scope of the grade level students are looking to skip, is not objectively scored, and lacks all transparency." The lawsuit also alleges that PAUSD violated the California Mathematics Placement Act of 2015, which requires districts to establish "a fair, objective, and transparent mathematics placement policy" for students entering ninth grade. The lawsuit ended in favor of the plaintiffs: on February 6, 2023, the judge ruled that PAUSD violated the Math Placement Act and that its "math placement policy must give parents and students a process for appealing their placements, and the district has to collect data on how the policy is working." However, parents and students alike remain dissatisfied with PAUSD policies around math, alleging that the district has done little to implement meaningful changes.

PAUSD is not the only school district facing controversy. In June 2022, the *New York Times'* podcast, *The Daily*, released an episode titled, "One Elite High School's Struggle Over Admissions."[24] In it, reporters covered the local school district's decision to replace the test-based admission system at Lowell High School, one of the top public schools in San Francisco, with a lottery system. The change was similarly implemented for reasons of equity: as it stood, the school did not reflect the racial identities of the population in the broader school district. Voicing their outrage at the change, Asian-American—often Chinese—parents ousted a school board member who was crucial to the policy change and replaced her with a candidate who supported test-based admission. Lowell High School has since reverted to its original, test-based admission system.

On one hand, it's likely that these cases represent a simple truth: parents want what is best for their children. Ensuring that they are placed in a classroom environment that appropriately challenges them would ensure that they have access to the best educational opportunities available. But on the other hand, notice that at the heart of these lawsuits is a familiar narrative—as in the Harvard case, parents feel that they are faced with unfair prospects when there is a perceived lack of objectivity typically granted by a standardized exam. Consider this from the perspective of the parents who themselves were not raised in an American system—how are you supposed to compete, let alone succeed, on subjective measures? Without years of experience that lends itself to intuitive knowledge, it is nearly impossible to ascertain what such measures might be. Objective measures provide a sense of security and clarity. Taken together, these cases have augured a shift in sentiment about the direction of education systems in the United States writ large. While at the national level, it has manifested in the Supreme Court's ruling against affirmative action, at the local level, these cases suggest that ranking and tests may be the way of the future. Not only that, but schools that had previously dropped standardized testing requirements, including Brown, Dartmouth, Harvard, Yale, Georgetown, MIT, Caltech, and the entire public university systems of Florida and Georgia, have begun to reinstate such requirements for student applicants.

The emphasis on education in these communities also influences other aspects of society, particularly in shaping housing trends and contributing to segregation patterns. Although Asian-White segregation is generally lower than Black-White segregation in the United States, the disparity has more than doubled in major school districts since the 1980s.[25] Neighborhoods like Palo Alto and Carmel Valley in San Diego illustrate this trend. Both areas are known for their highly rated school districts, significant Asian American populations (34 percent in Palo Alto and 32 percent in Carmel Valley), and high housing prices. The combination of desirable educational opportunities and demographic clustering frequently leads to heightened housing demand and inflated prices in these areas. Earlier research established a trend that has since been dubbed "white flight": the phenomenon of white people moving out of urban areas, particularly those with significant minority populations—usually African Americans or Hispanic individuals—and into suburban areas.[26] Now, however, as non-Asian families face challenges related to rising housing costs and educational competition related to the tournament, this results in patterns resembling white flight, where non-Asian families leave neighborhoods that become increasingly ethnically homogeneous.[27] This migration pattern ultimately contributes to growing social divisions.

THE EXAM EMPIRE

Even though US elite colleges may not offer rewards to the same extent as elite universities in China, the cases we have explored in this chapter suggest that Chinese families in the United States remain similarly obsessed with elite education. By immigrating, Chinese families make a challenging decision to leave behind their network of potential connections in favor of opportunities that the US may or may not have to offer. Through their eyes, the perceived advantages associated with obtaining an elite degree may alone be enough to offset the perceived disadvantages associated with life in a new country. And yet, the strategies employed by these families to get that degree—strategies that make perfect sense in the context of China—have sparked debates across the United States about what education should fundamentally prioritize. In the Harvard case and across PAUSD, you see that parents hope to implement score-based systems early in the middle school years that champion objectivity and transparency. They hope these systems will in turn facilitate their students' rise to the top of the academic hierarchy. The obsession has reworked national-level politics through affirmative action as well as local-level politics through curriculums that prioritize ranking initiatives. Not only that, but such systems have also caused increasing social divisions as parents who do not subscribe to the tournament mentality try to escape it altogether.

This obsession is longstanding. From its inception over a thousand years ago, the exam system underlying the obsession has remained a cornerstone of Chinese life, surviving even the rise and fall of China's most tumultuous dynasties and ruling parties. Having left its mark on hundreds of millions of families, served as a powerful tool of governance, and shaped institutions across China's society, the exam system is undeniably a powerful one. Now, with globalization facilitating unprecedented cross-border exchanges, it's clear that the system has the potential to impact families beyond China. Though we have focused almost exclusively on the relationship between China and the United States, other countries that similarly benefit from Chinese exchange, like the United Kingdom, Australia, and Canada are likely to experience similar tensions when faced with some of the harsher realities of exam culture.

But the exam system is not without its weaknesses. As we have discussed throughout the course of the last nine chapters, China's education system, political structure, and cultural norms are inextricably connected and mutually reinforcing, making the system particularly challenging to change. For the better part of the last thousand years, they have collectively shaped the destiny of generations of Chinese people. As China embarks on a new era characterized by the central government as witnessing "great changes unseen in a century," the strength and resilience of its system will be tested by the challenges ahead as China strives to reshape the global order.

IN REFLECTION

So which country's education system do we favor most?

After attending college and meeting people from different parts of the country, I, Ruixue, realized that my friends from my hometown—not to mention many other talented young Chinese—could not access the life-changing benefits of university due to systemic barriers. Instead, their fates were largely determined long before the gaokao by the primary, middle, and high schools to which they had access. These systemic barriers appear to only be growing stronger with economic development. While I can still find faculty older than me who hail from rural parts of China, I rarely meet any students with experiences like ours. This highlights a cruel reality: while previous generations still managed to overcome these barriers, increasing inequality means that fewer young people from disadvantaged backgrounds have those same opportunities today. In my opinion, the root of this problem is not the gaokao itself, but the pre-college education system. Instead of replacing the gaokao with a different system, like that in the US, I believe that improving the distribution and quality of educational resources before college would go further toward fostering equality in China.

I also believe it important to touch on the notion that China's education system stifles creativity and innovation. I do think it's fair to say that the exam-focused system discourages the development of certain skills, especially social skills that are extremely valuable and likely to become even more so as many tasks become automated.[28] Fostering these skills is undeniably a strength of the education system in the US. But social skills are not the same as creativity. I do not believe that one can blame the education system alone for stifling creativity or innovation. The root of these issues lies in a society structured as a centralized hierarchical tournament. Such a society rewards the types of behavior necessary to climb the hierarchy while disincentivizing behaviors that foster creative destruction. Many of the failures of the education system can be chalked up to broader societal structures, and it is these broader societal structures that would need to change to witness the same in the education system.

In reflecting on the education system, I, Hongbin, have found that many of my greatest takeaways are rooted in my experience as a parent. Making decisions about my own education and my children's education has been one of the great experiments of my life, and a wild one—after all, my most recent experimental subjects were my own children. Having traced the experiment back to its roots, my wife and I know that the experiment was simply a reality of changing circumstances. Our jobs took us from Hong Kong to mainland China to Palo Alto. But in the process, my two children collectively attended a dozen different schools before college, and through them I witnessed the strengths and weaknesses of the system across countries and cultures. I've often wondered how I might do it differently.

Few would doubt that the quality of an American college education exceeds that of a Chinese one. Given that both my children are and will be attending college in the US, any changes I would implement to their education journey would thus be to their pre-tertiary education opportunities. I've come to the following conclusion: I would likely send my children to a Chinese public school until seventh grade, and then switch them into the US for the last year of middle school and all of high school. In terms of hard skills, Chinese education emphasizes math and logic from the very beginning. Chinese is a much harder language to learn than English, and there are benefits to learning a difficult language early in life. In terms of soft skills, Chinese education emphasizes hard work, discipline, and competitive academics. Though not the full picture, these skills are useful in high school, college, and later, in the workplace.

Chinese education is also extremely narrow: by teaching to the test, students are neither afforded the opportunity nor encouraged to learn content beyond what appears on the pages of their highly regimented exams. As Ruixue pointed out, I have often considered whether such an environment stifled my children's curiosity at a time when maintaining their natural curiosity was my top priority. This possibility underscores why, in my view, eighth grade is the ideal time for a move to the US. At that point, they'd have a solid foundation in math and Chinese and disciplined working habits that would allow them to succeed in challenging courses in American high schools that push them to think outside of the box on an unrestricted set of topics and ideas. But each system has its own strengths and weaknesses, ones that may be more or less suited to certain children, my own included. It's impossible to say whether we made all the right decisions along the way, or even whether my own "ideal" combination would play to the strengths of my own children.

By now, readers likely have discerned our mixed feelings. In accessing the life-changing benefits of an elite college education in China, we benefited tremendously from the centralized hierarchical tournament. But having spent years in the system and over double that time studying it, we have become increasingly aware of the elements of the system that we believe may cause more harm than good. Above all, we know this to be true: there is no perfect education system, neither Chinese nor American, nor any other in the world. It is only through understanding China's exam culture and its context that we can embark on improving it.

Notes

Acknowledgments

Index

NOTES

1. OBSESSION

1. Barry Naughton, *The Chinese Economy: Adaptation and Growth*, 2nd ed. (Cambridge, MA: MIT Press, 2018); Yingyi Qian, "A Theory of Shortage in Socialist Economies Based on the 'Soft Budget Constraint,'" *American Economic Review* 84, no. 1 (1994): 145–156.

2. Jingzi Wu, Gladys Yang, and Xianyi Yang, *The Scholars* (Beijing: Foreign Languages Press, 2004).

3. The exam system, known as Keju, was in its nascent stage in Sui-Tang dynasties and got expanded around 1000 AD in the Song dynasty. For more information, see Peter Kees Bol, *"This Culture of Ours": Intellectual Transitions in T'ang and Sung China* (Stanford: Stanford University Press, 1992).

4. Benjamin A. Elman, *A Cultural History of Civil Examinations in Late Imperial China* (Berkeley: University of California Press, 2000); Chung-li Chang,, *The Chinese Gentry: Studies on Their Role in Nineteenth-Century Chinese Society*, with intro. by Franz Michael, (1955; Seattle: University of Washington Press, 1974).

5. Elman, *A Cultural History of Civil Examinations in Late Imperial China*.

6. Ying Bai and Ruixue Jia, "Elite Recruitment and Political Stability: The Impact of the Abolition of China's Civil Service Exam," *Econometrica* 84, no. 2 (2016): 677–733, https://doi.org/10.3982/ECTA13448.

7. The Republic had a "five-power" constitution, adding two Chinese institutions—the recently scrapped examination system and the censorate—to the legislative, executive, and judicial powers. The examination system was later institutionalized as the "Examination Branch" in the Republic of China and can still be seen in Taiwan today.

8. Hongbin Li, Mark Rosenzweig, and Junsen Zhang, "Altruism, Favoritism, and Guilt in the Allocation of Family Resources: Sophie's Choice in Mao's Mass Send-Down Movement," *Journal of Political Economy* 118, no. 1 (2010): 1–38, https://doi.org/10.1086/650315.

9. Andrew G. Walder, *China under Mao: A Revolution Derailed* (Cambridge, MA: Harvard University Press, 2017).

10. To understand how the Cultural Revolution changed the lives of many young people in China, see Xueguang Zhou and Liren Hou, "Children of the Cultural Revolution: The State and the Life Course in the People's Republic of China," *American Sociological Review* 64, no. 1 (1999): 12–36, https://doi.org/10.1177/000312249906400103.

11. Hongbin Li and Lingsheng Meng, "The Scarring Effects of College Education Deprivation During China's Cultural Revolution," *Economic Development and Cultural Change* 70, no. 3 (2022): 981–1016, https://doi.org/10.1086/713935.

12. Jacob Mincer, *Schooling, Experience, and Earnings* (New York: National Bureau of Economic Research, 1974).

13. Morley Gunderson and Philip Oreopoulos, "Returns to Education in Developed Countries," in *The Economics of Education,* 2nd ed., ed. Steve Bradley and Colin Green (Elsevier, 2020), 39–51, https://doi.org/10.1016/B978-0-12-815391-8.00003-3.

14. Xin Meng and Michael P. Kidd, "Labor Market Reform and the Changing Structure of Wage Determination in China's State Sector During the 1980s," *Journal of Comparative Economics* 25, no. 3 (1997): 403–421, https://doi.org/10.1006/jcec.1997.1481; Raymond P. Byron and Evelyn Q. Manaloto, "Returns to Education in China," *Economic Development and Cultural Change* 38, no. 4 (1990): 783–796, https://doi.org/10.1086/451833.

15. Hongbin Li, James Liang, and Binzhen Wu, "Labor Market Experience and Returns to College Education in Fast Growing Economies," *Journal of Human Resources,* June 10, 2022, 0421-11629R2, doi: https://doi.org/10.3368/jhr.0421-11629R2; Junsen Zhang et al., "Economic Returns to Schooling in Urban China, 1988 to 2001," *Journal of Comparative Economics* 33, no. 4 (2005): 730–752, https://doi.org/10.1016/j.jce.2005.05.008.

16. UNESCO Institute for Statistics, "School Enrollment, Tertiary (% Gross)—China, United States," World Bank Group, accessed April 24, 2024, https://data.worldbank.org/indicator/SE.TER.ENRR?locations=CN-US.

17. Dezhuang Hu et al., "The Burden of Education Costs in China: A Struggle for All, but Heavier for Lower-Income Families," manuscript, August 31, 2023, available at SSRN, https://doi.org/10.2139/ssrn.4558282.

18. One explanation would be that parents in more unequal countries invest more in their children's education. Matthias Doepke and Fabrizio Zilibotti, *Love, Money & Parenting: How Economics Explains the Way We Raise Our Kids* (Princeton: Princeton University Press, 2019).

19. Organisation for Economic Co-operation and Development, *PISA 2015 Results,* vol. 2, *Policies and Practices for Successful Schools* (Paris: OECD, 2016).

20. Amy Chua, *Battle Hymn of the Tiger Mother* (New York: Penguin, 2011).

21. There are ninety-six national first-tier colleges in college admission, which also overlaps with the Project-211 (meaning Top 100 in the twenty-first century) college.

22. Ruixue Jia and Hongbin Li, "Just Above the Exam Cutoff Score: Elite College Admission and Wages in China," *Journal of Public Economics* 196 (April 2021): 104371, https://doi.org/10.1016/j.jpubeco.2021.104371.

23. Sharon LaFraniere, "China's College Entry Test Is an Obsession," *New York Times,* June 12, 2009; Eva Dou, "In Flooded China Town, Students Cling to Tractors to Get to College Entrance Exam," *Washington Post,* July 8, 2020; Chao Deng, "China's Cutthroat School System Leads to Teen Suicides," *Wall Street Journal,* March 15, 2014; Yvette Tan, "Gaokao Season: China Embarks on Dreaded National Exams," *BBC,* June 7, 2016, https://www.bbc.com/news/world-asia-china-36457453; Ben Westcott and Nectar Gan, "10 Million Students in China Are Facing the Toughest Exam of Their Lives in a Pandemic," *CNN,* April 10, 2020, https://www.cnn.com/2020/04/09/asia/coronavirus-china-gaokao-student-intl-hnk/index.html.

24. *How Do Chinese Study for Exams? Day in The Life of a Chinese High School Student,* Youtube, 2020, https://www.youtube.com/watch?v=t1NNXInTVmo.

25. Ministry of Education, "1949–2013: Compilation of Statistical Data for Sixty-Five Years of New China [新中国65年统计资料汇编]," n.d.

26. National Bureau of Statistics of China, China Statistical Yearbook: 2022, https://www.stats.gov.cn/sj/ndsj/2022/indexeh.htm.

2. RULES OF THE TOURNAMENT

1. The hukou system is also a historical legacy of the Qin dynasty (221 BC–207 BC), the first unified and centralized Chinese dynasty. The policy was known as 编户齐民 (registered households and equal/common people). 杜正胜,编户齐民：传统政治社会结构之形成, 1990 [Du Zhengsheng, "Educating Households and Enabling the People: The Formation of Traditional Political and Social Structure"].

2. "2023 Admission Rates of 985 and 211 Universities in Provinces Across the Country [2023年全国各省985和211 录取率]," August 24, 2023, https://www.pagetu.com/2023/08/14/11/819/.

3. Ruixue Jia and Torsten Persson, "Choosing Ethnicity: The Interplay Between Individual and Social Motives," *Journal of the European*

Economic Association 19, no. 2 (2021): 1203–48, https://doi.org/10.1093/jeea/jvaa026.

4. 林毅夫, 蔡昉., and 李周, *The China Miracle: Development Strategy and Economic Reform [中国的奇迹: 发展战略与经济改革]*, Zeng ding ban, di 1 ban (Shanghai: 格致出版社 : 上海三联书店 : 上海人民出版社, 2012).

5. Scott Rozelle and Natalie Hell, *Invisible China: How the Urban-Rural Divide Threatens China's Rise* (Chicago: University of Chicago Press, 2020).

6. Hongbin Li and Binzhen Wu, "China's Educational Inequality: Facts from College Entrance Exams and Admissions," manuscript, 2023.

7. Hongbin Li et al., "Unequal Access to College in China: How Far Have Poor, Rural Students Been Left Behind?," *China Quarterly* 221 (March 2015): 185–207, https://doi.org/10.1017/S0305741015000314.

8. Ruixue Jia, Hongbin Li, and Lingsheng Meng, "Elite College Education and Social Mobility in China," *Economic Development and Cultural Change*, March 18, 2024, 730493, https://doi.org/10.1086/730493.

9. Dezhuang Hu et al., "The Burden of Education Costs in China: A Struggle for All, but Heavier for Lower-Income Families," manuscript, August 31, 2023, available at SSRN, https://doi.org/10.2139/ssrn.4558282.

10. Hu et al., "The Burden of Education Costs in China."

11. Jia, Li, and Meng, "Elite College Education and Social Mobility in China."

12. Ye Jin, Hongbin Li, and Binzhen Wu, "Income Inequality, Consumption, and Social-Status Seeking," *Journal of Comparative Economics* 39, no. 2 (2011): 191–204, https://doi.org/10.1016/j.jce.2010.12.004.

13. Jia, Li, and Meng, "Elite College Education and Social Mobility in China."

14. Hu et al., "The Burden of Education Costs in China."

15. Jia, Li, and Meng, "Elite College Education and Social Mobility in China"; Raj Chetty et al., "Income Segregation and Intergenerational Mobility Across Colleges in the United States," *Quarterly Journal of Economics* 135, no. 3 (2020): 1567–1633, https://doi.org/10.1093/qje/qjaa005.

3. THE PAYOFF

1. Gary S. Becker, *Human Capital: A Theoretical and Empirical Analysis, with Special Reference to Education,* 3rd ed. (Chicago: University of Chicago Press, 1993).

2. Organisation for Economic Co-operation and Development, *PISA 2018 Results,* vol. 1, *What Students Know and Can Do* (Paris: OECD Publishing, 2019). PISA 2022 results were released in December 2023. However, due to

COVID-19 restrictions, data from China's provinces—Beijing, Shanghai, Jiangsu, and Zhejiang—were not fully collected and thus not published.

3. Prashant Loyalka et al., "Skill Levels and Gains in University STEM Education in China, India, Russia and the United States," *Nature Human Behaviour* 5, no. 7 (2021): 892–904, https://doi.org/10.1038/s41562-021-01062-3.

4. Hongbin Li et al., "What Can Students Gain from China's Higher Education?" *Asian Economic Policy Review* 18, no. 2 (2023): 287–304, https://doi.org/10.1111/aepr.12426.

5. Organisation for Economic Co-operation and Development, *PISA 2015 Results*, vol. 2, *Policies and Practices for Successful Schools* (Paris: OECD, 2016).

6. Michael Spence, "Job Market Signaling," *Quarterly Journal of Economics* 87, no. 3 (1973): 354–374, 355, https://doi.org/10.2307/1882010.

7. Eric Fish, "Are China's Colleges Too Easy? Universities Lament Low Dropout Rate," *World Crunch*, April 9, 2013, https://worldcrunch.com/culture-society/are-china039s-colleges-too-easy-universities-lament-low-dropout-rate.

8. Hongbin Li, Pak Wai Liu, and Junsen Zhang, "Estimating Returns to Education Using Twins in Urban China," *Journal of Development Economics* 97, no. 2 (2012): 494–504, https://doi.org/10.1016/j.jdeveco.2011.05.009.

9. Jere R. Behrman, Mark R. Rosenzweig, and Paul Taubman, "Endowments and the Allocation of Schooling in the Family and in the Marriage Market: The Twins Experiment," *Journal of Political Economy* 102, no. 6 (1994): 1131–74, https://doi.org/10.1086/261966.

10. Ruixue Jia and Hongbin Li, "Just above the Exam Cutoff Score: Elite College Admission and Wages in China," *Journal of Public Economics* 196 (April 2021): 104371, https://doi.org/10.1016/j.jpubeco.2021.104371.

11. Stacy Dale and Alan Krueger, "Estimating the Effects of College Characteristics over the Career Using Administrative Earnings Data," *Journal of Human Resources* 49, no. 2 (2014): 328–358, https://doi.org/10.1353/jhr.2014.0015.

4. POLITICAL LOGIC

1. Javier Hernandez, "China Tries to Redistribute Education to the Poor, Igniting Class Conflict," *New York Times*, June 11, 2016.

2. 北京西城区顶级学区房被废，家长彻夜维权！所谓学区房就是政府精心设计的杀猪盘，收割的时候到了了 | 米国路边社 [*Housing in the Top School District in Beijing's Xicheng District Was Abolished, and Parents Stayed Up All Night to Defend Their Rights! The So-Called School District Housing Is a*

Pig-Killing Tray Carefully Designed by the Government. The Harvest Time Has Come | American Roadside Society], n.d., https://www.youtube.com /watch?v=Ve9dtA6Zmlc&t=373s; 北京新政出台取消学区房，西城区学区房日降50万 *[Beijing's New Deal Cancels School District Housing, and Xicheng District School District Housing Drops by 500,000 per Day]*, n.d., https://www .youtube.com/watch?v=mKn7yRlVKmM.

3. Education and social mobility are long-standing issues in the social sciences. Influential works include Pierre Bourdieu's work on education and culture capital. Pierre Bourdieu, *State Nobility: Elite Schools in the Field of Power,* trans. Lauretta C. Clough (Stanford, CA: Stanford University Press, 1998).

4. Christian Houle, "Social Mobility and Political Instability," *Journal of Conflict Resolution* 63, no. 1 (2019): 85–111, https://doi.org/10.1177/0022002717723434.

5. Even at its nascent stage around 650 AD, the system had already increased social mobility. Fangqi Wen, Erik H. Wang, and Michael Hout, "Social Mobility in the Tang Dynasty as the Imperial Examination Rose and Aristocratic Family Pedigree Declined, 618–907 CE," *Proceedings of the National Academy of Sciences* 121, no. 4 (2024): e2305564121, https://doi .org/10.1073/pnas.2305564121. More research has been published for the Ming and Qing dynasties, which generally shows that many of the officials came from nonaristocratic families. E. A. Kracke, Jr., "Family vs. Merit in Chinese Civil Service Examinations Under the Empire," *Harvard Journal of Asiatic Studies*, 10, no. 2 (1947): 103–123; Qin Jiang and James Kai-sing Kung, "Social Mobility in Late Imperial China: Reconsidering the 'Ladder of Success' Hypothesis," *Modern China* 47, no. 5 (2021): 628–661, https://doi.org/10 .1177/0097700420914529; Ping-Ti Ho, *The Ladder of Success in Imperial China: Aspects of Social Mobility, 1368–1911* (New York: Columbia University Press, 1962). Jia Ruixue and James Kung, "The Culture and Institutions of Confucianism," in *Handbook of Culture and Economic Behavior,* ed. Benjamin Enke, Paola Giuliano, Nathan Nunn, and Leonard Wantchekon (forthcoming).

6. Nicolas Tackett, *The Destruction of the Medieval Chinese Aristocracy* (Cambridge, MA: Harvard University Asia Center, 2014).

7. For a comprehensive discussion on this point, see Yasheng Huang, *The Rise and Fall of the East: How Exams, Autocracy, Stability, and Technology Brought China Success, and Why They Might Lead to Its Decline* (New Haven: Yale University Press, 2023).

8. Ruixue Jia, Gérard Roland, and Yang Xie, "A Theory of Power Structure and Institutional Compatibility: China versus Europe Revisited," *Journal of the European Economic Association* 22, no. 3 (2024): 1275–1318, https://doi.org/10 .1093/jeea/jvado50.

9. Huang and Yang also find that the civil service exam effectively constrained aristocratic power and contributed to the decline in intra-elite conflicts in imperial China. Yasheng Huang and Clair Yang, "A Longevity Mechanism of Chinese Absolutism," *Journal of Politics* 84, no. 2 (2022): 1165–75, https://doi.org/10.1086/714934.

10. 国家统计局人口和就业统计司,人力资源和社会保障部规划财务司编., *中国劳动统计年鉴 China labour statistical yearbook 2022*, Di 1 ban (Beijing: 中国统计出版社有限公司, 2022).

11. Hongbin Li et al., "Job Preferences and Outcomes for China's College Graduates," *China Quarterly* 258 (June 2024): 529–547, https://doi.org/10.1017/S0305741023001510.

12. Davide Cantoni et al., "Curriculum and Ideology," *Journal of Political Economy* 125, no. 2 (2017): 338–392, https://doi.org/10.1086/690951.

13. Hongbin Li, Sai Luo, and Yang Wang, "Curriculum, Political Participation, and Career Choice," manuscript, February 16, 2024, available at SSRN, https://doi.org/10.2139/ssrn.4707346.

14. Education and nationalism are broad issues relevant to many nations. Influential work includes Ernest Gellner, *Nations and Nationalism* (Ithaca, NY: Cornell University Press, 1983).

15. Wolfgang Franke, *The Reform and Abolition of the Traditional Chinese Examination System* (Cambridge, MA: Center for East Asian Studies, Harvard University; distributed by Harvard University Press, 1960).

16. Henrietta Harrison, *The Man Awakened from Dreams: One Man's Life in a North China Village, 1857–1942* (Stanford, CA: Stanford University Press, 2020).

17. Many scholars have conjectured that this focus on Confucian texts is the reason that China missed the Industrial Revolution. See influential work by Joseph Needham. Joseph Needham, *The Grand Titration* (London: Routledge, 2005).

18. Andrew G. Walder, *China under Mao: A Revolution Derailed* (Cambridge, MA: Harvard University Press, 2017).

19. Xueguang Zhou and Liren Hou, "Children of the Cultural Revolution: The State and the Life Course in the People's Republic of China," *American Sociological Review* 64, no. 1 (1999): 12–36, https://doi.org/10.1177/000312249906400103.

20. Hongbin Li and Lingsheng Meng, "The Scarring Effects of College Education Deprivation During China's Cultural Revolution," *Economic Development and Cultural Change* 70, no. 3 (2022): 981–2016, https://doi.org/10.1086/713935.

21. Party History Expo, "20世纪70年代末的知青返城浪潮 [The Wave of Educated Youth Returning to the City in the Late 1970s]," *中国改革信息*

库 [*China Reform Information Database*], n.d., http://www.reformdata.org/2004/0215/8092.shtml.

22. 青春湖北, "巨星陨落！湖北这位老人的一个建议，改变了全中国人...," *The Paper 澎湃新闻*, August 3, 2019, https://m.thepaper.cn/baijiahao_4083972?sdkver=e06426d6&clientprefetch=1.

23. Hernandez, "China Tries to Redistribute Education to the Poor."

24. Casey Hall and Laurie Chen, "China's Private Tutoring Firms Emerge from the Shadows after Crackdown," Reuters, October 27, 2024, https://www.reuters.com/world/china/chinas-private-tutoring-firms-emerge-shadows-after-crackdown-2024-10-28/.

5. CENTRALIZATION AND THE RISE OF STEM

1. "Degrees Conferred," Institutional Research and Decision Support, Stanford University, 2023, https://irds.stanford.edu/data-findings/degrees-conferred.

2. "Total Fall Enrollment of First-Time Degree/Certificate-Seeking Students in Degree-Granting Postsecondary Institutions, by Attendance Status, Sex of Student, and Level and Control of Institution: 1960 through 2031," Digest of Education Statistics, National Center for Education Statistics, Table 305.10, https://nces.ed.gov/programs/digest/d19/tables/dt19_305.10.asp; Ministry of Education, "Education Statistical Yearbooks," 2009–2021, http://www.moe.gov.cn/jyb_sjzl/moe_560/2020/.

3. Kjeld Erik Brødsgaard, "Institutional Reform and the *Bianzhi* System in China," *China Quarterly* 170 (June 2002): 361–386, https://doi.org/10.1017/S0009443902000232; Eva Huang, John Benson, and Ying Zhu, *Teacher Management in China: The Transformation of Educational Systems* (London: Routledge, 2016).

4. Liu Baocun and An Yalun, "Educational Administration and Leadership in China," in *Oxford Research Encyclopedia of Education*, May 29, 2020, https://doi.org/10.1093/acrefore/9780190264093.013.629.

5. Ruixue Jia, Huihua Nie, and Wei Xiao, "Power and Publications in Chinese Academia," *Journal of Comparative Economics* 47, no. 4 (December 2019): 792–805, https://doi.org/10.1016/j.jce.2019.08.006.

6. Hongbin Li et al., "What Can Students Gain from China's Higher Education?," *Asian Economic Policy Review* 18, no. 2 (2023): 287–304, https://doi.org/10.1111/aepr.12426.

7. This system is characterized as "decentralized authoritarianism" in Chenggang Xu, "The Fundamental Institutions of China's Reforms and

Development," *Journal of Economic Literature* 49, no. 4 (2011): 1076–1151, https://doi.org/10.1257/jel.49.4.1076; Hongbin Li and Li-An Zhou, "Political Turnover and Economic Performance: The Incentive Role of Personnel Control in China," *Journal of Public Economics* 89, no. 9–10 (2005): 1743–62, https://doi.org/10.1016/j.jpubeco.2004.06.009.

   8. Li and Zhou, "Political Turnover and Economic Performance."

   9. The influential cross-country study on this topic is by Robert J. Barro and Jong-Wha Lee, *Education Matters: Global Schooling Gains from the 19th to the 21st Century* (Oxford University Press, 2015).

   10. Suzanne Pepper, *Radicalism and Education Reform in 20th-Century China: The Search for an Ideal Development Model* (Cambridge: Cambridge University Press, 1996).

   11. Hongbin Li et al., "Skill Complementarities and Returns to Higher Education: Evidence from College Enrollment Expansion in China," *China Economic Review* 46 (December 2017): 10–26, https://doi.org/10.1016/j.chieco.2017.08.004.

   12. UNESCO Institute for Statistics, "School Enrollment, Tertiary (% Gross)—China, United States" (World Bank Group), accessed April 24, 2024, https://data.worldbank.org/indicator/SE.TER.ENRR?locations=CN-US; "College Enrollment Rates," National Center for Education Statistics, U.S. Department of Education, Institute of Education Sciences, May 2024, https://nces.ed.gov/programs/coe/indicator/cpb/college-enrollment-rate.

   13. Amani Core, "Chinese Universities Chip In to Narrow Semiconductor Talent Gap," *The China Guys*, June 10, 2021, https://thechinaguys.com/china-integrated-circuit-schools/.

   14. Limin Bai, "Monetary Reward versus the National Ideological Agenda: Career Choice among Chinese University Students," *Journal of Moral Education* 27, no. 4 (1998): 525–540, https://doi.org/10.1080/0305724980270406.

   15. Paul Anthony Samuelson and William D. Nordhaus, *Economics*, 19th ed. (Boston, MA: McGraw-Hill/Irwin, 2010).

   16. Ruixue Jia et al., "English's Significance: Exam Performance by Subject and Future Income in China," manuscript, University of California, San Diego and Stanford University, 2024.

6. EDUCATION AND GLOBAL POWER

   1. Loren Brandt and Xiaodong Zhu, "Accounting for China's Growth," IZA Discussion Paper No. 4764, Institute for the Study of Labor, February 2010, https://docs.iza.org/dp4764.pdf; Zheng Song, Kjetil Storesletten, and

Fabrizio Zilibotti, "Growing Like China," *American Economic Review* 101, no. 1 (2011): 196–233, https://doi.org/10.1257/aer.101.1.196; Hongbin Li et al., "Human Capital and China's Future Growth," *Journal of Economic Perspectives* 31, no. 1 (2017): 25–48, https://doi.org/10.1257/jep.31.1.25.

2. National Bureau of Statistics of China, Annual Statistical Yearbooks, 2001 and 2021, https://www.stats.gov.cn/english/Statisticaldata/yearbook/; National Bureau of Statistics of China, China Statistical Yearbook: 2021, https://www.stats.gov.cn/sj/ndsj/2021/indexeh.htm.

3. Li et al., "Human Capital and China's Future Growth."

4. For an earlier study of the relationship between education and economic growth, see Robert Barro, "Economic Growth in a Cross Section of Countries," *Quarterly Journal of Economics* 106, no. 2 (1991): 407–443, https://doi.org/10.2307/2937943; for how education quality affects growth, see Eric Alan Hanushek and Ludger Woessmann, *The Knowledge Capital of Nations: Education and the Economics of Growth* (Cambridge, MA: MIT Press, 2015).

5. For a summary of China's reforms, see Yingyi Qian, "The Process of China's Market Transition (1978–1998): The Evolutionary, Historical, and Comparative Perspectives," *Journal of Institutional and Theoretical Economics* 156, no. 1 (2000): 151–171, http://www.jstor.org/stable/40752194.

6. Hongbin Li, Mark Rosenzweig, and Junsen Zhang, "Altruism, Favoritism, and Guilt in the Allocation of Family Resources: Sophie's Choice in Mao's Mass Send-Down Movement," *Journal of Political Economy* 118, no. 1 (2010): 1–38, https://doi.org/10.1086/650315.

7. Robert C. Feenstra and Shang-jin Wei, eds., *China's Growing Role in World Trade* (Chicago: University of Chicago Press, 2010).

8. Barro, "Economic Growth in a Cross Section of Countries."

9. Xiao Ma, "College Expansion, Trade, and Innovation: Evidence from China," *International Economic Review* 65, no. 1 (2024): 315–351, https://doi.org/10.1111/iere.12670.

10. John David Minnich, "Scaling the Commanding Heights: The Logic of Technology Transfer Policy in Rising China," MIT Political Science Department Research Paper No. 2023–2, June 29, 2023, available at SSRN, https://papers.ssrn.com/sol3/papers.cfm?abstract_id=4496386.

11. Caroline S. Wagner, Lin Zhang, and Loet Leydesdorff, "A Discussion of Measuring the Top-1% Most-Highly Cited Publications: Quality and Impact of Chinese Papers," *Scientometrics* 127, no. 4 (2022): 1825–39, https://doi.org/10.1007/s11192-022-04291-z.

12. *Nature Index,* Institution tables, April 1, 2023, https://www.nature.com/nature-index/institution-outputs/generate/all/global/all.

13. Chong-En Bai et al., "Entrepreneurial Reluctance: Talent and Firm Creation in China," NBER Working Paper 28865 (National Bureau of Economic Research, May 2021), https://doi.org/10.3386/w28865.

14. Ruixue Jia, Huihua Nie, and Wei Xiao, "Power and Publications in Chinese Academia," *Journal of Comparative Economics* 47, no. 4 (2019): 792–805, https://doi.org/10.1016/j.jce.2019.08.006.

15. Yigong Shi and Yi Rao, "China's Research Culture," *Science* 329, no. 5996 (2010): 1128, https://doi.org/10.1126/science.1196916.

7. VALUES AND INSTITUTIONS

1. Michael Young, *The Rise of Meritocracy* (London: Routledge, 1958).

2. Michael Young, "Down with Meritocracy," *The Guardian*, June 28, 2001.

3. Lani Guinier, *The Tyranny of the Meritocracy: Democratizing Higher Education in America* (Boston: Beacon Press, 2016).

4. Alberto Alesina and George-Marios Angeletos, "Fairness and Redistribution," *American Economic Review* 95, no. 4 (2005): 960–980, https://doi.org/10.1257/0002828054825655.

5. David S. G. Goodman, *Class in Contemporary China* (Cambridge: Polity Press, 2014).

6. The World Values Survey was founded by the political scientist Ronald Inglehart. In his influential book, he finds that East Asian cultures exhibit some distinct values. Ronald Inglehart, *Modernization and Postmodernization: Cultural, Economic, and Political Change in 43 Societies* (Princeton, NJ: Princeton University Press, 2020), https://doi.org/10.2307/j.ctv1ovm2ns.

7. World Values Survey Association, "World Values Survey Wave 7 (2017–2022)," https://www.worldvaluessurvey.org/WVSDocumentationWV7.jsp.

8. Alberto Alesina, Edward Glaeser, and Bruce Sacerdote, "Work and Leisure in the U.S. and Europe: Why So Different?" NBER Working Paper 11278 (National Bureau of Economic Research, April 2005), https://doi.org/10.3386/w11278.

9. Martin King Whyte, "China's Dormant and Active Social Volcanoes," *China Journal* 75 (January 2016): 9–37, https://doi.org/10.1086/683124.

10. Jia Ruixue and James Kung, "The Culture and Institutions of Confucianism," in *Handbook of Culture and Economic Behavior*, ed. Benjamin Enke, Paola Giuliano, Nathan Nunn, and Leonard Wantchekon (forthcoming).

11. Prasad Krishnnamurthy, "Harvard's Cult of Personality," *The Hill*, October 26, 2022, opinion, https://thehill.com/opinion/education/3704542

-harvards-cult-of-personality/#:~:text=Harvard%27s%20admissions%20
officers%20determine%20personality,race%20can%20be%20a%20factor.

12. Hongbin Cai, Hanming Fang, and Lixin Colin Xu, "Eat, Drink, Firms, Government: An Investigation of Corruption from the Entertainment and Travel Costs of Chinese Firms," *Journal of Law and Economics* 54, no. 1 (2011): 55–78, https://doi.org/10.1086/651201; Andrew Wedeman, "The Intensification of Corruption in China," in *Critical Readings on the Communist Party of China*, ed. Kjeld Erik Brodsgaard (London: Brill, 2017), 1242–72, https://doi.org /10.1163/9789004302488_045.

13. Hongbin Li et al., "Job Preferences and Outcomes for China's College Graduates," *China Quarterly* 258 (June 2024): 529–547, https://doi.org/10.1017 /S0305741023001510.

14. Ruixue Jia, Xiaohuan Lan, and Gerard Padró I Miquel, "Doing Business in China: Parental Background and Government Intervention Determine Who Owns Business," *Journal of Development Economics* 151 (June 2021): 102670, https://doi.org/10.1016/j.jdeveco.2021.102670.

15. Hongbin Li et al., "Does Having a Cadre Parent Pay? Evidence from the First Job Offers of Chinese College Graduates," *Journal of Development Economics* 99, no. 2 (2012): 513–520, https://doi.org/10.1016/j.jdeveco.2012.06.005.

16. Loren Brandt and Hongbin Li, "Bank Discrimination in Transition Economies: Ideology, Information, or Incentives?," *Journal of Comparative Economics* 31, no. 3 (2003): 387–413, https://doi.org/10.1016/S0147–5967 (03)00080–5; Hongbin Li et al., "Political Connections, Financing and Firm Performance: Evidence from Chinese Private Firms," *Journal of Development Economics* 87, no. 2 (2008): 283–299, https://doi.org/10.1016/j.jdeveco.2007 .03.001.

17. "In China, Parents Bribe to Get Students into Top Schools, Despite Campaign Against Corruption," *Washington Post*, October 7, 2013; Dan Levin, "A Chinese Education, for a Price," *New York Times*, November 22, 2012.

18. Liu Jiaying et al., "Doctors and Red Envelopes: How Corruption Has Blighted China's Public Health System," *Caixin Global*, January 20, 2017, https://www.caixinglobal.com/2017–01–20/doctors-and-red-envelopes-how -corruption-has-blighted-chinas-public-health-system-101047316.html.

19. Huang Yanzhong, "Anti-Corruption Campaign in China's Medical Sector: Unmasking the Hidden Agenda," blogpost, Council on Foreign Relations, August 18, 2023, https://www.cfr.org/blog/anti-corruption-campaign-chinas -medical-sector-unmasking-hidden-agenda.

20. Chun Han Wang and Clarence Leong, "In China, a Completely Different Approach to Lowering Healthcare Costs," *Wall Street Journal*, September

13, 2023; Simone McCarthy, "China Is Launching an 'Unprecedented' Crackdown on Corruption in Its Health Industry as Economic Woes Pile Up," *CNN*, August 25, 2023, https://www.cnn.com/2023/08/24/china/china-healthcare-corruption-crackdown-intl-hnk/index.html.

21. Edward Wong, "Test That Can Determine the Course of Life in China Gets a Closer Examination," *New York Times*, June 30, 2012; Javier C. Hernandez, "China Threatens Jail Time For College Entrance Exam Cheaters," *New York Times*, June 7, 2016.

22. Hongbin Li et al., "Poverty in China's Colleges and the Targeting of Financial Aid," *China Quarterly* 216 (December 2013): 970–992, https://doi.org/10.1017/S0305741013001082.

23. Thomas Piketty, Li Yang, and Gabriel Zucman, "Capital Accumulation, Private Property, and Rising Inequality in China, 1978–2015," *American Economic Review* 109, no. 7 (2019): 2469–96, https://doi.org/10.1257/aer.20170973; Li Hongbin, Meng Lingsheng, and Zhang Yunbin, "How Common Is the Prosperity? The Trends and Nature of China's Income Inequality, 1988–2018," manuscript, 2023.

24. Li, Meng, and Zhang, "How Common Is the Prosperity?"

25. Shen Lu, "America Had 'Quiet Quitting.' In China, Young People Are 'Letting It Rot,'" *Wall Street Journal*, December 18, 2023; Elsie Chen, "These Chinese Millennials Are 'Chilling,' and Beijing Isn't Happy," *New York Times*, July 3, 2021.

26. Jane Cai, "China's Path to Common Prosperity Puts Pressure on Private Enterprise," *South China Morning Post*, November 10, 2021.

27. Andrew Mullen, "What Is China's Common-Prosperity Strategy?," *South China Morning Post*, August 26, 2021; Kevin Yao, "What Is China's 'Common Prosperity' Drive and Why Does It Matter?," Reuters, September 2, 2021, https://www.reuters.com/world/china/what-is-chinas-common-prosperity-drive-why-does-it-matter-2021–09–02/.

8. A MIRROR OF SOCIETY

1. Hongbin and Li-An Zhou benefited greatly from earlier theoretical work, including the following: Eric Maskin, Yingyi Qian, and Chenggang Xu, "Incentives, Information, and Organizational Form," *Review of Economic Studies* 67, no. 2 (2000): 359–378, https://doi.org/10.1111/1467-937X.00135.

2. Chenggang Xu, "The Fundamental Institutions of China's Reforms and Development," *Journal of Economic Literature* 49, no. 4 (2011): 1076–1151, https://doi.org/10.1257/jel.49.4.1076.

3. Hongbin Li and Li-An Zhou, "Political Turnover and Economic Performance: The Incentive Role of Personnel Control in China," *Journal of Public Economics* 89, no. 9–10 (2005): 1743–62, https://doi.org/10.1016/j.jpubeco.2004.06.009.

4. Ye Chen, Hongbin Li, and Li-An Zhou, "Relative Performance Evaluation and the Turnover of Provincial Leaders in China," *Economics Letters* 88, no. 3 (2005): 421–425, https://doi.org/10.1016/j.econlet.2005.05.003.

5. "A Big Chinese Province Admits Faking Its Economic Data," *The Economist*, January 26, 2017.

6. Ruixue Jia, Masayuki Kudamatsu, and David Seim, "Political Selection in China: The Complementary Roles of Connections and Performance," *Journal of the European Economic Association* 13, no. 4 (2015): 631–668, https://doi.org/10.1111/jeea.12124.

7. Central Committee of the Communist Party of China, "Decision of the Central Committee of the Communist Party of China on Several Major Issues Concerning Comprehensively Deepening Reform [中共中央关于全面深化改革若干重大问题的决定]," November 12, 2013. Emphasis added.

8. Ruixue Jia and Yiqing Xu, "Rotating to the Top: How Career Tracks Matter in the Chinese Communist Party," manuscript, 2018, available at SSRN, https://doi.org/10.2139/ssrn.3613276; Zheng (Michael) Song and Wei Xiong, "The Mandarin Model of Growth," manuscript, October 2024, https://wxiong.mycpanel.princeton.edu/papers/Mandarin.pdf.

9. Emily Weinstein, "Chinese Talent Program Tracker," Center for Security and Emerging Technology, November 2020, https://chinatalenttracker.cset.tech.

10. Raymond Fisman et al., "Social Ties and Favoritism in Chinese Science," *Journal of Political Economy* 126, no. 3 (2018): 1134–71, https://doi.org/10.1086/697086.

11. Smriti Mallapaty, "Killing at Chinese University Highlights Tensions over Tenure System," *Nature* 595, no. 7866 (2021): 158–159, https://doi.org/10.1038/d41586-021-01716-2. Luo Yahan and Wang Jingyang, "Up or Out: The Ruthless Tenure Race for Young Chinese Scholars," *Sixth Tone*, July 3, 2024, https://www.sixthtone.com/news/1015445.

12. 澎湃新闻 [The Paper], "高校教师读博后违约离职 校方拒办档案索赔79万 [University Teacher Breached Postdoctoral Agreement by Resigning, the School Refused to Process the File, Demanding 790,000 Yuan in Compensation]," 凤凰网 [Phoenix.com], accessed October 31, 2024, https://news.ifeng.com/c/8Bbuhnjlo23.

13. Viola Zhou, "TSMC's Debacle in the American Desert," *Rest of the World*, April 23, 2024, https://restofworld.org/2024/tsmc-arizona-expansion/.

14. Celia Chen and Iris Deng, "Tencent Seeks to Kill Silo Culture That Gave It WeChat as It Expands into AI, Big Data," *South China Morning Post*, November 14, 2018.

15. Hongbin Li et al., "Bureaucratic Incentives and Effectiveness of the One Child Policy in China," manuscript, October 31, 2024.

16. Minxin Pei, *China's Crony Capitalism: The Dynamics of Regime Decay* (Cambridge, MA: Harvard University Press, 2016).

17. C. A. E. Goodhart, "Problems of Monetary Management: The UK Experience," ch. 3 in *Monetary Theory and Practice* (London: Macmillan Education, 1984), 91–121, https://doi.org/10.1007/978-1-349-17295-5_4; Lewis Elton, "Goodhart's Law and Performance Indicators in Higher Education," *Evaluation & Research in Education* 18, no. 1–2 (2004): 120–128, https://doi.org/10.1080/09500790408668312.

9. THE EXAM EMPIRE EXPANDS

1. "China 'Overtakes' US as World's Largest Goods Trader," *BBC News*, January 10, 2014.

2. David H. Autor, David Dorn, and Gordon H. Hanson, "The China Syndrome: Local Labor Market Effects of Import Competition in the United States," *American Economic Review* 103, no. 6 (2013): 2121–68, https://doi.org/10.1257/aer.103.6.2121.

3. Yu Xie et al., "Caught in the Crossfire: Fears of Chinese-American Scientists," *Proceedings of the National Academy of Sciences* 120, no. 27 (2023): e2216248120, https://doi.org/10.1073/pnas.2216248120.

4. Albert Park is currently the chief economist of the Asian Development Bank and professor at the Hong Kong University of Science and Technology.

5. Gaurav Khanna et al., "Trade Liberalization and Chinese Students in U.S. Higher Education," *Review of Economics and Statistics* (October 23, 2023): 1–46, https://doi.org/10.1162/rest_a_01378.

6. Ruixue Jia et al., "The Ripple Effect of China's College Expansion on American Universities," University of California, San Diego, and Stanford University manuscript.

7. Migration Policy Institute, "Countries of Birth for U.S. Immigrants, 1960–Present," accessed January 23, 2025, https://www.migrationpolicy.org

/programs/data-hub/charts/immigrants-countries-birth-over-time?width=900 &height=850&iframe=true.

8. Madelyn Ross, Harris Doshay, and Young Yang, "Three Decades of Chinese Students in America, 1991–2021," China Datalab, School of Global Policy and Strategy, UC San Diego, n.d., https://chinadatalab.ucsd.edu/uscet /three-decades-of-chinese-students-in-america-1991-2021/.

9. Ruixue Jia et al., "The Impact of US–China Tensions on US Science: Evidence from the NIH Investigations," *Proceedings of the National Academy of Sciences* 121, no. 19 (2024): e2301436121, https://doi.org/10.1073/pnas.2301436121.

10. Lei Guang et al., "Chinese Talent, American Enterprise: Five Takeaways of How Chinese Talent Contributes to Biotech Innovation in the U.S.," blogpost, China Datalab, School of Global Policy and Strategy, UC San Diego, February 21, 2021, https://chinadatalab.ucsd.edu/viz-blog/chinese-talent-american -enterprise-five-takeaways-of-how-chinese-talent-contributes-to-biotech -innovation-in-the-u-s/.

11. John Bound et al., "The Globalization of Postsecondary Education: The Role of International Students in the US Higher Education System," *Journal of Economic Perspectives* 35, no. 1 (2021): 163–184, https://doi.org/10.1257/jep .35.1.163.

12. Bethany Allen-Ebrahimian, "A U.S. University Insured Itself against a Drop in Chinese Students," *Axios*, August 8, 2020, https://www.axios.com /2020/08/18/university-illinois-chinese-students.

13. Migration Policy Institute, "Countries of Birth for U.S. Immigrants, 1960–Present."

14. Abby Budiman, "Chinese in the U.S. Fact Sheet," Pew Research Center, April 29, 2021, https://www.pewresearch.org/fact-sheet/asian-americans -chinese-in-the-u-s/.

15. Natasha Kumar Warikoo, *Race at the Top: Asian Americans and Whites in Pursuit of the American Dream in Suburban Schools* (Chicago: University of Chicago Press, 2022).

16. Rick Smith, "Your Elite School Is Not Worth the Cost, Studies Say," *Forbes*, November 24, 2014.

17. zhangfei123, "华人为什么要爬藤？," April 12, 2021, https://huaren .us/showtopic.html?topicid=2834016.

18. "United States District Court District of Massachusetts: Students for Fair Admissions, Inc., v. President and Fellows of Harvard College (Harvard Corporation)," accessed October 31, 2024, https://int.nyt.com/data/documenthelper /1865-harvard-admissions-process/fcb2b57c15f154b139df/optimized/full

.pdf; Peter Arcidiacono, Josh Kinsler, and Tyler Ransom, "Asian American Discrimination in Harvard Admissions," NBER Working Paper 27068, National Bureau of Economic Research, April 2020, https://doi.org/10.3386/w27068.

19. Warikoo, *Race at the Top*.

20. University of California, "Admissions by Source School," April 17, 2024, https://www.universityofcalifornia.edu/about-us/information-center/admissions-source-school; California Department of Education, "Data and Statistics," accessed January 23, 2024, https://www.cde.ca.gov/ds/.

21. "Mathematics—Palo Alto Unified School District," accessed October 31, 2024, https://www.pausd.org/learning/curriculum/math.

22. Grace Gao, "Controversy over Math Policies: PAUSD Implements New Changes Following Math Lawsuit," *Midpeninsula Post*, May 23, 2023, https://midpenpost.org/2023/05/23/controversy-over-math-policies-pausd-implements-new-changes-following-math-lawsuit/; Grace Gao, "Students Speak Out on Math Issues at Palo Alto School Board Meeting," Palo Alto Online, August 29, 2023, http://www.paloaltoonline.com/news/2023/08/29/students-speak-out-on-math-issues-at-palo-alto-school-board-meeting/; Sue Dremann, "District: Advanced Math Class Will Earn College, but Not High School, Credit," Palo Alto Online, May 24, 2023, http://www.paloaltoonline.com/news/2023/05/24/district-advanced-math-class-will-earn-college-but-not-high-school-credit/; Carolyn Walworth, "Paly Student Tells of School Stress: 'Students Are Gasping for Air,'" *The Almanac*, March 26, 2015.

23. Cayden Gu, "Falling Behind the Curve," *The Campanile* (Palo Alto High School Student News), accessed November 1, 2024, https://thecampanile.org/24966/spotlight/falling-behind-the-curve/; Elaine Goodman, "Lawsuit Claims PAUSD's Math Placement Tests Are Biased Against Girls," *Palo Alto Daily Post*, October 24, 2021; Allyson Aleksey, "The Lawsuit That Could Change California Math Education," *San Francisco Examiner*, February 20, 2023.

24. Jessica Cheung, Chaturvedi Asthaa, and Rob Szypko, "One Elite High School's Struggle Over Admissions," *The Daily, New York Times*, June 24, 2022.

25. Stanford Education Data Archive, "The Educational Opportunity Project at Stanford University," accessed January 23, 2025, https://edopportunity.org/about/.

26. David Card, Alexandre Mas, and Jesse Rothstein, "Tipping and the Dynamics of Segregation," *Quarterly Journal of Economics* 123, no. 1 (2008): 177–218, https://doi.org/10.1162/qjec.2008.123.1.177; Elizabeth U. Cascio and

Ethan G. Lewis, "Cracks in the Melting Pot: Immigration, School Choice, and Segregation," *American Economic Journal: Economic Policy* 4, no. 3 (2012): 91–117, https://doi.org/10.1257/pol.4.3.91; Allison Shertzer and Randall P. Walsh, "Racial Sorting and the Emergence of Segregation in American Cities," *Review of Economics and Statistics* 101, no. 3 (2019): 415–427, https://doi .org/10.1162/rest_a_00786.

27. Leah Boustan, Christine Cai, and Tammy Tseng, "JUE Insight: White Flight from Asian Immigration: Evidence from California Public Schools," *Journal of Urban Economics* 141 (May 2024): 103541, https://doi.org/10.1016/j .jue.2023.103541.

28. David J. Deming, "The Growing Importance of Social Skills in the Labor Market," *Quarterly Journal of Economics* 132, no. 4 (2017): 1593–1640, https://doi.org/10.1093/qje/qjx022.

ACKNOWLEDGMENTS

Hongbin and Ruixue would like to thank those with whom they have collaborated over the years. Each has offered an invaluable contribution to the research we have referenced throughout this manuscript: Chong-En Bai, Ying Bai, Matthew Boswell, Loren Brandt, Ye Chen, Sinclair Cook, Dezhuang Hu, Gaurav Khanna, James Kung, Masa Kudamatsu, Tang Li, James Liang, Pak Wai Liu, Prashant Loyalka, Sai Luo, Yueyuan Ma, Lingsheng Meng, Grant Miller, Huihua Nie, Binh Thai Nguyen, Torsten Persson, Yu Qin, Xue Qiao, Molly Roberts, Gerard Roland, Mark Rosenzweig, Scott Rozelle, David Seim, Huan Wang, Qian Wang, Qiuyi Wang, Xin Wang, Yang Wang, Ye Wang, Binzhen Wu, Jing Wu, Wei Xiao, Jieyu Xie, Yang Xie, Yanyan Xiong, Eddie Yang, Hanmo Yang, Yiqing Xu, Yuli Xu, Junsen Zhang, and Li-An Zhou.

We would also like to thank Zhiwu Chen, Xiaoying Liao, Lingsheng Meng, and Guoguang Wu for reading earlier versions of the manuscript and providing comments that helped improve the quality of the book. We also thank two anonymous reviewers for reading the earlier draft and providing constructive feedback.

Ruixue extends her gratitude to her UCSD colleagues—Lei Guang, Gordon Hanson, Barry Naughton, Molly Roberts, and Susan Shirk—for many stimulating conversations about Chinese and American societies, as well as for the support provided by the School of Global Policy and Strategy and the 21st Century China Center.

Hongbin and Claire would like to extend their gratitude to their Stanford colleagues and friends (in addition to those mentioned above) for consistently enriching interactions and generous support, including Belinda Byrne, Jennifer Choo, Mark Duggan, Karen Eggleston, Todd Ewing, Ronda Fenton, Tom Fingar, David Flash, Gregory Gamble,

Eric Hanushek, Yue Hou, Ragina Johnson, Matthew Kohrman, Jessica Leino, Yue Ma, Michael McFaul, Alexis Medina, Jean Oi, Jennifer Pan, Shih-Wei Peng, Xinyao Qiu, Heather Rahimi, Frank Scioscia, Tina Shi, Steve Suda, Michelle Townsend, Andy Walder, Chenggang Xu, Hanmo Yang, Yang Yang, Xinmin Zhao, and Xueguang Zhou.

Hongbin also thanks those who have generously supported the research and writing of this book.

Claire would like to thank all those who passed through Prospect Place, including Tressa Fallon, Christopher Gernon, Zach Levitt, and Cora Rose, who collectively served as invaluable sounding boards throughout the drafting process. She would also like to thank Matthew Boswell, for his continued support and willingness to lend an ear, and Charley Burlock, for her words of encouragement on an original draft that made writing a book feel within reach. Lastly, Claire would like to thank both of her parents for their continued support across all her endeavors—educational and otherwise.

We would like to extend our gratitude to our agent, Jill Marsal, for seamlessly guiding us through the earliest stages of our process; to our editor, Grigory Tovbis, whose insight and careful readings made for a better manuscript; to Kate Brick for her extreme care and excellent editing; to Jamie Armstrong for her attention to detail in shepherding our manuscript through production; and to Harvard University Press for their support in publishing our work. All remaining errors are the responsibility of the authors.

INDEX

"academician" title, 178

acceptance rates, 39–40, 61, 203. *See also* admissions process, university

ACT, 7, 8, 73, 157, 198

admissions process, university, 7–10, 13–14, 39–40, 74, 80; ethnic minorities, 54–55, 60–62; for immigrants to United States, 193–194; meritocracy and, 157–158; in United States, 71–74, 84, 157, 196–198; as zero-sum game, 7. *See also* gaokao; quota system

advanced placement (AP) exams, 109

affirmative action, 4, 60, 152, 197, 207, 209. *See also Students for Fair Admissions, Inc., v. President and Fellows of Harvard College*

American Dream, 151–152

artificial intelligence (AI), 136, 137, 147

Australia, 83, 85

Battle Hymn of the Tiger Mother (Chua), 39

Beijing: Ba Bao Shan Cemetery, 15; CCP's 100th anniversary, 94; college admission rates and, 61, 62–63; COVID-19 pandemic in, 93–94; education tournament and, 56–58, 68; elementary schools in, 67; Forbidden City, 93; No. 4 High School, 94; as provincial-level city,

10, 170; quota system and, 10, 102; state sector employment in, 42–43; student aspirations for, 4, 6, 22, 26–27, 29–31, 52–53, 171; Tiananmen Square protests, 29, 93, 94; Xicheng District parent protests, 93–97, 104, 110, 111; Youth Education Alley (Yuyou Alley), 94–95; Zhongnanhai, 93

Bergman, Ingmar, 191

broken windows fallacy, 185

Brown University, 207

California Mathematics Placement Act of 2015, 206

Caltech, 207

Canada, 154, 209

centralized hierarchical tournaments: education system, 7, 13–15, 89, 141–142, 144, 169–170, 176–184, 195–198, 203–204; journal ranking system, 181–183; political system, 174–176, 184–186; zero-COVID policy, 186–187. *See also* centralized systems; hierarchical systems; tournament systems

centralized systems, 8; Chinese GDP and, 137; Chinese politics, 170–171, 174; control over human capital, 121–125, 179; control over people, 117–119; control over resources, 119–120; education in China,